MIRACLES
In The Naked Light

THE
EXTRAORDINARY LIFE
IN EVERY MOMENT

KIMBERLY BRAUN

Copyright © 2023 by Kimberly Braun

Miracles in the Naked Light
The Extraordinary Life in Every Moment

All rights reserved.

No part of this work may be used or reproduced, transmitted, stored, or used in any form or by any means graphic, electronic, or mechanical, including but not limited to photocopying, recording, scanning, digitizing, taping, Web distribution, information networks or information storage and retrieval systems, or in any manner whatsoever without prior written permission from the publisher.

In this world of digital information and rapidly-changing technology, some citations do not provide exact page numbers or credit the original source. We regret any errors, which are a result of the ease with which we consume information.

Disclaimer: This book is a memoir. It reflects the author's present recollections of experiences over time. Some names and characteristics have been changed, some events have been compressed, and some dialogue has been recreated. This is a book of memory, and memory has its own story to tell.

Edited by Laurie Knight
Cover Design by Kristina Edstrom

An Imprint for GracePoint Publishing (www.GracePointPublishing.com)

GracePoint Matrix, LLC
624 S. Cascade Ave, Suite 201
Colorado Springs, CO 80903
www.GracePointMatrix.com
Email: Admin@GracePointMatrix.com

SAN # 991-6032

A Library of Congress Control Number has been requested and is pending.

ISBN: (Paperback) 978-1-961347-16-8
eISBN: 978-1-961347-17-5

Books may be purchased for educational, business, or sales promotional use. For bulk order requests and price schedule contact:
Orders@GracePointPublishing.com

Contents

Introduction ix
    Foundations xii
Prologue... xvi
    The Encounter with Mary: January of 1995 xvii
Guided Steps into the Unknown 1
The Breath of Inspiration Arises Within All 36
Soil of Creative Impulse Is Tilled 98
Signs Align 124
Anchoring Deep 146
Manifold Ways of Spirit 171
The Face of the Beloved Everywhere 187
Destruction of Form by the Formless One 208
The Dance of Dissolution and Emergence 225
Ending Message to the Reader 247
Connect with Kimberly 251
Acknowledgements 253
About the Author 255

Praise for *Miracles in the Naked Light*

Sometimes the immortal light of consciousness strikes a person like gentle lightning, and they become lit up from the inside and forever. And some find themselves impelled to share the story of this illumination. We all can't go away for ten years on a meditation retreat, living in prayer continuously, becoming a nun. Here is the story of a daring, spiritual adventurer who did just that. And she has stories to tell.

> Lorin Roche, PhD.
> Author of *The Radiance Sutras,*
> Instinctive Meditation® and Pranava Meditation Training
> meditationtt.com and lorinroche.com

With delight and depth Kimberly illustrates how miracles shape our world; how they are born of open hearts that are attuned to the intelligent source of love and who are willing to act upon that love. Enjoy this tale as it weaves a home for the holy in humanity, and for humanity in the holy.

> Mukti Gray
> Co-Founder of Open Gate Sangha with husband Adyashanti
> Audio presenter *The Self in Full Bloom* and *The One of Us*

Kimberly Braun is a skillful teacher whose unique personal journey is as moving as it is inspiring. The combination makes *Miracles in the Naked Light* an illuminating companion for anyone on a spiritual path, whether traditional or non-traditional, mainstream or unconventional.

> Philip Goldberg
> Author of *American Veda* and
> *Spiritual Practice for Crazy Times*

This book is dedicated

To the One Beauty who is,
who was, and
who will always be.

To You
who read this message.

To each and every individual who participated in the
building of the monastery
whether your story is here in this book,
or contained in the stones of the building,
You are cherished by me
and your goodness does not go unseen.

Wrap your fingers around the rim of your heart
pounding… pounding… pounding…

It is the only way to feel the exultant throb
that edges your toes to the cliff
It is the only way to jump
to exhale descent into the Kali mystery

'Why' keeps dripping down our chins
But the eternal heart is
beating… beating… beating…

Reminding you, me, us, friends,
That we are too far gone
Freedom crests like curling waves
Steadily reaching its fingers
To grab us and take us

High… high…
So high…
Into the erotic embrace
Of the One Beauty

Introduction

There is a magnificent and difficult story in this book. In it contains the seeds of freedom and love for every reader. My story has its setting in history but is intended to pull back the veil to reveal the Divine story taking place within me, every other person, and within creation individually and collectively.

So, this story is your story as well because it reveals a path that is universal. It is a path providing timeless stability in an ever-changing world, inspiring ineffable insight leading to wisdom and clarity in a world climate where confusion abounds, and revealing a Source (I call Beloved) that is ever-present, loving us unconditionally through and in this existence we call life.

It is imperative for each of us to discover our way, and when we do, new horizons open, new solutions appear, new meaning is experienced. And when we do not discover the way—our way—life becomes narrow, meaningless, and can be fraught with a level of suffering that leads to despair and even destruction.

The storyline is a period of four years in my life as a young Carmelite monastic nun. My life had changed radically from living in my chosen monastery for five years prior to joining a small group of nuns who had been forming a new community in a new state for six years. As a young nun I was moved to say YES to build our permanent monastery, a wholly unanticipated turn of events in a life I thought was going to be cloistered and contemplative. The story recounts the first half of this building project. My memory is rich in detail, so in one way it is historical, but my focus is not upon accuracy to provide you a play-by-play for the sake of the events.

My focus is upon foundational messages that have been my own source of continual healing, transformation, and love.

Let yourself draw close to the many individuals here; they each were and are on their own path to wholeness. Every person here is one to whom I bow in respect, for I know very little of the inner workings of their own souls and Spirit in their lives. I only know we were part of a sacred journey together. In a way, there is a piece of each one of us in all the characters. I express my thoughts, feelings, observations, and actions as I share events. I have formed events and elements to reflect my internal experience and the inspiration of Spirit happening there.

The story also celebrates the amazing contribution of hundreds of people and companies that made the building project possible. Originally this manuscript was more than nine hundred pages, so there were many stories I could not include and many more that will be included in the book to publish after this one. I was witness to countless daily miracles all worthy of remembrance, even more than what I have written. As the general contractor for the project, and managing the large scope of donations, there was not enough time in the day to also record the incredible miracles and happenings day by day. Our community was small and there was also no one to assist me on this level.

All the company and contractor names that I remember have been retained, since these are public records, and the book is a way to celebrate their generous contribution. I have changed all my sisters' names to preserve privacy, and I have changed the names of volunteers, benefactors, and contractors where I share more in-depth personal stories except those I was able to locate and obtain permission from. In my desire to honor those who gave so much of themselves, it was difficult to change the names of those I could not find, but I made this choice to honor them and their families.

Two individuals whose names are changed deserve a special moment of recognition here. Frank Preusser is the name I use for the amazing architect who is responsible for the mission concept. I was unable to find him after all these years. Frank, if you read this, know that your generous contribution is celebrated through-out this story. The second person has passed away—I use the name Ava—and I was unable to locate family. She was our largest financial benefactor and a pioneer worthy of commendation and gratitude. Thank you, Ava, for your life's dedication to supporting your community in so many ways. You continue making a difference even today.

I am not attempting to create a finely tuned historical accounting; I am telling a story of miracles for the sake of inspiration. Where I have dialogue, it is only to give you a sense of an interaction as I experienced it; I did not take notes when people spoke and make no claim to accuracy. If you read this book and see yourself and would like your name to be known, I want you to be known as well. Let me know and I will add you to my website landing page for the book. And if you have a story to share, or want me to share, let me know and I can write it into my blog.

At the dedication ceremony of this monastery, I was not given a voice to celebrate all the amazing people of the project. I was a young nun, and it would have been out of custom to allow me to speak on behalf of the project during a ceremony that had so many priests and religious. As I sat there during the dedication of this miracle, there was a longing to publicly recognize the many contractors and companies, since I alone knew who they were. I was the custodian of the great event. At that time, I did not know my next step would be to leave monastic life, so I closed my eyes and celebrated them all with my friends of other realms, like Jesus, Mary, Therese, Teresa, and all the rest. I knew that they could see the larger picture that had less pomp and more human devotion. This is not to say the pomp and ritual did not have a heavenly aspect as well.

To all who generously participated, I celebrate you and thank you, whether you are in this final publication or whether you are here implicitly. Each of you remains in my heart; you have been etched there in love.

Foundations

Why I wrote the book does not need to be why you read the book or what you get out of the book. In fact, I prefer not to tell you what I hope you will receive other than I hope it is healing, transformational, inspiring, and *good*.

There are foundational messages and operating assumptions I want you to know so you can understand a little about me as we take this journey together.

I am aware that all words fall short when talking about what is greater than time and space and what is unquantifiable. I am also aware that poetry, for me, speaks most directly and penetratingly to these mysteries. For these two reasons I use many different words to speak of, or point to, the Uncreated Ground of Being. My favorite word is Beloved, for my own path is a love affair and I have found myself pursued by, embraced in, and supported unceasingly by an all-encompassing God. Where you see the use of a capital, such as Source, Essence, Presence, God, Conscious-ness, it is intentional. My use of many different words reveals many different aspects of the One. Hopefully, it lets you find your own entry point as well.

This language or belief does not have to be your truth for you to experience the magnanimous work of Spirit in this text. I invite you to overlook the words, for I fall short to adequately speak to these mysteries. Let yourself be touched by the power of the events alone. I am not taking a stand for or against how to speak about this Beloved, if speaking about it at all, I am only singing the song that Spirit sang in the form of the project.

The first foundational message contained here is that God (Consciousness or Life Force) is emerging in form in the very process of life, is the Source from which that emergence happens, and is celebrating the awakening of itself to Itself. This emergence contains all sorts of paradoxes. Contrasting words such as *dark* and *light* may engender a desire for one and not the other, but it is in both experiences the Beloved is found. Other words like *good* and *bad* take on a subtle nuance giving way to compassion when we realize that all life is held by God. This divine dance, therefore, has endless distinctions and individuations creating a tapestry of unique expressions of eternal Essence. We are invited to consciously participate in this dance, which is like coming home.

This cosmology existed for me as a monastic, even if my language was quite different than it exists for me now.

This leads to my next foundational message: Everything is grace.

It is a tricky postulation to claim as true. At face value it could be used to diminish, bypass, repress, or deny the human experience of suffering.

Drawing close to life through this statement, however, can reveal a very different kind of reality—one where all the joys and sorrows, manifold blessings, and horrific atrocities are seen and held. And this *being seen and held* opens horizons to new ways of being and seeing.

The title of the book points to this message. I was listening one day to "Sounds of Silence" by Simon and Garfunkel and was struck by the phrase, "and in the naked light I saw."

A certain delight ran through me as I envisioned us all walking around in this world, each one of us open to the reality of being alive in different ways, and existing continuously in naked light. Miracles abound all around us, in naked light. Sometimes we see these miracles, and at other times we do not. In some moments we are surprised at the synchronicities, in other moments we dip into an angst of feeling out of sorts or out of our flow, and at other times, we are so in the flow that we are not surprised but enjoy child-like wonder and joy.

To put it in other words, we walk in this naked light sometimes aware of what is happening and at other times ignorant of the grace that is always present. Realizing that every human being is on this same path and is somewhere along the spectrum of conscious or unconscious participation can open our hearts to a compassion that knows no limits, for we have received it ourselves. We can also rise into the potential of what is possible with God. Our inquiries take on different subtle nuances, leading us down a path of unknowing and dismantling all we thought we knew to reveal a more solid nonverbal knowing which leads to freedom.

The story is not intended to stop there. I hold the sincerest intentions that you will not read the story and think *wow, that was an amazing project*, but rather, I hope you will taste that same miraculous essence inside of you and you will walk more fully awake to the miracles happening in the naked light in your own life.

To see everything as grace was my lens and my inquiry. It was how I wrestled with what was confusing and how I danced with what was exhilarating.

Don't take what I have to say as true, find your truth. Be willing to get naked and throw off your defense. I believe you will discover the essence of everlasting life in some new way that is your own.

The third foundational message: It was Source that accomplished everything. My participation in the project as a nun opened for me this continual experience. Yes, it is quite miraculous that I participated as a young woman with no experience, and that miracle ran through me like a current of eternal light. All of me was ignited, tapping known and unknown parts of my mind, heart, body, and soul. I held no expectation of reward—the reward was in being the instrument and seeing it happen for my community.

Each player in this book had their own unique path. Each player was influenced, as we are, by their beliefs, their conditioning, their development, and their availability. This led each player to participate, more or less, in the miracles that were happening within us and before our eyes.

When we develop the ability to respect the experience of another, we open a door to a true understanding of them, which ultimately leads to greater intimacy. The intimacy may or may not lead us closer to the person, but it always leads us closer to ourselves and to the Beloved.

We are so often in need of encouragement, for life challenges us. Life pushes us toward the edge of our knowing repeatedly, and relief is found by stepping into the unknown, again. I hope this story provides you that encouragement.

Let's wake up together upon the page. Let's be broken open by the story like I was more than twenty-six years ago. Let us together find consolation in the words of Isaiah 55:11 "I will send forth my word to the earth, and it will not return to me void but will accomplish all for which I sent it."

Your friend in the journey,

Kimberly

Prologue

This book starts just two weeks after I had taken solemn vows (vows of consecration for life) as a Carmelite monastic nun. Up to this point I had lived in community in a monastery in North Dakota from my entrance on February 11, 1991, having moved through novitiate (formation) for four and a half years until I was invited to profess my solemn vows on July 16, 1995.

My entrance into the monastic life was met with overwhelming gratitude. For five years leading up to this entrance, my life was like a honeymoon with what I name the Beloved. Rushes of spirit, long states of bliss, miracles, visions, and more had become my daily experience. Illuminations, people shape-shifting into Christ, angels, saints, and guides were just as common. And even more importantly, I was being healed and transformed, and moments became sacraments of the presence of the Beloved. Words are elusive to describe how I was finding myself pursued by the Lover, and being taken up was nothing short of making love with God. To say I was seeking union was not a phrase that was true for me, for I was being sought beyond what my imagination and desire could conjure.

Three years before entering the monastery, Teresa of Avila, Therese of Lisieux, Titus Brandsma, Edith Stein, John of the Cross, and Mary Magdalene de Pazzi all introduced themselves to me through friends giving me books, other friends introducing me through devotionals and stories, and just as much, if not more, through spontaneous prayer. All these individuals are Carmelite, and they quickly became my friends. It was a natural urge to want to be

Carmelite, to join my friends, to open myself to the depth of mystical adventure, and to have more of what was my sole source of happiness, that is, time in solitude with my Love.

I was not let down. The lifestyle of being taken up into Divine Embrace, and poured out as ceaseless prayer for the world, was activated through chant, prayer, meditation, farming, community sharing, and silence. Mysteriously I realized my cocreative assent to the One whose longings are the source of all grace. Together, I was led along a luminous path.

My response to this call left me quite content in North Dakota and I would not have considered leaving if the following vision had not happened. It was the invitation of Mary alone that led me to say yes to leaving my home and traversing into the desert of Texas to join a small group of Carmelites creating a new community there. The following is what happened.

The Encounter with Mary: January of 1995

The floors of our corridors in North Dakota were painted concrete. It was a fascinating pattern, imitating white flagstone, and it always made me smile and think of cows. One long corridor was mine to scrub every week on Tuesday afternoons. Today was that day, so I was on my knees with a small bucket of hot, sudsy water, a cloth the size of a washcloth, and a toothbrush. The toothbrush helped to scrub the edges of the white spots and harnessed my focus on the task. It was never complete; I never made it all the way down the corridor in one day, which gave me the opportunity to let go of any goal. This non-attachment was an incredible source of fun and play for me.

About half an hour into my scrubbing I heard the buzzer coming through the intercom. To assist the community observing silence, each nun had a code and when that code was buzzed, we knew we were being called to the prioress's office. *Buzzzzzz-buzzzzzz-buzzzzz-buzz-buzz*. That was my code!

What happened next is difficult to put into words, as timeless, Spirit-infused moments are for any of us. I will describe it with the hopes you can enter into the energy of the encounter.

I dropped my toothbrush next to the bucket and headed to the office at the end of the corridor. As I walked, my entire inward state shifted, losing a sense of physical boundaries and I became clear and silent, like a large white canvas ready to receive paint. *Knock-knock*, my hand acted of its own accord.

"Come in," the familiar voice of our leader said. It was Mother Gemma who had been elected to be prioress the year before and had formerly been my novice mistress for the first year and a half of my formation as a Carmelite.

My body glided to her desk while she looked at me and stated quite matter-of-factly, "Sister Annunciata, we would like you to consider joining the Texas community after your solemn vows." As she finished the sentence the room became shades of white light and a painted image of Mary that was leaning against another desk came alive. It became only Mary and me in the room, though I was aware of Gemma speaking words as you might be aware of background music happening while you are focused upon something else. Mary communicated to me, "I have a special love for this community. I want you to go, and I promise to carry you," she finished. Her presence and message filled me as a painting takes over a canvas and becomes a beautiful piece of art.

Because of this experience, I did not need to discern a response, but the prioress did not know what had just happened and I didn't feel like telling her. I was dismissed with the encouragement to think and pray about it.

I waited a few weeks until another leader, the nun who was prioress before Gemma, Mother Maria Teresa, asked me if I knew what I wanted to do. She confided that she wanted the monastery closed and did not want me to go for fear I would lose my vocation due to the challenges that had happened over the years of its existence. I did not know what these challenges were at the time and did not have too much concern about them in light of the encounter with Mary. "I believe it is God's will for me to go." Her face sank but she nodded.

The decision was made quickly that my departure would happen on July 27th, six months after the decision and two weeks after my solemn vows.

The six months were rigorous. Mother Maria Teresa gave me a crash course in multiple skills so I could be a support to Mother Gemma. I did not realize they were considering me anything more than a young nun there to scrub toilets and be a dedicated younger sister.

North Dakota was founded (that is the word used when a new community comes into an area and begins to live there) in the late sixties from a group of nuns in Allentown, Pennsylvania. One of the leaders from Pennsylvania was Mother Anna, who remained in leadership throughout her entire life in North Dakota. When I entered in 1991, she was the spiritual director since she had reached an age where she could no longer be the prioress or novice mistress anymore. She still bore a strong influence in the observance of the community. Mother Maria Teresa entered the North Dakota monastery when she was quite young, though this was not uncommon in earlier generations of monastic life. She was in her teens. Because of her natural musical talents, the community was able to preserve the rich musical rituals that Carmelites had enjoyed for hundreds of years. Maria Teresa was also groomed for leadership and became a prioress at a very young age. The two of them were elected year after year for the positions of prioress and/or novice mistress. The latter role takes care of the formation of women who enter all the way up to solemn vows which usually takes place after four and a half years but can be as long as six years into a vocation.

Sister Gemma had moved into leadership as a novice mistress before I entered in 1991. While she was deeply charismatic and loving, she also confided how much she felt like a puppet in her role, carrying out only what she was told. When she was elected as prioress while I was still in formation, it was the first opportunity she had been given to be a leader forming her own style and using her own voice. Early on in my own vocation, we had a special connection that was quite life giving, but this had faded for me after about one year. I avoided her advances to develop a friendship. Part of this was because it felt unhealthy, and part was because it was in opposition to our observance in North Dakota. Her understandable attraction to me came about because Spirit spoke through me once and she was healed of something that had caused her great internal pain. I never knew what this was, but I do remember energy going out from me on the feast of the conversion of St. Paul one year as she left my cell after morning check-in.

Unknown to most of the nuns, including me, the community in Texas was having serious difficulties. The challenges were so great that at one point the leader there had purchased tickets for each sister to fly to their family and dissolve the community altogether. I only learned of these details much later, during my final year as part of the Texas community.

When the North Dakota leadership learned about what was happening, they intervened. Canonically (this is the internal law of the Catholic church), the Texas community was still attached to the mother ship in North Dakota; they had not grown large enough to be autonomous. Once Sister Gemma was elected prioress of North Dakota she took over leadership in Texas as well, making her prioress of both communities. She flew down to Texas and decided she wanted to stay there and only flew back to North Dakota as needed.

My encounter with Mary that I have just shared happened during this time. This double reign of Mother Gemma would last up to the next elections in 1996. The flight of Gemma and me to Texas inaugurated the choice by North Dakota to give Texas a chance to survive, a motive unknown by me. While I knew the former leader had left, I was not told she had joined one of our sister communities. There was an air of heavy mystery around the charismatic woman I had met when she visited the year before. At various moments my heart sank as I heard my leaders speak unkindly to our community about our southern foundation, and each time I would privately defend them without having met them. From where I stood, the community had been through a lot. They had lost their leader, chanced losing their new foundation, and Mary wanted me to go to love them and be their sister. This was enough for me.

Guided Steps into the Unknown

The Fargo airport was an hour's drive from Wahpeton, but it felt like just a few moments. I walked in relative disbelief that I was leaving my North Dakota home. I had just taken my solemn vows (vows for life). My feet were barely touching the ground so much was my state of bliss after my ceremony. In addition, I was absorbed in the magnitude of the change presently happening to which I had given my assent. I have no remembrance of arriving at the airport, checking in, or even getting to our gate. Sister Gemma, the prioress, had made all the arrangements.

I do remember boarding the plane.

Our seats were about halfway down on the right. We buckled ourselves in and said a few spontaneous prayers. Much to my surprise, as the plane began to move, so did my stomach. The years void of travel had caused me to feel uneasy with this unfamiliar movement. *At one point in my life, I had considered being an airline stewardess,* I ruminated, *and now here I am sick on a plane.* Mother Gemma very sweetly reached her hand to take mine into her own and together we entrusted the trip into the hands of Jesus and Mary.

As soon as the plane accomplished its ascent and rested at a cruising altitude, my stomach rested as well. My attention, harbored to land for so long, was taken up into the magnificent views. It was marvelous how new everything felt even though my exit from the world had only been five years prior. I was also a different person than the woman who entered the monastery doors in 1991.

The nonstop flight seemed to end as soon as it had begun, landing in a small Texas airport where a metal staircase on wheels was quickly butted up to the door and latched into place. Eagerly we stepped onto the platform where my breath was literally taken away by the hot, heavy heat that wrapped its arms around us. *At least we are warmly embraced by our new hometown*, I smiled to myself.

There was no wind on this summer day, and no humidity either, only heat all around us. Clad in so many layers of clothes, my 104-pound body felt as heavy as the air around me. *Haaaaah, huhhhhhh, haaaaaah, huhhhhhh,* my inhale and exhale felt as thick as a wool blanket.

Two big joyous grins waited for us at the bottom of the metal stairs. It turned out to be two Carmelite hermits, good friends of Mother Gemma, Father Tomas and Brother Mathias. Mother Gemma's joy escalated and the three of them launched into friendly banter.

I immediately felt a part of the happiness and the four of us laughed and talked without a moment's pause. The warmth of informal conversation stood in stark contrast to the community from which I had just departed, where the decorum was almost always proper and measured and rarely spontaneous. *This moment feels refreshing,* I noticed.

For years as a monastic I had kept my own counsel, preserving my family heritage of playfulness and gumption, inwardly staying true to the essential call to be a person of joy even when the prevailing manner was full of propriety and gravity. In this moment there was no need to be reserved and Mother Gemma's charm and humor drew me in immediately. It seemed in the presence of these brothers she was able to be herself as well.

Father Tomas was foundational to the Texas monastery. He was the driving force bringing the first small group of nuns from North Dakota to create a new community in San Angelo in 1989. He secured the house that the nuns converted into a modest monastery, he offered friendship and counsel every step of the way, and was still here, faithfully supporting the nuns as he poured himself into the development of his own community of male hermits.

There is a helpful distinction to make between his community and the nuns when it comes to what is called observance. An *observance* is the word used to describe how *the life is lived* by a particular community. It includes everything from the larger aspects, like the overarching charism and mission of the religious community, to the way the community is structured with roles and responsibilities, all the way to the smaller aspects of ritual and daily practice.

Father Tomas's community members were, and are, hermits. A hermit usually spends most, and in some cases all, of his or her time alone in abiding contemplation. The word for this lifestyle is *eremitical*. The choices of the community, including where each individual sleeps, what the daily schedule is, and how relationships and work are organized support and encourage the call to silence and solitude as a hermit.

Our community of nuns were eremitical in emphasis with a coenobitical aspect. This means our life was a dance of living in silence and solitude while in community. We would more likely work beside each other but do it without speaking. Our time of meditation usually happened together versus all being in our own cell (the place where we sleep alone). Solitude was still a strong part of the life, but the hermit observes a stricter form of solitude. And our cells were more often dormitory style while hermits would have—this probably will not surprise you—hermitages.

While the ride from the airport was not long, it was late once we made it to our monastery door. Mother Gemma asked Father Tomas to bless us. This is a common practice to receive a blessing from a priest or a superior. A superior is either a teacher, elder, or leader in the community.

We quickly got on our knees as he laid one hand on Gemma's head and one hand on mine. Tears welled up within me as his words evoked a rushing sensation moving through my body and heart bearing a sweetness and peace. I still remember the focus of his words and the conscious choice I made as he spoke. "God, surround and protect these servants, fill them with blessing for this community," he began. My heart opened widely, but this wideness did not last long. As he continued my body contracted tightly, "Give them grace as they save this community and guide the sisters back into the light."

No, no, no, I silently spoke to God, *No. The sisters do not need a savior, I am here to be one with them and them with me. They will be my teachers and my friends, and together we will build a strong community.* I overrode his blessing with my own.

The monastery was a small, converted house, tan colored with a dark roof; the only clear designation of its sacred purpose was a wooden sign that read Our Lady of Grace, Carmelite Monastery. Fitting for this miniature monastery the statues were household size, nestled into corners near rose bushes. The scene was endearing.

As I stood there, flashbacks of childhood came to me of the times when our beds became forts, or the kitchen became a faraway land, or the front yard became a zoo. *This little house made it feel like we were playing monastery*, the thought tickled me.

After our blessing, Mother Gemma rang the bell so the door could be opened for us. Joyful scurrying could be heard, *Oh my gosh, I am finally going to meet these sisters that are mine to love*, I thought.

My heart beat rapidly. Three sisters greeted us like bubbles at the top of a whirlpool, quickly ushering us through the small entry-way.

A speakroom in a monastery is the place visitors enter to meet with the nuns or leave items. It is called such because it is the one room where nuns within the monastery (called a cloister) can speak by entering an adjacent room. There is an open space in the dividing wall the size of a super wide window allowing for an in-person meeting.

For centuries this opening had an iron grate called a grille and even a curtain that would sometimes be pulled back and at other times left in place, stressing the separation between the consecrated nun and visitor. The division was an outward symbol of the nun's commitment to a life set apart from the normal rhythms of society and wholly devoted to prayer, meditation, and silence in service of the world.

The joy carried us like a raft on a stream down the short, dark hallway into a large room that served as our refectory. It was about ten-by-twenty feet, so quaint compared to North Dakota where the refectory loomed like a large conference hall. The back wall had large windows creating a pleasant connection with the acres of open land behind our home. The sun had already set, but the dark night sky of stars and the shafts of light bouncing off the grass made their way through the windows. It occurred to me that most my evenings in North Dakota were void of the night sky and all at once my time there, for close to five years, felt incredibly insulated compared to this new home.

At first my joy met my sisters with a sense of unboundedness. Then a disturbing jolt took place. I looked over to meet smiles with Mother Gemma, but she did not have a smile on her face, her brow was furrowed, and a frown had replaced the smile I had just enjoyed for the past hours. The dramatic difference between our time with Father Tomas and this moment caused chills to ride up my spine. I had no idea how to interpret the Jekyll and Hyde behavior before me and my gut revolted, making me want to leave. The instant was like a warning flag, although no one else in the community paid attention, or perhaps they ignored the cold, distant way she stood there.

Standing there silently aghast, my memory flashed to the day I experienced Mary, and I renewed my yes to coming here. *My call is to be a source of joy in the community, to pour myself out in love, and to create playfulness*, I said to myself. There is nothing keeping me from putting my youthful energy into this service since I was twenty-plus years younger than my sisters. This freed me of my distress.

Sister Elisha had very sweetly made me not one but two of the best cheese sandwiches I think I had ever had, with cheddar cheese, soft bread, mayonnaise, and tomatoes. I devoured both sandwiches partly out of hunger and partly out of overwhelming emotion.

She had been a part of the monastery up north when I was there but had decided to join the community in Texas. She longed to be chosen as a leader; it was a desire that had gone unfulfilled in the larger mother house.

Sisters Elizabeth and Catherine were the other two nuns standing before me. I felt I already knew them through the letters they wrote to us when I was in North Dakota. Meeting Sister Catherine felt like I was finally meeting a true mystic; how I admired her from her letters where she spoke of her deep contemplation as she would sweep the floor.

Not long after our welcome visit I was escorted about fifteen short steps, from the refectory through the kitchen. The left side had a stove and the right had two sinks. The kitchen door had been open during our visit letting cool air come through a screen. The monastery did not have air conditioning or fans even though we were in the desert.

The Texas night brushed my face with a balmy kiss and open skies cast their shining lights like a tapestry falling behind the covered corridor. The dormitory was a separate building from the house, added on shortly after the nuns had moved in about six years prior. It felt like summer camp as we made our way the short distance to the wing.

Three doors faced the sidewalk; mine would be the middle door considered the novitiate though we had no novices, and I was no longer a novice. I didn't mind as it gave me my own personal wing, which meant I could use the bathroom without having to get dressed to leave my cell. Each door facing the outdoor corridor opened to a collection of four cells, two on each side of the hallway, and one bathroom that was a straight walk down the hall from the outside door.

There was an added joy to being relegated to the novitiate wing. My dear friend Therese of Lisieux (a nineteenth century French Carmelite nun) never left the novitiate (and unknown to me then, this would be the case for me as well).

My cell was the second door down the hall on the left and offered me a large window looking out onto the open land. The furnishings mimicked North Dakota: a low bed sitting upon wooden boards which in turn sat upon sawhorses about eighteen inches high, a small metal desk with a wooden chair, and a set of four small shelves. The mattresses were thin and flat, keeping things austere and simple.

Even though exhaustion led my feet immediately to bed, the first night was sleepless. The thick hot air hung like a wet blanket all around me. The wing had been built without air conditioning, probably due to cost and the intention to build the permanent monastery. Lying there, alternating between casting the sheets off for coolness, which felt uncomfortable not to have covering, to covering back up, which would trap the hot air against my body, the night hours wore on with sleep eluding me.

It was comical. *Who would have known??* I thought. Night after night the sleeplessness wore on until my lightheartedness gave way to tired wandering thoughts, *Will I ever sleep again??? No, no, it is just a matter of time.* My mind persisted in seeing a way through. Acceptance. I accepted what was, and peace was mine whether I slept or not.

Without any noticeable change, change happened. Just like children grow up before your eyes fast as lightning, so change happens without formal assent. After about two weeks slumber fell upon me, pulling me back into the sweet rhythms of my body.

Texas life was simple compared to the complex observance of North Dakota. It was surprising to me how much it felt like a breath of fresh air considering how much I loved the layers that formed the daily routines of the latter. What influenced the observance in Texas most dramatically was the ways the monastic practices were adapted to the size of the tiny, converted house, and the smaller number of nuns who were older in age and not as able to keep rigorous practices.

One morning kneeling in our choir before lauds the warm Texas air rolled through the screen door. *The screen door,* I thought. *Oh my gosh, I am living a monastic life meditating in a converted garage with a screen door allowing the sweet songs of birds to accompany me.* Deep love for both lifestyles existed in my heart. It remained easy to sing the love of North Dakota's rich life of ritual where all the senses were involved while simultaneously expanding into a more Zen, Buddhist-like monastic life. The smaller space, instead of suffocating me, refashioned me, creating larger spaces within, shifting attention from detailed observance to presence.

What was even more of a surprise was that my body and heart expanded into the simplicity. There was an inner awareness that I would never go back to the complexity of North Dakota.

Years of unnoticed pressures from North Dakota's rigors washed out of me. I had not realized what was being held within from the years of consistent effort, keeping a tight sense of time and duty while rarely being given a moment's rest. There were two days a year when we were given a window of free time that usually lasted about one to two hours. In my youthful zeal seeking every opportunity to be poured out as love for Love, I did not know my body held a tightness that could now be released.

The schedule of prayer and meditation were the same, but the time in between was organized dramatically different. What tasks and when you did them would be defined down to ten minutes up north, while how you organized your time in Texas was entrusted to you, so long as you accomplished the roles and tasks assigned to you.

As the only one with substantial musical ability, the role of liturgist was given to me. We did not have a piano or pipe organ, but we did have an electric organ and a guitar. The former was an acceptable instrument for Liturgy and the latter was relegated to any songs sung outside of chapel. Admittedly, this assignment gave me great joy. It was quite a privilege to accompany these sisters who had developed the ability to chant intricate tones even though they were not musicians.

Our recreations were always filled with joy. This was the one time of day we would all sit and talk and enjoy time together freely. The interests of my older sisters there in Texas were vastly different from the topics of my novice years with women my age; most of our topics had held mild interest for me. This gave me the chance to let go of my own desires and contributions and devote all my attention to entering into the interests and joys of my sisters. Our evenings became ones of service. And even more than service, I practiced entering so deeply into the interests of others that they became my own, and the sweetness of finding the Divine in all resulted.

Our schedule was as follows:

>Midnight Matins (vigil prayer)
>6:00 a.m. Lauds (morning prayer)
>6:30-7:30 Morning meditation
>7:30 Liturgy
>8:30 Breakfast if we were not fasting
>9:00 Terce (midmorning prayer)
>9:30 Work and/or spiritual reading
>11:15 Sext (midday prayer)
>11:45 Dinner (main meal)
>2:00 p.m. None (midafternoon prayer)
>2:30-4:30 Work
>4:30 Vespers (evening prayer)

    5:00-6:00 Evening meditation
    6:00 Supper (small repast)
    7:30 Recreation
    8:30 Compline (night prayer)

In monastic life there is always some kind of celebration, because the year was a standing schedule of rituals falling even if you are celebrating ordinary time (a time that bridges between seasons like Christmas and Easter). However, feast days were days of special attention.

Over and again the layers of feasts and remembrances of sacred moments, people, and places harnessed my attention to some aspect of God. It formed in me a heightened awareness of the sacredness of each moment and the insight that all that is needed to experience sacredness is opening to it, becoming aware of it, and participating in it.

Feast days were of many varieties. Some are celebrated by all Christians, like Christmas and Easter. Some, like the Transfiguration, are celebrated by many because of the basis of the story coming from the Bible; some were particularly Carmelite just for the Order, and the rest were particularly ours, like the celebration of one of our sisters' religious names.

My first feast day was the Transfiguration about nine days after joining the community. I loved this day because of what it taught me about impermanence.

The feast day name, Transfiguration, is inspired by the passage in the Bible where Jesus takes John and Peter to a mountain to pray and before their eyes he becomes as bright as white light, while Elijah and Moses appear in luminous form on both sides of him. It is so glorious for Peter that he says to Jesus, "Lord, it is good to be here; let us erect three tents." A dark cloud appears that represents God, the Divine, and Jesus's friends are struck with fear even though the message coming from the cloud is one of consolation.

The moment ends, like all moments do, and Jesus shifts back to his normal appearance and descends the mountain with his friends.

How often in my own life, I reflected during the feast day like I often did, *do I want a special moment to go on without ending, or at least to go on for longer than it does? And how often do I grasp after or try to hold onto the occasion, whether it is an ecstatic inner state or a happy moment with a loved one, which only creates tension?* My own life was intimate with loss from an early age, and it created an awareness in me that losing something wonderful can be painful. The adjustment is tough, whether the loss is a big one, like when I lost my grandma when I was three, or the loss of something much smaller like the end of a party filled with love. I was no stranger to the many times I held onto something when it needed to be let go, holding on for all the right reasons even if the only reason that mattered indicated it was time to let go.

That feast day also left me reflecting on how far I had come. How much my own development had eased into the deeper freedom of realizing that those special moments increased my capacity to experience other moments to be sacred as well, rather than minimize or trivialize them.

The day seemed to be filled with all sorts of new joys. It was the first feast day to witness Sister Catherine's joy cooking for our community. When the Mass ended, I glanced over at her, even though I was supposed to be rapt in reflection with eyes closed, and saw her face infused with joy. I could not resist watching her. With spring in her step, she genuflected to leave the chapel to prepare breakfast, whirling to get to the kitchen. If she wasn't bound to keep silence, I think she would have giggled with glee.

Not long after, we processed (walking quietly while reciting a psalm) to the refectory. Catherine had loaded the table with special goodies like butter, homemade coffee cake, jam, cream, and honey, festively arranged on our Formica table. She was confident and humble as she bustled to get the fresh-made coffee to the table. This woman had lived monastic life since she was sixteen, which meant she was close to sixty years as a nun, and she was a shining example of the newness of life that comes from an innocent heart.

Quick prayers flew from our mouths, plates were loaded, and within moments Mother Gemma rang the bell for table recreation. For some reason it surprised me, it always did. Even though there was no obligation for the leader to ring the bell for us to speak during our normally silent meals, it was predictable that feast days were days we spoke at table. I had developed a strong habit of not expecting certain liberties, or holding longings either, however, which meant I was always surprised, like a child opening a gift they had longed to receive.

My small community of nuns felt like a ragtag collection of miscellaneous quilt pieces, all different shapes, colors, and textures, thrown together to figure out life in community. Our personal call to be Carmelite drew each of us together for a noble purpose and included an implicit invitation to connect with and embrace each other as sisters. Impressions quickly came to me. Elizabeth was a living smile; even when she was sad or stressed, a smile occupied the majority of her face. She walked with a gait that was both exuberant and unexpected. Perhaps it was that her veil would oftentimes be a bit off, communicating an air of, *I just came from digging for hours with both hands in the garden and didn't have time to freshen up,* as she entered the chapel. Sister Catherine was quiet yet anchored strong like a pillar going deep into the earth. Her expression could be both sweet and fiery in the same glance. Mother Gemma was charismatic and quick-witted, and I was getting to see her act from a new-found place of confidence and freedom there in Texas. Sister Elisha felt more hidden. She seemed deeply reflective, taking everything in, and she held a reserved stature most of the time. It felt like she was holding discontentment, but I couldn't tell for sure until we gathered to plan our first feast day celebration for Mother Gemma which happened soon after the Transfiguration.

Mother Gemma's full consecrated name was Mother Gemma of the Angels, and her special day was celebrated on September 30th. I had no idea it was the custom to privately prepare a special day for her, and even less realization that I would be asked to lead these meetings. The tradition was exciting. We were given the freedom to create an entire day to honor her in any way we chose. The first evening Catherine, Elizabeth, and I waited for Elisha to join us in one of the offices. About five minutes late, she came in with her face set and sat abruptly down into a chair with arms crossed. I felt a little shudder move through me. It seemed that she was not happy I was given the role to lead the meeting, but we were not given permission to talk for me to know for sure.

I had my pen and paper and opened the discussion, "What would we like to do? Who has ideas?" Catherine and Elizabeth started speaking at once while Elisha stared. As I was writing down their ideas and adding on to them, Elisha made a loud, *Hmmmmph.* "I'm not going to put up with this," she blurted out, stood up, and abruptly left the room, shutting the door loudly.

I was shaken, and returned to the thought that it was because of me that she was upset. I asked Mother Gemma if Elisha and I could talk. "No, you have to trust the silence and that God is working," she said. This felt entirely wrong; the unspoken tension had the makings to result in even greater discord.

Thinking to myself, *If she and I could talk I could hear what it was that she wanted and she could hear that I wanted her to be happy. I want her to know that I did not choose to lead, and if this was the source of her unhappiness, I am sorry.* I asked my Love to communicate this to her if I was not permitted to use my own words. This did not happen. Each meeting before Gemma's feast day I would strive to support *any* idea Elisha might have in a gesture of showing her she mattered. The more I tried to serve Elisha the more she became irritated. My heart beat rapidly with the stress of each meeting, while I preserved the spirit of excitement as the project lead. *How am I going to persevere through the years if this only gets worse?* I regretfully worried.

Texas may have been void of luscious green leaves and chocolate-like soil for crops like North Dakota, but it was overflowing with dusty paths hosting cacti, mesquite trees, and bristly plants that needed very little water, and was bathed in broad blue skies, open land, and pleasant air. The arid land felt wave-like as it spilled out behind our monastery; it mirrored the wave-like movement of the chant we offered hour after hour.

For the first time in years, I had contact with men in our cloister almost every week. They would assist us with our long to-do list. Our faithful workforce was led by a man named Roy, who would show up late morning. Gemma would open the gate for them, and they would tumble into the back full of laughter and comments. You could hear them talking about their families, dogs, hunting, and just about every other topic as they tackled the to-do list we kept regularly updated.

Since I was working in the kitchen with Catherine preparing our main meal, it quickly became my personal duty to be sure they were hydrated and well-fed. This task was unnerving and delightful at the same time. I hadn't been around men in years, other than the yearly visits from my dad.

"Hello," I quietly said as I carried a tray overloaded with sandwiches, lemonade, and cookies.

"Well," Roy took charge, "Hello! You must be Sister Annunciata," and he quickly introduced me to everyone. I had no idea what to do next, *Do I engage conversation? Do I exit quickly?* As a naturally outgoing person I was torn between what would be my idea of what was charitable and what might be the protocol as a Carmelite. Since I was not given advice either way, I decided to follow what was charitable and respond with openness to them.

They immediately dug into the lunch while asking me questions. "Wow, these are the best sandwiches ever!" one of the workmen exclaimed. After the initial uncertainty, and the awkwardness of using my voice to talk with men, joy resulted.

Day after day communication grew. We didn't talk for long, maybe ten minutes, but what a rich ten minutes they would be. They would talk about their families, or how the job they were doing for us was going, we would undoubtedly laugh, and words began to brightly flow from me. This return to conversation touched a place within myself that I had let go. Like playing a piano after a ten-year hiatus or riding a bike after years of walking, exhilarating sensations ran through me as I remembered a part of life before the monastery.

Unconsciously my soul began to sing again the melody of joyous conversation and new friends. I took a certain pride that we nuns would open ourselves to build relationships with our community. We did this in many ways, one of which was to be the host place for our Hispanic community to celebrate their rituals with all the trimmings. One big ritual was the feast of Our Lady of Guadalupe on December 12th. The day before, our doors would remain open into the evening so they could set up pedestals of roses and other decorations to honor this apparition of Mary that happened in Mexico in 1531. The songs would all be traditional to their customs, beginning before dawn the morning of the feast. Our speakroom turn (a turn is a large wooden turn style with shelves to pass items from the visitor's side to the nun's side without seeing each other) would be filled with homemade tamales, slow cooked chili verde, and fresh baked delicacies. It didn't take long for my 104-pound body to plump up to 130.

The only downside to this level of intimacy was the imbalance it introduced into our monastic schedule. We did not have a nun dedicated to be our daily connection with all our local friends.

Who would guess that such a simple sound like a doorbell could become a distraction, yet it did. Starting after Mass and sometimes going as late as 9 p.m., the button outside our door would begin its reverberating *diiiing-doooooong*, echoing for moments, bouncing through each corner of the house. Since we did not have an internal speaker system, the bell was rigged to ring even into the separate dormitory and sidewalk area around the perimeter. *Diiiiing-*

dooooooooong, friend after friend seeking prayer, benefactor after benefactor donating to us, a stream of talking ensued most days in the small room. We valued each one of them, loved them dearly. They were why we were here, and our role was to support them with our presence and our prayer. Yet, it was exhausting at times because our home was not designed to keep the sounds contained.

Sister Gemma, as leader of the community, would immerse herself in the flurry of visits that would happen after Mass while we ate our breakfast with the joyful noise floating through the thin walls. The echoes simultaneously punctuated our silence and excluded us from the conversation.

At first, I resisted the sound, it felt like an intrusion upon recollected space. A certain protectiveness of our silence rose up in me. However, it did not take long for my inner guidance to interrupt the ways I was taking up my sword, *God's will is what IS and my union with God is within my hands, just accept what IS.*

The acceptance reframed the reverberating conversations. They became like a backdrop to my own reflection, like an orchestra might paint the tapestry of sound upon which the aria might fly. My vows created such an inward flexibility.

It wasn't ultimately about the vows themselves though there was a sensible shift in every cell of my being for both my simple and solemn ceremonies. They were the container that amplified my focus, attention, and surrender. All people coming across my path were part of the Divine plan, all duties were the vehicle giving me the chance to love God alone; all circumstances were mysteriously ordained, and it was my journey to unearth the Presence in all its power and beauty. My Beloved was all that could be found.

Before entering the monastery, this lived perspective became my daily bread due to my mystical experiences; the veils of reality were oftentimes pulled back to reveal deeper truths to me through the moments of my day. However, my vows created in me the uninterrupted knowing and disposition. Nothing was outside of this formal consecration.

When some event did not make sense, the natural question was not *Why?* but rather, *How?* is God working.

How liberating it was in that moment to look at the speakroom noise through this lens. Why it was loud was not really any of my business. But the personal questions between me and the Beloved were imperative to how I handled myself and the situation. *What are you asking of me my Beloved? How can I respond from a place of Presence?* This was my set of questions that provided answers that truly satisfied my soul's desire for peace and shifted the energy to a path of joy.

This direct experience revealed to me that each one of us has the capacity to look at life this way, that is, we must learn to stay very close to what we really want, and then to ask the kinds of questions that give us the kinds of answers that will provide peace, freedom, and joy.

It did not have to happen through vows like mine, I reflected. The only ingredient needed was a dynamic and vital assent to the relationship between self and Source. Within this stance, I found, over and again, all secondary relationships to be illumined by Source.

I have found over the years that monastic life is romanticized to be a peaceful and easy life. A life that is relieved from all the stresses of society. There is some truth there. The lifestyle is constructed to take care of survival needs and to provide a rich fertile environment for the deeper experience to take place. But when it comes to challenges, the opposite is true. Renowned Carmelite Teresa of Avila talks at length in her writings about how the greatest challenges come to those who are on the path to true realization. To encounter the hidden places of the self takes courage. In monastic life you are with yourself, in silence.

Life is laid bare. We can hide from ourselves even in silence, but in such a devotionally oriented community, what we are below the surface shows up. It could be easy to believe that what is below the surface is only scary, but what is below the surface is also more beautiful than could possibly be put into words. All the aspects of ourselves come forward and there is nowhere to go except where we are. It is a rigorous life. While this aspect of the lifestyle was not my primary reason for entering the monastery, I loved it. It was so attractive to think I could encounter myself day in and day out and encounter the Divine day in and day out. Alone. If I lost my peace inside, it may have been prompted because something external triggered me, but I am the only reason I remained without peace.

One morning Mother Gemma asked me to join her in the speakroom to meet two visitors who were sisters, Claire and Sandy Schmidt. It was my first time being invited to go from the speakroom din being the background to my cooking and cleaning, to being part of the din itself.

The door opened to these two sisters sitting quietly and respectfully on the chairs. Physically they didn't look like sisters until they said hello with mirrored exuberance. Yes, they were siblings. Claire struck me as articulate and driven; Sandy seemed gracious and creative. Both were clearly and deliberately generous. Even though Claire would become integral to our fundraising down the road, the next few years would be a time of becoming friends with Sandy.

Conversation overflowed. The sisters shared about their husbands and children, their faith, and their connection to the community. The Schmidt family line were longtime ranch owners in San Angelo, huge forces in the community, and very strong Catholics. They were deeply passionate about everything in their lives, including us.

One of Sandy's loves was cooking. Her face would light up as she described the meals she spent days preparing for her family. She hesitatingly offered an idea: "Could I cook an entire meal for your community? It could be for one of your feast days."

"Of course!" Mother Gemma responded happily while my own face silently mirrored the same sentiment.

Her first meal arrived the night before one of our feast days. She needed to bring it early so the main dish could be in the refrigerator overnight to be ready for the oven the next day. The doorbell rang about 7 p.m. and there stood Sandy giddily holding her first load. She never prepared less than a feast that could feed ten hungry mouths even though we were only five light eaters.

"For the main dish, I prepared brie strata," Sandy proudly told us. We had no idea what she was talking about, and the wrapped casserole pan she presented swished with liquid reaching close to the edges. "So, this dish is made with dried bread broken into cubed pieces scattered alongside pieces of brie broken across the bottom of the baking dish. I whipped eight eggs by hand, added whole milk and salt, then added basil leaves, torn in half by hand to unleash the seasoning, and poured the mixture into the casserole dish." She happily explained each dish prepared before setting it upon the turn. Her love was palpable.

Her next extraordinary culinary surprise was pumpkin stew. Inside the carved-out pumpkin, vegetables and seasonings floated in a sea of milk and blue cheese. I gasped with wonder. I can still remember her sweet explanation of her stew. "In the morning you will need to take it out of the oven, then at 10 a.m. take out all but the bottom rack in the oven and preheat to 200 degrees. Place the pumpkin on a cookie sheet in the oven and leave it to cook for one hour without opening the door to look. After one hour remove the pumpkin, take off the cap, and very slowly stir the ingredients. Scrape the sides lightly, letting only the layer of pumpkin that is cooked to be pulled into the milk. Replace the pumpkin and cook another half hour." She carefully explained the incremental steps. The pumpkin was so heavy it took both Catherine and me to lift it out of the oven. She was not alone in offering us such tenderness; it would have been quite difficult to doubt divine providence with the loving solicitude coming to us each day through our friends.

Monastic communities are usually hoping new women will discover the lifestyle and find themselves called to join. Many times, this process happens through word of mouth or when a woman lives in a community where a monastery exists. More frequently over the years women find monasteries through brochures, websites, or even directories.

Usually there are two parts to the call. The first is the experience of a call to monastic life and second a call to a particular community because of its charism or its practices. The charism is the defining mission and vision of a particular order such as Carmelite, Franciscan, Dominican, or Benedictine (just to name a few).

A conversation begins between the interested woman and the leader of the community or designated nun. During my years this happened through handwritten letters, phone calls, and visits. I am not sure how we let the world know of our existence since I was not involved, but it seemed we almost always had some correspondence going on.

If Mother Gemma discerned a potential vocation, she would invite them to visit for a couple days. They would not join us in the monastery but would rather join us in long conversations in the speakroom. During my six years with the community, I remember five women trying the lifestyle and one of them moving all the way through solemn vows.

Privately I wondered if we were in a place to accept new women, because with the unbalanced lifestyle and makeshift cloister it was not an optimal experience. Then again, I had come from a well-established community that impressed upon me an image of what monastic rhythm was meant to be.

One woman's letters gave Mother Gemma a deep sense of sincerity and prompted her to come for a visit. To my surprise I was invited to join Gemma in the interview process. I remember the day she crossed our threshold and greeted us. Her solid framed figure was already cloaked in the postulant garb of brown skirt and white shirt.

She had a matronly presence though her conversation revealed a younger woman with a low voice.

The morning visit sped by, so we planned to reconvene for lunch. The second conversation lasted for quite a long time and its impressions even longer. Her personal journey was filled with Spirit and grace. I found myself hoping she would choose us, and we would choose her. The tenderness of her devotion was steady and her stories of God's grace in her life moved me to tears.

During a pause her voice haltingly interjected, "I have some-thing… uh…. important to tell you." Looking down at her folded hands her body tensed as she set herself to speak. My body welled up slightly, feeling the emotional vulnerability. "I grew up as a boy," her face now red as she burst forward, "but felt all my life that I was really a girl," tears now in her eyes. Her courageous disclosure drew my chest wide open along with her while division filled the space as Mother Gemma bristled and contracted. "It was torturous to go through high school and feel like my body didn't express me," she went on. A tear ran down her cheek, evoking a tear down mine as well, like a mirror. The story went on, leading finally to details about her sex change. What a courageous woman. All night I tried to put myself in her shoes, to feel what it would be like to question your own gender and sexuality.

Mother Gemma didn't connect to her courage; instead, she closed off. The loneliness of our private exchange that night after the visit wrapped itself around me. My own desire to talk about her courage, to touch the heart of her dilemma and her choice, was buried beneath Gemma's bias.

The reflective night brought us into a morning, and still no deep dialogue about her visit. I prepared to go into the speakroom to have our second day of visits with her already knowing the discussion was over. Perhaps she felt it too. Awkwardly we all sat down. During the night I had prayed to somehow convey to her my sentiments without opposing my superior. The moment came and a few words flowed from my lips. It was unclear whether she heard my heart as it was overshadowed by the emotion coming from Mother Gemma denying her desire to join us.

It was a dilemma that caused me great stress. What do I do around my desire for meaningful conversation about this person and their call? I was being required to silently stand behind a decision that I did not agree with and seemed to be coming from a place of prejudice. I had been invited into the discernment but went unheard in private and was denied a voice when we met her.

My emotions stirred me, *We were there in the world to be love, where was the love? We were the last ones that should stand in a place of judgment.* My thoughts were not revolving around whether she was called or not, but around the narrowed way we addressed the whole question of her vocation. Her sex change was *the deciding factor*, instead of it being a factor among many, and the magnitude of her courage to share openly with us was brushed aside and never discussed between Sister Gemma and me.

It was one of the first times I encountered loneliness in my life of solitude.

That evening after Compline with its chant, reading, reflection on the day, and closing chant devoted to Mary, the final knock by Mother Gemma signaled us to kneel on the ground and kiss our scapular before rising to proceed to bed. The scapular was given to one of Carmel's leaders in 1251 by Mary to assure him the Order would make it through its rough times.

I left the chapel in the procession but returned to play the organ and sing once all were in their cells. It was my way to release emotions and have unstructured time. That night I played and cried until it felt the tears were complete.

Late-night music was good for my soul. The workload was heavy, and the days were short. But in this small gap of time, I could enjoy a feeling of freedom. Sometimes I would even dance since no one was around. Spontaneous prayer rose up through me, abounding sometimes all the way to matins at midnight.

Smiles arose from my legs, my gut, my heart, my shoulders, and my face as it bent backward in gratitude. It was a secret rendezvous of lovers, holding themselves back all day, then flinging themselves into each other's arms once they had privacy. *Ah, my Beloved providing for all I needed again.* I would flip through my charismatic song books that had come with me into the monastery and play every song that resonated.

It seemed impossible to quench the divine thirst rising within me at each phrase. The words would rise like a tidal wave, then subside into a receding shoreline. This would go on for hours.

With Therese of Lisieux my soul cried out, "O Lord your love has gone before me, it has carried me, and now it is an abyss whose depths I cannot fathom, my Lord my love leaps up to you…" (*The Story of a Soul, The Autobiography of Therese of Lisieux*, Chapter nine.)

Another page, another book, an old hymnal with prayers sounding more like marching tunes, another page, another book, a perusal of love songs written in North Dakota.

"Mary how sweetly falls that word, on my enraptured ear… oft do I sing in accents low that song when none are near…" Starting off as a whisper, feeling the tones move out into the cosmos, climbing higher and building momentum, "sing oh my soul and loudly proclaim," and yes, loudly my voice proclaimed, "O Mary, O Mary how sweet is thy name…" (Anonymous. St Basil Hymnal)

It would not be long before I would imitate my dad whose everlingering song contained lyrics that were nonsensical, or at least made up on the spot. Phrases gushed, making me laugh to know Mary heard me and enjoyed this silly love gesture. Sometimes the made-up lines had poetic merit and a fleeting thought arose, *write them down so you can sing them again*, which never happened; it would have turned the moment of presence into a moment of record.

This nighttime communion left me feeling how much I was living as a mother to all. I could feel the line taken from our Constitutions:

"A Carmelite's heart holds all the joys and sorrows, the hopes and disappointments of all humanity." The first day I received this Carmelite book, that broke open the meaning of how to live our Carmelite rule, this one line became my mantra. So much so, I wrote it on a piece of scrap paper and kept it on my metal desk all my years.

Not long after our transgender candidate visited, Mother Gemma told me another woman had been writing with interest in being Carmelite. Since she was both prioress (leader of the community) and novice mistress (leader of the formation of new women up until their solemn vows), she rarely confided to us nuns about interested candidates.

It was exciting to think we were going to have another visitor. Her name was Donna. She arranged to spend a weekend in town, joining us in the visitor side of the chapel each day during our many hours of prayer, meditation, and chant, and then meeting in the speakroom primarily with Gemma (but a few times with me). Donna was well established in her career as a nurse. Mother Gemma felt she had enough internal movements of Spirit that it warranted a postulancy, while I learned about the process silently. *Postulancy* is the time when the woman lives as part of the community, and everyone gets to see how it goes. There is no long-term commitment at this point.

Aspects of the monastic life held challenges for her from the start. Our life had an established rhythm along with steadfast practices that were aligned with our vows of poverty, chastity, and obedience. The prioress was the only one among us who could talk anywhere she saw fit, and for the most part we followed all her choices.

Gemma was quite busy and asked me to oftentimes be the point person for Donna, suggesting I act as assistant novice mistress. This was dreadfully uncomfortable for me. It meant I had to be in the hierarchical structure, which I could accept so long as I was the one who followed and not the one who directed or led.

Donna proved to be a powerful teacher for me. She asked direct questions, giving witness to a self-realized woman who had navigated her life as a professional and one responsible for her choices.

One day she knocked on my office door, her mind clearly distressed. We stood before each other as she laid out her first concern about this life. It revolved around the vow of poverty. She hadn't realized what this vow meant. "You mean you give up all your possessions by giving them to family, friends, or the monastery?" she asked with alarm. "Is this right to give up all I have worked hard to establish and create? What if something happens to me as a Carmelite and I leave, and then, I don't have any money to take care of myself?" Her voice betrayed the deep emotion within her heart.

It was a fair question. It was a big deal for her to hand it all over. Her quandary evoked great respect from me and got me thinking. I was incredibly happy to live this vow, so my experience was radically different. I loved the surrender and trust it took to know I would be taken care of by God in non-societal ways through my order. My soul sang like John of the Cross:

"Mine are the heavens and mine is the earth. Mine are the nations, the just are mine, and mine the sinners. The angels are mine, and the Mother of God, and all things are mine; and God himself is mine and for me, because Christ is mine and all for me. What do you ask, then, and seek, my soul? Yours is all of this, and all is for you" (from John of the Cross, Sayings of Light and Love).

Donna didn't see it that way. She shed light on how powerful the gift of ownership is in our process here on earth, not as a crutch, but as a right. Her concerns were valid. Inspired by her I reflected, *Does one need to give up material things, and even take a vow where ownership only happens communally to experience the type of spiritual abundance spoken of in the poem?*

I could only say for sure what was so for me. "Donna, this is a path that is a calling, and where there is a calling, there is grace," I put out there. "All paths are unique and holy, so there is not a right or a wrong but those of us in vows have felt that saying yes would give us freedom in new spiritual ways."

It wasn't clear whether she felt any better and I was uncertain whether what I said was said well enough or was felt as support. It could have just felt like, "That's the way it is," though this was not what I meant.

Not long after this conversation, a disturbing moment happened for us all. It was a normal evening in the refectory transitioning from Vespers and evening meditation to our light meal. One observance we had was to kneel in the refectory to acknowledge personal failings to the community and receive some kind of reparative act as decided by Mother Gemma. This practice jolted my psyche when I first entered but in time had become playful, a gentle act of being reminded we are all weak and we all fail every day. Acknowledging failures publicly gave me an opportunity to develop non-attachment and ease around ideas of self and image.

The practice was understandably challenging for Donna, a truly self-made woman, to accept, and this evening was particularly challenging for us all. Sister Elizabeth was kneeling in our refectory, ready to acknowledge some minor failing. We all stood there expecting her to speak and Mother Gemma to respond without much ado as things normally went.

Mother Gemma's face grew intense and red. She began to speak harshly to Elizabeth, railing her for this failing without ceasing. Her fingers were looped in her leather belt which sat somewhat low as her belly jutted over it slightly. The words continued and I could feel Elizabeth sinking in her heart; my entire body was bristling, and tears were welling up in my eyes. The harsh words continued as we all stood there in shock.

Each phrase subjected us to riding her internal wave of anger as it hit the shore of this woman kneeling before us. My stomach began to sink, my heart ached, and it seemed all of us were becoming gravely sad at what was happening, but we all stood there out of obedience.

It was terrible and I stood there feeling powerless. We had been trained that this was part of God's will to accept what your leader did and how she did it. Generally, each of us felt unreserved patience with our leaders, recognizing that so much was on their shoulders, and when they were edgy or impatient it was only due to all they were doing for us.

I began to question, *What could I do? Could I break silence and stop her?*

Mother Gemma continued as Elizabeth's body slowly bent forward, and her face grew more ashen.

Grave silence.

No one moved.

Eventually we moved, following Mother Gemma's lead to dish up our meal.

But it was not possible to taste the food, I could barely put anything on my plate. My eyes followed Sister Elizabeth in hopes they could reach out and hug her.

Not long after the meal was done, as we were doing dishes, Donna pulled my arm to speak with me in the office. The door had hardly shut before her face turned red, "How could I stay when that happened? You mean if I take vows, I am submitting to THAT?!"

I wanted to say, "What happened was not okay," then I remembered that I was there to help her decide what she wanted to do.

Her justified anger triggered my own growing dilemma; the only difference between us was that I was already in solemn vows. Her anger was refreshing. "When we take vows," I commented from experience, "we trust that God is working for our good; we trust that all will be well even as the darker sides of humanity show themselves."

It felt like she wanted me to say something that would help her have peace about what just happened, but what happened was not okay. Our silence as a community was not because we thought it was okay, but because our practice was to accept what our leader decided. I felt a terrible divide within me between our custom that had me excuse or let it go and charity, which ignited a desire to stand up for Elizabeth.

"No," she admitted, "I cannot believe that level of submission is a good thing."

Resignation replaced the anger on her face. "I understand Donna, truly," my heart-wrenched words reached out to her. Inwardly, doubt crept up leaving me wondering if I navigated the moment with wisdom.

Donna stayed another few months then left us shortly before Thanksgiving, unable to reconcile our practices to what she believed was best for herself. She was a prime example of exploring possibility, finding truth, and then staying faithful to make her choices accordingly. She was a true teacher for me.

At this point Gemma's outbursts happened occasionally and were generally unexpected. She seemed to be struggling deeply. I could see her growing tired and irritable, but I did not think it was appropriate for me, as a young nun, to open this conversation with her at first. One day, while working in the main office filing papers, I heard, like the whisper of an angel, "Soon she will direct her anger toward you." As a new addition to the community, brought down at her bidding, she expressed only kindness to me up to this point. I was a bit rustled by the whisper and wondered, *If this happens what can I do as a young, vowed nun?*

One way I knew I could support her was by making her feast day as special as possible. And this day turned out to be just that with love notes on her stall, the refectory decorated, and special flowers placed near her napkin. We had all learned a charismatic song from one of my songbooks, to open the Mass, a song she would remember from her time when she and I were in North Dakota.

Everyone had a valued spot and we treated her like a queen. We had created a homemade card with a spiritual bouquet, prepared her favorite foods, and crafted homemade feast day songs. Heightened moments were part of our life outside feast days, and they opened me to daily magic. The day after that, Catherine was coming out of the laundry with a full basket, and she tripped. Elizabeth and I were right there and without any reflection my body swung around and caught her in my arms. We looked at each other with a twinkle and moved on.

Another close fall resulted in a joyful moment soon after this one. Mother Gemma and I were escorting Sister Elisha to a car after morning Liturgy. She had to go to the doctor and was incredibly weak. She needed help but refused it from me with a huff and sentiment that left me feeling unwanted. As she maneuvered herself to twist and lower into the car seat her balance was lost, and she started to topple! Without hesitation my body moved in such a way to reach, catch her, twist, and lower her with ease and gentleness into the seat. We both looked at each other in complete surprise, and she nodded a thanks that was soft and made me want to hug her (I didn't).

She was on her way to see our personal physician, Dr. Stolsky, and his nurse, Debbie. They took our health into their own hands with great devotion and care, arranging visits and connecting us with any extra care we may need. Sister Elisha suffered with MS, so her need for this level of dedicated care was invaluable. I remember going to the office once and being asked by Debbie, "How can we make you more comfortable?" I drew a complete blank; I had not been asked about personal comfort for five years.

During this time, I thought a way Elisha and I could grow in friendship would be for me to spend time learning from her. Maybe she would feel my care and understand that I valued her and her skills. Even if my hands were tied around what roles she was assigned in community, they were not tied in that respect.

Since she was very gifted at tending plants and making bread, I sought to learn these two skills from her. The bread making fascinated me. We had been given an abundant supply of canned whole wheat berries that had sat dormant for months, side by side like little soldiers, upon the top back corner shelf of our food cooler. She and I started blending them into flour, subbing them into a recipe she knew well. Our first loaf was a monumental success! The crust was golden, and the dough had risen to the perfect loaf size giving us a moist middle. From there I tried a second loaf on my own and quickly realized that the magic ingredient was Sister Elisha's sense of how much water. She did it by feeling. My loaves were less than a success, but at least they were edible like a heavy Germanic bread you sink your teeth into and tear vigorously.

It took months, sticking close to her recipe, until it clicked, and the bread came out of the oven golden.

After that moment I could play with ingredients like sunflower seeds and herbs and even changed up the honey to molasses or added cinnamon and walnuts. And dependably the loaves would come out golden and delicious.

The plant endeavor did not reap the same success. The gap between our natural capacities was too great but it was fun to try. I looked for courage when it came to Sister Elisha, and I was always reminded of my former spiritual director Mother Anna who said months before I moved south, "It will be a solitary road down in Texas and you will be tested on every level." These words gave me comfort that the Divine saw my efforts.

After Mother Gemma's feast day, we were ushered into a month of Marian devotion. October was the month of the rosary. It was my first year in Texas, only a couple months into my solemn vows, and I was still in the bliss that comes from being expanded and upleveled in love. The rosary, in conjunction with Mass so our local friends could participate if they wished, would be truly ecstatic.

The chapel was always full during this month. It would start with the feast of Therese on October 1st, a double reason for our friends to fill the chapel with roses throughout the month. On this first day of the month, we knelt as friend after friend brought roses into the space. The air became intoxicating, and we prepared to begin the rosary.

With a nod of Mother Gemma's head, the five of us started while about 200 locals quickly joined their voices to ours. "In the name of the Father and the Son and the Holy Spirit," we began, crossing ourselves with our rosaries. The gesture and words opened a floodgate of consolation pouring through my heart *Whooooosh.* Mary's presence invaded my soul. The sense of boundary called my physical body seemed to disappear and all was sweet as honey and wide as the ocean. The hues were white and bluish and while time whisked forward, words hung suspended like billowing clouds.

The absorption was pulsing with each phrase of the prayers, interpenetrating me from within and without at the same time. It felt like two waves climaxing into a kiss reaching high into the sky.

The familiar sensation was welcomed by my hungry heart. "Hail Mary, full of grace, the Lord is with you, blessed are you among women and blessed is the fruit of your womb, Jesus," Mother Gemma led, and I swooned unable to speak, pierced with sweetness. The response was dumbfounding, as it poured forth like a freight train on full throttle by 200 unseen guests in the public part of our chapel, "Holy Mary Mother of God pray for us sinners now and at the hour of our death, amen."

With the rush of Spirit upon me it became too difficult to remain kneeling, the feeling of delightful drunkenness forced me to sit back upon my feet to steady. Each voice participating felt like a personal kiss of Mary. While not losing my individuality, Mary was in me and I, in Her. It was utterly delightful and painful all at the same time.

Once the rosary finished, I had no idea if standing was possible. Mother Gemma had a sense of my dilemma and came over to give me a kind hand up. I swayed in a giggly sort of way. She escorted me up the steps and all the way to her office, with Sister Elisha trailing close behind with a worried countenance. Once the door was closed, I leaned against the cabinet in sheer glee. I was drunk, "Thaaaat rosary was sooooo great! Wow, wow." Sister Elisha lobbied to get me food, feeling it had to be low blood sugar, but Mother Gemma knew.

"Oh, no…" Gemma laughed, "this is Mary within her, Sister Elisha." I added a joyful glint while looking her way. She looked at Mother Gemma in complete disbelief.

Each day of that month, the rosary started after Mass. "In the name of the Father and of the Son and of the Holy Spirit," and each day my heart space would *Whoooooosh*, open with a flooding of feminine sweetness. But each day I grew a little stronger, more capable of holding my own as it happened while not repressing it. The ecstasy became a private affair, thank goodness. One of these rosary days the doorbell rang, and Mother Gemma motioned to me to go. *Tap*, my knee quickly hit the chapel floor in genuflection and my quiet Birkenstocks, a gift from my family each year, carried me without disruption out the door.

As I entered the speakroom, one of our close friends was standing there. Marta. Her expression changed the moment she looked at me. She forgot her question, and tears began to pour from her eyes. "You, you look just like Mary!" she exclaimed. Mary's presence was pulsing in me, so I was not surprised but I was embarrassed, like I got caught without my clothes.

Caught in this vulnerable moment I quickly responded, "Ah, thank you Marta, I feel her so strongly perhaps you were meant to be consoled by her, like I am feeling right now."

This was the blessing of monastic life, the purity of focus gave space, literally. Boundaries and selective channeling fell away for us all to the degree we allowed. It was true intimacy; we could be communing in the safe space of our eremitical community, vulnerable in ways that would be challenging to live in the constructs of the world.

Mother Gemma called me into her office one day. "Guess what came in for me from Father Tomas?" she joyfully invited.

"Hmmmm," I was at a loss.

"My very own hair shirt; all the brothers wear them." She pulled the small article from a box. It was much smaller than I ever imagined; honestly, I didn't know they still existed. The texture was like a rough hemp, woven into two small squares about eight inches by four inches each, one for the front of the body and one for the back. The straps connecting them were of the same material and sat upon the shoulders, like a small scapular.

Even though the idea repulsed me, I also found myself wanting to be like Sister Gemma. Hair shirts reminded me of the discipline (a wax coated macramé whip with three arms creating a flagellation device) we were given once we received our religious name. When I first received the gift of the discipline, I tried so hard to use it every Friday. I united myself with all the other sisters, but the attempts I made to use it from a place of love evoked tears, until I finally gave up. I would spend the dedicated time each evening on Friday praying on my knees instead. My desire to imitate Gemma trumped my repulsion, so I found a few gunnysacks in our shed. *This would make an amazing hair shirt,* I thought, and I spent hours of sewing and cutting it into a large undershirt.

For one short evening after compline, I sat at the organ attempting to play songs of love and worship with this item upon my body, but tears of sadness flowed down my cheeks. My heart contracted and it felt impossible to sing songs of love, *No, this path is not for me. Mine is the path of love.*

The next day I showed Sister Gemma my creation. "I want one; it is so much larger!" she exclaimed, "I had no idea you could figure out how to make one, this is great." Not confiding in her that the gunnysack creation went into a box somewhere, I was waiting to burn it the next time we had a fire and fortunately she forgot about her request for me to make her one.

Months flew by filled with the sounding of chant and the sweetness of silence. I was charmed as we moved through the liturgical year.

Tap, tap, tap, the light knock upon my door at 11:45 p.m. came sweetly each evening, and I awakened with joy each evening for matins. This midnight gathering contained recitations of psalms, readings from inspired writers, and silent prayer. Lying briefly upon my thin mattress in the heat of Texas, memories of North Dakota washed through me.

Clap-CLAP, clap-CLAP, clap-CLAP, starting soft and far away gaining momentum and vigor as the sound arrived outside my door, was how we were awakened in the mother community, Carmel of Mary. My response was always an eager jump out of bed to commune with God while the world around me slept. I felt so fortunate to be there, to be one of those that lived in community and rose for such a sublime purpose. This meaning and romance never diminished throughout the ten and a half years of my life as a Carmelite. The handheld clapper, appropriately named after its sound, was the method used to wake the twenty-sister community not only at midnight, but again at 5:45 a.m. for lauds and the start of the day. At first the sound seemed brash and impersonal, accustomed as I was to hear the radio alarm of my favorite music arouse me for years before entering the monastery, but soon after my sensibilities shifted and its rhythm and regularity became the romantic beckon of God, my Love, waking me to join him in conscious contemplation.

The clapper had to be invented in the earliest religious communities, perhaps even Babylonian times 5,000 years ago, the construction was THAT basic. One main piece of wood was fashioned like a small paddle easily held in your hand. Adjoined to it were two identical pieces of wood the size of the paddle end. They straddled the main paddle, held loosely in place by two small metal rings running through the end closest to the handle. The rhythm of the *clap-CLAP* was wholly dependent on the coordination of the sister using it, which allowed for quite a variety of sound in the middle of the night. The clapper duty was rotated each week, like many other duties already mentioned. It was utterly efficient, allowing a sister to walk the long corridors with ease until she saw every door ajar, our silent signal we were up and getting ready. Lights were never turned on, barring emergencies, so we dressed in the dark taking only five minutes or so.

Some of our funniest stories are of fellow tired sisters who arrived in chapel without veils, or with extra layers and aprons; one sister even forgot our main garment, the long brown tunic that goes over everything!

My mind returned to the present and I jumped to be dressed and in chapel before starting time. Without any long corridors in Texas the clapper was replaced by the soft knock, much warmer and more intimate.

Matins ended as quickly as it had begun, and we returned to our cells. Morning came, lauds, mental prayer (meditation), Mass, breakfast, and terce (midmorning chant and prayer).

This celebration of terce would change our lives.

The Breath of Inspiration Arises Within All

The prioress blew the pitch pipe for the opening chant and the doorbell chimed in discordantly on the tail end of the pitch pipe. Seconds later the bell rang again as our prioress quickly tabbed her place in the chant book, half genuflected, and scurried to answer the door. We continued, absent one of our strongest voices. With only five sisters, our chant felt hollow when one was missing from our most important occupation.

Mother Gemma soon returned, joining her voice with ours upon entering the chapel and again, fullness resounded. Minutes into terce, the doorbell rang again and then another time. Barely had she opened her book when she closed it abruptly and loudly sighed as she briskly half genuflected and rushed to the front door.

For some reason, this day the doorbell rang nonstop and for some reason I found myself longing for complete silence. This challenge ushered in a pivotal experience of my Beloved just hours later.

During the evening I traversed out back for my time of meditation at 5 p.m. A sea of wildflowers greeted me. Moving among them, they swayed like the waves of the ocean, dusting my habit in bright yellow, engulfing me as they swelled up to my waist.

Looking out into the expanse of land behind us, my heart shed the tensions of distractions and interruptions. Silence. Solitude. These sentiments arose within me like a burning desire and a wordless prayer. An informed yearning exploded, and I heard my Beloved say to me "build our permanent monastery."

The prayer had erupted within me in ways I knew well; as it bubbled forth, I knew it would be answered.

I said yes.

Not long after, maybe a week at most, the question of whether to build our permanent monastery was added to the agenda of our weekly chapter meetings. I laughed inside at the speed of the Divine and the synchronicity of my recent meditation experience. I had not mentioned what I heard to Sister Gemma yet. Mostly because it felt like an answer to a personal prayer and not like a request to do something.

Of one mind and one heart we voted YES!

This vote set everything in motion.

This vote was built upon a vote that had taken place years prior when the community first sent nuns, responding to the invitation of the San Angelo Diocese and Father Tomas.

Father Tomas, already a Carmelite hermit who established his community in San Angelo, presented the idea of bringing Carmelite nuns into the Diocese. He even offered to participate actively in the process of making it happen. And so he did. He was always clothed in his full Carmelite habit and stood tall and solid. His thick Cuban accent, curly brown beard, and warm, expressive gestures tempered his strong-willed nature, making him influential and well-liked.

Since he belonged to the Carmelites of the Ancient Observance (O.Carm), his search was for nuns of the same observance. In the US at the time, there were only three of these communities, so his options were limited. The monastery in Allentown was the original foundation from Europe. From there, two monasteries were birthed, one in Hudson, Wisconsin and one in Wahpeton, North Dakota. Had he chosen the Discalced branch (same rule, different constitutions), there would have been about sixty-six different communities to consider at that time.

Tomas chose Carmel of Mary in North Dakota. Not present to the process personally, it seems initial inquiries were sent by both Father Tomas and the Bishop to the leadership counsel of North Dakota who responded with interest.

Visits were arranged in both directions, ending with the decision to go forward. Agreements were set in place defining the relationship and responsibilities of both the Bishop/Diocese and the new nuns. The community then discerned who would go, and who would be the interim prioress operating under the direction of the North Dakota community.

He secured many of the details needed to bring in the nuns, including the donation of a small house as temporary residence, one that bordered open land for added quiet. He was also very involved with renovations creating a chapel for the public connected to, but visually separate from, the nuns. The modifications worked well, creating a quaint residence. Generous hearted, Father Tomas remained an endeared friend all along our journey, at least while I was there.

This happened in 1989, and our vote in 1996 was built upon it.

During their first five years, one of the solemn professed sisters had left the community along with their prioress Mother Angelica leaving a little later. Before she left Texas, she visited North Dakota; it was my only time seeing her and I liked her. There was something about her spirit that made my heart smile.

The Carmelites are part of a branch of the Catholic church called *mendicant* orders. Mendicant orders were formally instituted by the Pope approximately eight hundred years earlier. At the time, many groups had emerged seeking reform and grass roots Christian spirituality free from the lofty trappings of pomp and circumstance highly ingrained in the reigning church hierarchy and common society.

These groups of men and women, usually under the inspiration of a founder, lived in poverty, chastity, and obedience, and were marked by their dependence upon donations for survival. Since there were so many groups popping up like mushrooms, the Pope chose four to continue at that time as ordained mendicant organizations. In doing this, the way of life was given a stamp of approval within the church structure, and the practitioners were channeled into a more manageable (or controllable) system.

These four are the Augustinians (the oldest group), the Francis-cans, the Dominicans, and the Carmelites. Today mendicant orders strive to preserve a spirit of poverty by holding all things in common, while oftentimes making a more traditional salary or living. And since the 1200s, variants on these four and other charisms and communities have emerged.

The Carmelite nuns of North Dakota and Texas chose to maintain the primary focus of contemplation and relied upon the generosity of benefactors for their needs. Even though the nuns are under the governance of the male branch of the order, they are also autonomous in how they provide for themselves and maintain stability.

Our vote to build the permanent monastery opened the floodgates of the universe and pieces fell quickly in place. Like wildfire the word of our intention quickly reached the local community. We did not even have time to actively look for a place to build or form a fundraising initiative, before two people stepped into our lives and hearts, Pierce and Deanna Holt.

The Holts rang the doorbell of our San Angelo house-turned-monastery one evening with an offer that would change the lives of our community. Respecting our normal hours, they had called ahead for a special appointment. Once they came through the door, Mother Gemma and I met them from our side of the grille. I could tell by their excitement they knew it was a big moment but wondered if they felt how much it would impact us for years to come. Deanna and Pierce owned a ranch outside of San Angelo, like many other residents of the area. They were generous people, kind to everyone they met. On this day their kindness took no exception.

Straightforwardly they spoke, straightforwardly they offered, "We want to give you land from our ranch to build your permanent monastery." We were stunned, thrilled, and speechless. They continued with voices that were trembling with both excitement and honest shyness.

They wanted to give us a whole section, 640 acres, and would allow us to choose which land we desired. One square mile would be ours to do what we wanted. Deanna's face was lit with hope we would say yes.

Dumbfounded, we both stumbled with words expressing how amazing this would be and that we were sure our community would be happy to accept their gift. We confided that decisions like this are always discussed and voted upon by the community. Mother Gemma confirmed that she would call within a couple days after the community discussed the idea and voted.

While this offer came from nowhere, it had been seeded by a side comment Gemma had inserted during a visit earlier that month. Deanna Holt had booked an appointment for her daughter's confirmation class to visit and learn about Carmelite life. Gemma, not giving much emphasis, mentioned we were looking to build our monastery. Deanna took it to heart and undoubtedly sat down with Pierce where they envisioned their gift to us.

Unanimously, we voted and accepted the offer from the Holts, even though we had been contemplating moving closer to Fr. Tomas.

Tomas and his hermits had roughly one hundred acres from which they offered us ten acres on the edge of his property. This held a lot of attraction for us to be close to Carmelite brothers and to assist each other while maintaining our own lifestyles. Surveying the land with him, listening to the realistic factors involved, I could see it would be challenging and costly to build there. The three factors prohibitive in my mind were the dense growth of trees that would need to be cleared, the steep grade of the land that would require much leveling, and the absence of any dependable water source.

My mind quickly assessed the cost of these three factors, realizing it would and could be a long-term challenge for my community. Water was the last need I wanted my sisters to have to worry about. This investigation was great information as we prepared to look at the Holts' land. It honed my awareness of some of the essentials to have in place when we brought the options before the community. It also helped me understand the value of so much land being given to us and the long-range potential for the community to expand and utilize the space. Six-hundred forty acres is a large canvas on which to grow.

I had not imagined that Gemma would involve me in the process, and I don't think she had imagined it either. It was more a happenstance occurrence out of the need she had for support and the fact that I was young and energetic. And even in her bringing me along there was no self-appointed thought in my mind that I was responsible for anything more than gathering information. That being said, my mind put itself at the service of my sisters as a protectress and advocate.

Pierce picked us up in his large pickup truck, opening the door and giving us both a hand up into the seat. The drive took about forty-five minutes. It was both beautiful and worrisome in its distance from the city of San Angelo.

We started with a luxurious lunch prepared by Deanna. Unaccustomed to entering someone's house, Mother Gemma and I were absolutely giddy to be given a tour ending in a banquet. Deanna had prepared a layered salad with chopped eggs, lettuce, peas, and other goodies, all topped with a homemade creamy dressing. My mouth salivated just looking at it in the clear crystal bowl.

Alongside the main dish were shrimp miraculously breaded and fried, yet not greasy, and bursting with lemon seasoned flavors.

We lingered as stories of their life when Pierce played pro-football seasoned our lunch; it was as though we had always been friends. Eventually we all hopped in Pierce's truck to survey the land, big full bellies in tow. They gave us a map showing the size and shape of the five plots, and of another option further away should one of these sections not work out. We all hoped to find a good place close to them, so our search began. We bobbed and jostled as Pierce's pickup navigated the rocky roadless soil. Deanna dedicated her time to taking pictures and videos for our sisters back home. While this afternoon would have seemed quite normal to anyone outside a cloistered wall, we were walking a completely new, non-traditional path by engaging our construction project so actively. This type of focused and deliberate spontaneity, being open to the moment, was an elixir for my soul and plunged me into a state of envisioning without boundaries.

First we looked at the land they thought might be best. It was situated on the road leading to their house slightly off the main road from San Angelo to Eldorado. The location was perfect. We got out of the car and walked the property, a bit discouraged to find the terrain was quite irregular. Our feet hit long flat sheets of solid rock, over and over again, adding to our disappointment. To build on this land would take dynamite and endless amounts of soil, in addition to posing long-term challenges to gardening. If the layers of flagstone could be seen, we knew that there was even more rock we could not see. We pressed on.

The last property caught our eye. We visited it last because it was the furthest off the main road and would require a road to be built the entire length of the plot and then of course inland as far as we ventured off the fence line.

However, it had so many great qualities we were quickly drawn to it and our conversation moved from *if* to *how*. On this property alone there were many places that could work well for the monastery—lots of flat open surfaces, amid the mesquite trees.

The bumpy drive along the fence line took a good hour to reach one end. Pierce wanted to drive the entire way around the perimeter and give us as much detail about the center section as possible. Reaching the back end along the left side of the property, a slight incline carried us to the top of a small hill. It was magical. One of Pierce's wells was situated there with dependable water and a retaining tank. He told us that the well reached the main aquafer of the region.

We jumped out of the truck to walk over to the well which had an aboveground wall about twenty feet in diameter and four feet high. The thought of us never having an issue around water was a huge endorsement to choose this plot.

The center of the hill was a natural, flat clearing, standing ready. I could almost imagine it saying, "Build upon me! Choose me! I have been waiting." A soft breeze swayed the sporadic clumps of grass, and I could see it, see it all: The monastery was already sitting there, like a powerful sacred fortress upon sacred land. Over the back edge of the hill was a gentle view for miles on end and I could see each of the sister's hermitages (we called them cells) perched there like nests looking out onto endless land, away from the chapel and section for visitors.

We took video and pictures to take back to everyone. It seemed so easy, so fluid. Bringing the decision before community meant trusting that the vote would be God's will. All was peace and a sense of confident detachment reigned in my heart as I balanced my growing excitement about building there and my deep wisdom of knowing if it was meant to be, it would be. The confirmation that Spirit was moving was this interior sense of true possession without control or grasping.

The meeting started with the video of the land as Gemma and I narrated and filled in to give the bigger picture. Then questions were welcomed and there were many of them. We answered them all slowly and with as much detail as we possibly could.

After an hour-long discussion the time to vote came.

I had the same undaunted confidence that I had when I stood upon this piece of land. It felt like it was going to be, but I didn't have to hope for it or try for it.

Mother Gemma asked who was in favor and one by one every hand went up! The excitement was palpable aside from Sister Elisha's face. She was voting yes but her face did not back up her action.

We did it! We trusted the process and we were going forward with an adventure of a lifetime.

This vote opened something very light-filled in me. It was like the vote broke open a portal that had been closed until that point and with it my whole soul opened as well. A new sacred event was officially in motion.

We called the Holts immediately and could hear Deanna on the other line shout out joyously.

These beginnings did not start with established roles. We didn't sit down and talk about *how* we were going to do this and *who* was going to take what role. We didn't even talk about the need to have discussions, or any type of process or strategy. My assumption was that Gemma was the project lead since she was the leader of the community and if she asked for support, I would give it; and if she didn't, that was fine as well.

The next step before finalizing the agreement into a contract was to meet with the bishop. We were under his jurisdiction so if we moved out of the city of San Angelo onto rural ranchland into another county, the details of our relationship would need to be redefined.

One of the most impactful details of our agreement was his commitment to supply us with priests for daily mass and other rituals and sacraments. He had promised this service as part of the negotiation when the nuns were deciding whether to found a monastery back in 1989. What would he have to say if we were moving about an hour out of town? We discussed this as a community since there had been a little trouble with priests showing up and decided we were going to be okay if we released the bishop from this part of our agreement.

Quickly Mother Gemma submitted our request to the bishop, and we were added to the next Diocesan meeting of the council of priests. We were told there would be a discussion and then a vote requiring a majority approval for the move.

Since Mother Gemma was our leader and spokesperson I gathered information for her, kind of like a speech writer, though she added her charming delivery and own inspiration. I had been doing enough research to put together a vast amount of detail to show that we understood what we were undertaking. Pierce and Deanna drove us to the meeting.

The four of us sat there in the foyer of the Diocesan center until Mother Gemma and I were ushered into a conference room. I looked back to see their bright eager eyes look to us with great hope.

What an exciting moment this was for us and for me. Having been in the cloister for five and a half years and being part of a formal business meeting of men in a conference room felt like I had stepped onto another planet. In a way I suppose that is true.

There was a paradox going on in my body. Confidence pulsed and sustained me; I could *feel* God's presence while intimidation made my heart skip a beat as we entered the room where the large oval table was already filled to overflowing with priests in their clerical garb. Fortunately, I took the chair next to a jovial stout priest who had clearly been around for a while. Throughout the meeting he would lean over and whisper a chuckling side comment into my ear while his belly shook and his eyes sparkled.

God's will would happen for us. I was confident of this. This alone would be the source of true inspiration for new horizons.

Soon into the meeting our presentation was queued. Silence pervaded the room as the bishop pondered all we shared. Mother Gemma went on at length laying out the offer, our desires, how we proposed to accomplish the project, and the redefined expectations. I was not invited to speak since I was a younger nun, so I sat uniting all my intentions to her words.

We were not surprised when the bishop turned our attention to the issue of having priests for our rituals. "I cannot continue to ask my priests to support you if you move so far away, so you will be on your own." Having anticipated this issue we were already ready to say as a unified community that we officially released the Diocese of this service and would figure it out on our own.

The bishop moved back into his quiet listening posture.

He was not one who was easily read, his face was completely placid though you could see he was thinking. His small stocky hands twirled the pen sitting on the presentation details we had printed for him and placed in a manila folder.

He asked a few more small questions, and I could see we had impressed the bishop with our level of preparation and the account of grace and synchronicity in the story we recounted to the room leading us into this project.

Once the presentation and discussion were over, the room became pregnant with silence. I think I was holding my breath at that point as I watched his profile with eyes gazing down at his hands.

Finally, he looked up and said, "Clearly God's will is happening here. Who are we to stand in His way?" And he looked right at me with sweetness.

My soul filled with euphoria and tears came into my eyes with his reflection of what I knew so well.

Perhaps it was a confirmation of what he said as true, or perhaps what he said was a confirmation of what we knew was true. Whichever was the case being irrelevant, the vote was unanimously in favor of the move; we bolted out of our seats, joyously shaking hands with them all. Mother Gemma and I were so high we jumped up and down in each other's arms and took our leave rushing and shouting out to Deanna and Pierce who joined their tears and hugs with ours. The four of us exclaimed, "We can't believe it! We can't believe it!"

Getting back in time for lunch, sweet and faithful Sister Catherine turned the meal into a feast day. We talked at the table and recounted everything. Everyone laughed and rejoiced at the ease with which our desire was manifesting. With all the challenges the community had endured for so long, this was a source of great hope and an indication that all was going to be okay, even better than okay.

Personally, this YES from the Diocese amplified all the yeses up to this point and gave me wings to fly into the manifestation of the monastery. My mind, heart, and body all became highly tuned instruments for the project. Something in me opened beyond boundaries. The first yes: In the field of our backyard standing in the swaying yellow wildflowers. This yes came from me to the Beloved. The second yes: The inspiration of the community to say *it is time*. The third yes: Deanna being inspired and then Pierce. Yes after yes paved the way to this moment and it opened the gates as far and wide as you can imagine. Something in me became boundless, with my mind and heart and body all calibrated to the manifestation of the monastery.

The next important step was two-fold. First, Pierce and Deanna focused on the paperwork for the transaction and second, we needed to decide the location on the land we chose. Even though building on the open hilltop near the well was obvious, we still thought it would be smart to have a sense of the entire 640 acres. Maybe there was an area that would be even better. But we wondered, how do we see it all? Pierce took us for another ride, but it was hard to get a real sense of such a large amount of land, and honestly things looked very similar since it was mainly desert land with mesquites and brush and lots of rocks.

I wanted to look more deeply into many considerations such as the harmony with the land both visually and physically, proximity to potential neighbors, land elevation, water source, and land formation. We strove to do this by driving the perimeter of the property again. We laughed at how we had to inch along in so many patches over embedded boulders. At a certain point we drove randomly across the land keeping in mind all our questions. We were like ants trying to get a bird's eye perspective. There were clearly places that were too rocky or had too many trees needing to be cleared to make it a suitable site.

After this drive through the property, I obtained an elevation chart and topographical map for the section from SK Engineering which proved very helpful in isolating the subtle lowlands, places we wouldn't want to build just in case water would drain toward us instead of away from us. *We have so much luxury in not only choosing our land but choosing exactly what we want. Every question imaginable was posed to help us make the best choice*, I thought from a place of gratitude. I would try to cram in all the technical details to help the sisters contribute informed comments. The details still led us to choose the high point, but we were concerned about the distance from the main road. *Hmmm. I want a bird's eye view. How can I have a bird's eye view?*

It was not long before my silent wish was granted, and we were offered a free ride in a small plane to look from above!

Even small desires are not too mundane to the Beloved.

The pilot offered to take Pierce, my prioress, and me for a leisurely ride over the 640 acres; it was a perfect solution for the uncertainty still in my heart. The morning arrived for us to take the plane ride and sweet joy pervaded even my nostrils. My being given the honor to participate so intimately in the project is a gift I feel even to this day. This moment sparked a memory from my postulancy (the first five to six months in the monastery just five years earlier). In August of 1991, I entered a painfully dark time of doubting my vocation. The doubt had nothing to do with the contemplative lifestyle, it had everything to do with observance, obedience, and the conservative community I called home. The strict attention to the minutest details seemed to reign supreme as a mark of being spiritual, yet it felt artificial and contrived to me at times. I also longed to develop my gifts, to use my mind, to expand in my music, to use the vibrant physical energy I had for living, all of which were subjugated to my observance that looked with a utilitarianism point of view toward what we did in the community. It wasn't just my personal desires, it was a genuine worry and wondering, *Am I failing to have the gifts given me buried and never used or expressed?*

In the silence I wondered if I should leave. Embracing the life had to happen if I was going to stay. I wanted to learn from my sisters and let them be my teachers, I wanted to give myself to this observance to see where it would take me. I felt I should trust the system over trusting myself. I wanted to see what it was like to experience God's hand involved in everything. I wanted to learn humility and freedom. I wanted to be a mystic like my friends Teresa of Avila and John of the Cross.

Coming through this hell of a temptation took a radical surrender into the unknown. During this crisis I lamented to a priest in the confessional, hoping to hear some words of guidance to give rest to my weary searching and his words often came to me. He encouraged me, "You need to trust God. Even though you are not being given an opportunity to use your gifts now, you need to trust that once you truly surrender, every gift you were born with will be used." On January 2, 1992, the birthday of dear friend Therese of Lisieux, the top of my head opened, and white light flooded me like a waterfall. In that grace my concerns were alleviated, and I was able to surrender and trust and say yes to being a Carmelite.

He was right these many years later. Not only did the project give a place for my natural untapped, unforeseen skills to emerge, but it also unleashed the opportunity to live by the power of belief and to see with my own eyes what happens when we let go and say yes to Spirit.

The offer for the plane reconnoitering was another gentle gesture from God to me. Trust. Trust that all is well; trust that you are where you are meant to be.

The day for our plane ride arrived, so I joyfully knocked on Mother Gemma's door for us to leave. The sweet joy pervading me was replaced with uncertainty the moment she responded. Chills ran through me at the tone of her voice. She was in a bad mood. Mother Gemma had a difficult time being approached in moments like these; she desired to be left alone. But a prioress has many responsibilities where she needs to be involved with people. It was a tricky and fear-inducing situation for me. The stress was magnified since I couldn't act on anything without her direct involvement, so I had to think of the project needs as well. Already I was in contact with contractors to build cattle guards and bring in fencing and engineering groups to survey and test the soil. Once we chose the spot on which to build, many balls would go up in the air at once.

Changing gears by putting all the items on my list that could wait until a better moment, I gathered a deep breath, said somewhat futilely to myself, *I'll concentrate on being an instrument of joy*, and entered. With trepidation I rattled off the necessary questions. The quickness of my pace or the tone of my nervous voice irritated her, and she began yelling at me. I took it and knelt to kiss the floor because that was our custom when corrected by a superior, then rose. In an angry tone she struck out, "I'm not going, you can just go by yourself."

I was mortified. "This is such a great gift, and your being there is an important part; it would be sad if you weren't there."

She muttered, "Sister Elizabeth can go." The anger crushed my joy. I left to my office.

A few moments later, she changed her mind though the scowl on her face did not change. By the time Pierce and Deanna had arrived, I had gathered my things trying to recover my enthusiasm and followed Mother Gemma out the door. As we walked through the door to greet them, she became jovial and light. It felt so fake. And I was stuck striving to restore my squashed joy.

By the time we met the pilot, I was still reeling from the anger expressed but excitement began to make its way in around the edges. He spoke with us about the trip and took us to the plane. The plane had four small seats so tiny anyone could have reached the controls to fly if need be. Mother Gemma and I sat in the back and Pierce took the right-hand position.

The engine started. We edged forward. The plane was so small it could turn on its axis. The propeller sped faster and faster. Moments later our pilot put it in full speed ahead and we began to ascend; nausea ascended my digestive tract as well and the predominant thought was, *Get me out of here!* Quickly the thought morphed into exhilaration and self-forgetfulness. Coasting over the land, we were high enough to see far distances and low enough to feel we could almost touch the land with our fingertips.

At this point I found myself leaning way out the window to feel the wind on my face as I snapped as many pictures as possible. Amidst our laughter it was difficult to know how long the flight really lasted, but we were all sad when the job was done, and it was time to head back. The pictures once developed provided us the final piece of information, giving us confidence in our choice of where to build. We also used these shots to help us design the road and plan for future development. The community voted to build upon the high point of the land and was happy to learn that the very center was the highest point on the entire property. While it had spiritual significance, I was more thrilled at the practical implications.

I was effortlessly remembering names and numbers without paper, quickly assimilating architectural, management, and engineering details, and found myself able to speak with enthusiasm and confidence about the project. By sheer virtue of it happening *through* me, Mother Gemma laid more and more in my lap.

It was no surprise that word about our project spread like wildfire through the community. Our friends called and rang our doorbell offering their help. One of our first needs was a fundraising group. This one came together instantly though we ourselves were a bit uncertain about our plan. In response to our open invite, Claire Schmidt, Casey Williams, Debbie Hansen, and a few other friends gave an open *yes* without any description of the commitment. We left the organization of their meetings and goals in their hands figuring we would meet frequently enough that our relationship would define itself over time. The first meeting was exciting and full of ideas.

The women were each so unique: Casey Williams, a quiet true-blue woman who gave of her time so liberally; Debbie Hansen, intelligent and committed; Claire, the powerhouse about whom you have already learned.

Claire called us soon after the fundraising committee had formed, "Do you have an architect yet?" She inquired in a way that sounded more like a pause before the next part of her sentence than an actual question.

We did not.

We had no other plan in motion other than finalizing the paperwork for the property and getting the land ready in a general way. "Well, I know just the architect for you," she went on brightly. "His name is Frank Preusser and he specializes in artistically rich architecture projects. He just finished a project I was a part of for San Angelo. Do you want me to call him?"

"Absolutely," Mother Gemma responded. I added, "Could you let him know we do not have a budget for the project at this point. And ask him if he would be open to donating some of his work?"

"I think he would really like that," she said. "He works for many wealthy clients who hire him without concern about funds; he likes to give back and this is just his kind of project." We liked that he was friends with our friends and that he was a devotional Catholic, which meant he would have a sacramental sensibility in his design if we did indeed work with him.

She called him that day and his intrigue led him to ask about a meeting with us. Excitedly she called us that night, "He wants to meet with you! When can you go?"

We had no idea. This was a first for us to consider leaving the monastery to travel to a different city for a business meeting. Everything felt surreal. I had just gone from days of silence and speaking only with two to three other people to being plunged into unending calls and plans and then travel. It was exciting and I was ready for it.

We reached out to Carmen and Pedro Herrera to see if they would drive us to Dallas. At this point the community in North Dakota did not endorse us having driver's licenses. They were thrilled to be invited to help us. We made a plan for them to pick us up at 4 a.m. to drive four hours to Dallas the following week. We built in extra time since we weren't sure where we were going and if we would need to stop. Frank worked us into his schedule.

A good hour or two before sunrise Mother Gemma and I quietly slipped out the monastery door. I can still see Pedro and Carmen sitting in their car with the interior light on. Their tired eyes lit up with joy as we approached them. Pedro jumped out to open the door for us.

We traveled with just two things, our breviaries, and a printout of any details we had for the project up to this point.

The car slowly pulled out of the lot in front of our monastery and Gemma began, "In the name of the Father and of the Son and of the Holy Spirit," followed by a spontaneous prayer inviting the protection of Jesus, Mary, and Joseph and all the angels and saints with special mention of our beloved Carmelites Therese, Teresa, John, and a few others. Before discussion could ensue, she asked if they would mind if we prayed lauds. They were fascinated to be a part of our ritual and eagerly awaited us to begin.

I pulled out our two flashlights, handing one to Mother Gemma, and flipped pages to the day's opening song and psalms.

Together we sang the opening hymn in English. Ethereally the chant rose like the light before us as we drove east to have a meeting of destiny.

Silence came next. Of one heart we enjoyed the overflow of sweetness that had come from the chant.

At some point not long after, Pedro stopped to fill up on gas. We walked into the attached market where Carmen encouraged us to get something to drink. On the back wall there were spigots of every imaginable soft drink and cups ranging in size up to 132 ounces. It was 1996; I was speechless. *When did this happen? Only six years into the monastery and the world has changed so much.* We stood there in our brown habits marveling at the site.

Mother Gemma and I decided to get one of the super large drinks. The soda fell on our tongues like a delicacy. It was not really *delicious*, but rather seemed delicious because I hadn't had soda for years. How a baby must feel the first time they taste the icing on a cupcake.

Carmen got one of these large sized drinks as well and we got back on the road. Not only were they driving, and paying for gas, but also insisting on paying for these kinds of treats for us as well. Back then the paradigm of receiving gifts as vowed nuns seemed so natural.

For every kindness like this that happened in the project we would create special cards, poems, and spiritual bouquets of prayer for our benefactors. We gave what we had to give, prayer and tokens of love.

About half an hour after stopping for gas and monster-sized drinks, the dusky dawn approached us on the horizon. The last time being on the road for sunrise was taking the greyhound bus in the early morning in February 1991 to travel to North Dakota to join the monastery. We began a rosary, filling the morning air with beautiful words of love for Mary. The blissful moment was suddenly replaced with stress. We had all sucked down these drinks and our bladders went from empty to full beyond capacity without warning.

I looked to Mother Gemma and she nodded, then Carmen looked back at us with distress as well. Here we were trying to find a bathroom in a very rural part of Texas, trying to control our laughter and our abdomens to keep from peeing our pants. In all our modesty it didn't occur to us to just get out of the car and pee on the side of the road. About half an hour later we found a bathroom and had the greatest relief imaginable.

Then we were free to laugh, and laugh we did!

We launched back into the rosary with full morning daylight shining directly into the car window. Forty-five minutes passed. Bladders filled again during that time and once again we had to turn all our attention to finding a bathroom. *Never again*, I lamented about buying that super-sized drink.

This was our last stop before the outskirts of Dallas and Fort Worth. We were there at morning traffic hour but fortunately did not have to go too far through it to reach Frank's office.

The Herreras dropped us at the office and immediately took off to visit a relative. We were ushered with kindness and a certain formality and awe by one of the other architects into the large conference room. Wonder filled me. *How am I here right now? How was I chosen by you my Beloved for this moment?* The doorknob turned with notable gentleness not long after we had taken a seat. The face and gait of the man who entered matched the soft yet firm hand that opened the door and extended to take our hands in his own. I liked him instantly; it was easy to see he was kind, playful, and extremely competent.

Without any delay he invited us to tell him what we were looking for in a monastery. Both of us proceeded to share our heart's desire for a home where we could live like contemplatives. With Gemma's permission and encouragement, I fleshed out the details of rooms and needs that had been collected through the com-munity, along with the standard rooms needed such as chapel, refectory, cells, offices, kitchen and work rooms, and the relation-ship between all of these spaces.

Frank admired our aerial photos showing the spot we had chosen and the overall lay of the land.

Then he shared his inspiration, a notable moment of grace. He had been thinking about this monastery project ever since Claire had called him.

As he began, he asked if we knew the difference between Roman and Greek architecture. "No, but I would love to learn," he nodded to my response, quickly launching into the difference between the two perspectives.

Roman architecture seeks to stand out; it says, "Look at me." Its magnificence seeks to be different than its surroundings, to draw attention. Greek architecture, on the other hand, seeks to compliment and live in harmony with the world around it. Also committed to magnificence, it seems to enhance the area around it by keeping with materials and design that draw upon its surroundings. As I sat in fascination, Mother Gemma nodded off a little in sleep but came back around after a little doze.

We quickly decided to commit ourselves to the Greek perspective and design a structure that would be in harmony with our land. Frank went on to broach the idea of a mission-style monastery. I was pleased to see him so eager with ideas. He showed us pictures and talked about various designs and materials used. We agreed on the principal design and set goals for our next meeting. We also asked to create the buildings on an axis that would lead to the sanctuary, and to have the chapel doors face to or from the east symbolizing the coming of Christ as the Sun rising in our hearts.

Next, both Mother Gemma and I told Frank the inspiration we had about hermitages. "We were reflecting upon our Carmelite rule, chapter three, that says," Mother Gemma started, "each one of you is to have a separate cell, situated as the lie of the land you propose to occupy may dictate, and allotted by disposition of the Prior with the agreement of the other brothers, or the more mature of them."

"So we were thinking," I chimed in, "we have 640 acres. Why not build each sister her own hermitage so she can be like the original hermits on Mount Carmel, and also have a place that inspires the beauty of God?"

Privately we had talked about walking away from the old paradigm of poverty wherein nuns lived dormitory style to save money and limit anything that might seem excessive. We knew we were on the edge with our choice.

"All the sisters voted unanimously, so we hoped you would be able to help us with this design as well," Mother Gemma continued.

Frank loved the idea. With the broad strokes of the envisioning process done, the next step would be to create a conceptual rendition and a floor plan. The design would include an artistic yet practical set of sketches for each space and the floor plan for the overall monastery project. While details such as pitch lines, windows, and stonework would all be included, the main purpose of the conceptual drawings was to define the design aesthetically and practically.

While Frank took all the information we had printed for him to incorporate and use to inform his design, I would continue the work of getting soil tests done for underground design, securing a storage shed, find masons to stone the well, and interview potential engineers, subcontractors, and suppliers. This would be alongside fundraising campaigns beginning. We had a true beginning and would meet again in two weeks.

I did not mind that Mother Gemma left the dialogue to me. It was stimulating and exciting. My heart and soul poured into the exchanges effortlessly, and knowing my service was for our community provided wind beneath my wings.

Pedro and Carmen knew we would end close to dinnertime and had prepared something for us to eat along the way. Even though we had our breviaries out to pray vespers, the meeting had to be talked about first. I gushed all about Roman and Greek architecture and how perfect Frank was for our monastery.

It was interesting that Spirit introduced him to us and us to him without delay. We didn't have to go through interviewing a multitude of architects or monastery designs. Within the space of a few weeks, we had the right person who had the time and had the creative genius to guide us and provide for us.

We had traveled that day from dark to light into a new step for our community, and we traveled home from light to dark. Once we began vespers, the sun had set so we used our flashlights and ended the day as we had begun, "In the name of the Father and of the Son and of the Holy Spirit," we toned without reservation. Carmen and Pedro, their hearts palpably filling the air beside our chant, prayed silently with us.

We arrived home after all the sisters were in bed. After getting a little something to eat Gemma and I headed in separate directions, me to the chapel to get the music ready for the morning Liturgy and her to her office to filter through the daily mail.

Keeping silence the next morning was hard for all of us. The few hours between Mass and our midday meal seemed to go so slowly. I filled my time researching project details and making lots of phone calls until all track of time was lost. The bell for sext sliced through my focus and I placed my pen down.

At the end of sext, we knelt for seven minutes to reflect upon our day (it is called examination of conscience). The original intent was to look deeply at mistakes made but Carmelite spirituality looked more graciously. We were encouraged to see where we enjoyed God's presence and surrendered into this state and where we got caught in worry or thought or anything that took us away from presence. We knew that the greatest gift that could be given is the gift of true presence.

I understood through experience that everything affects every-thing, and that the more one part of the whole is illumined the more the rest are benefited and uplifted.

Once this seven-minute period was over Mother Gemma knocked on her stall and we all shifted off our kneelers onto the floor, kissed our scapular as it lay upon the kneeler, and rose to leave the chapel.

We walked the twenty or so steps to the refectory, stood in front of our place at table and said the prayers of the day before the meal. Within moments we were dishing up the food Sister Catherine had prepared and sitting at our places. Once the last sister was seated, Mother Gemma rang the bell, and everyone started chatting and asking questions.

Gemma shared mostly, but I found easy ways to add to the conversation, slipping in details here and there without detracting from the focus upon her. She let everyone know that we would bring all the details of the project to the weekly chapter meetings and anything that needed a vote would be tended to at that time.

This project brought renewal to us. Not only because it was a new adventure but also because it gave us hope around our little foundation becoming autonomous and existing for a long time. Our first chapter meeting took place the next day.

My excitement and my unexpected ease with a massive amount of detail resulted in an overwhelming amount of information for them. I laid out the processes for the storage shed, masons, engineering, soil tests, grade analyses, fencing, supply needs, fundraising, quotes on road options, and so many more details. Everyone sat there and looked at me with eyes glazed over. I jumped into architectural design, but they were not really interested in this either.

While quotes on block and rebar and lists of who would donate and how we would receive it fascinated me, they were clearly not interested. Quickly I learned it was of much greater service to them to keep my reports to only what interested them, like the practical aspects of the rooms, and what was needed to help them vote.

There was a part of me as well that just wanted to bond and share with them, so I had to accept this may or may not be a desire that would be fulfilled.

After I finished my report, Gemma opened a new topic.

"Well sisters, I have great news, we have a woman who is going to become a postulant!" Surprise rippled through the meeting, none of us knew she had been talking with anyone.

Nicole was her name and Gemma felt so confident the traditional visit was bypassed. She was coming directly to join us. We were all so excited to have another young soul join our life of prayer, and everyone buzzed with side comments of what to do and how to get ready.

Mother Gemma had chosen her date to enter, October 15th, the Feast of Teresa of Avila.

Elizabeth offered to prepare her bedroom, Elisha committed to sew her postulant veil, skirt, and vest, Catherine said she would rearrange the refectory, the place where we ate, so she could fit right in, and I offered to prepare her stall with chant and prayer books, along with creating copies of the entrance ritual for each of us.

Once the chapter meeting had ended, Mother Gemma and I headed to her office. "Mother Gemma," I began, "I noticed that the sisters were extremely interested in the practical elements such as closet space, kitchen and sewing room layout, and flow of the corridors for processions, when can I meet with each of them to get their ideas?"

"We do not have conversations like this in Carmel," she said strongly with no room for dialogue.

I was shocked, *We have the chance to design our entire monastery and the community is not going to be directly involved?* I had no idea this would be the case. I assumed when I was in Novitiate that the hierarchical structure was loosened once a nun was in solemn vows. Growing up in a family, at a school, and in a culture that valued dialogue, this was a jolting moment for me. It was even more so because I was involved as the project lead (at least at this point) and was denied dialogue with the sisters for whom I was building the monastery.

I prevailed upon her to allow everyone to give me sketches and ideas on paper. This way I was honoring her by not having continuous individual discussions, and I was honoring them by creating a window through which I could incorporate their ideas.

The day for Nicole to join us came rapidly. We gathered in the chapel that morning, none of us having met her except Mother Gemma the night before. Once the Mass had ended, we all stayed there kneeling. I could hear the bustling of many of our friends in the public side of the chapel. Elisha opened the grille. Beside the grille was a small table with the white veil neatly placed upon it. A young woman came forward, looking in at us with a sweetness that was curious and intent. She knelt in front of the grille while Gemma moved to stand on our side of the opening. The ceremony was simple and short. Our presiding priest sent from the diocese read his words off the paper consecrating Nicole as she took this step. His next words pronounced a blessing upon the veil she would wear while Gemma placed it on her head, then he blessed us all as we accepted her with open arms.

Nicole moved quietly through the grille into the embrace of Mother Gemma. She was motioned to come to each one of us, starting on her right with Catherine, so each of us could welcome her personally. While Nicole did that, Gemma closed the grille.

Keeping silence was difficult, the joy of welcoming her leaked out of our mouths through laughing whispering comments into her ears as she smiled and looked us straight in the eyes. Gemma motioned her to her kneeler and stall, and we all resumed posture by kneeling until the knock came. United, we dropped to kiss the kneeler with Nicole awkwardly looking around to follow us. She then rose to process to the refectory. We all knew this awkward-ness upon entering and being immersed in the many rituals and movements for the first time along with the overwhelming emotion of the event.

Not long after we were enjoying breakfast and talking with Nicole to learn all about her, and she us.

She picked up on the rhythm of life quickly and was musically gifted, which added vibrance to our soft chanting.

Having someone new to our community made time go even more quickly, and before long our elections came. It was late in the fall of 1996. Every three years we elected or re-elected a prioress and two counselors. Mother Gemma would cease to be prioress of both monasteries after this set of elections.

With North Dakota's stability, it was easy for her to be away even though she was technically still the prioress there too. Now one year later, Mother Gemma was taking the risk of not being elected to either leadership position, but fortunately she was chosen by our southern Carmel. This separated her from North Dakota and shifted her role into one of reporting to the prioress there. She spoke frequently with the elected prioress, Mother Maria Teresa, more as a friend and confident than as a superior.

Gemma had grown endeared to the simpler lifestyle and since she was the logical choice for leader, she had the chance to effect change here, to make a foundation that reflected some of her own preferences.

She appointed herself as novice mistress, giving her a chance to teach, which was one of her gifts. I used to love her classes in North

Dakota for their insightfulness and humor, and I missed having classes with all my duties.

The project expanded quickly into new relationships. I quickly began to feel like I had two lives. All of the sudden I was developing friends and having positive conversations and happy encounters. Instantly, eager volunteers from the local community stepped forward to form two groups. The first offered to be our official fundraising committee and the second, a loosely organized list of friends, offered to help with the little things like driving to appointments, picking up supplies, and aiding in the unexpected needs that would arise. Both proved to be angels. Both were channels for connections and contacts. There were a few that straddled both and became individuals we called close friends. Jean Ann LeGrand was one of them.

Jean Ann formed an integral part of the tapestry of our monastery project. She was one of those angels who appeared out of the woodwork. We had never met her before the building project. She moved with grace into my life as a friend and with us as a whole community as one of our major benefactors.

We both had projects going on at the same time. She hired our architect, and we hired her timber truss company, the lines of connection overlapping as we shared ideas. Jean Ann showed us her dream home being built on the water where her creative vision was coming into form and drove me many times to take in our project, sharing with me her journey and inspiring me with her unassuming strength that shined brightly upon me.

As our fundraising committee was working on a few ideas, the bishop offered us a one-time gift of 10,000 Catholic diocesan addresses to conduct a mail-out. This was the first time for us to create an appeal letter. In it we focused on our mission and service in the diocese, leading to the building project and support of the bishop, and ending with a direct appeal.

Our monastery turned into a post office and became a bubbling frenzy of chaos. Stacks of letters and envelopes were staged in each room, on tables and floors, organized by zip code.

We printed 10,000 copies and ordered mailing and return envelopes. Our friend Manuel Rangel printed the addresses on labels. I was not the accountant and never knew what the cost of supplies ran, but the endeavor drew in the entire community in ways that would be few and far between given the nature of the project. Hours and hours were spent licking and sealing, sorting, and bundling into zones. There was a buzz in the air. Bins were everywhere: under tables, scattered through rooms, and covering tables. Simultaneously, we also approached Ava Decker, a deeply kind and wise philanthropic woman, asking for the first large donation.

She was sophisticated yet simple, a woman of deep faith. She was one of the most well-known philanthropists in San Angelo, and a strong Catholic. She became our largest donor. The story of our friendship with her began like so many others that entered into the building project, through one of our friends.

Mother Gemma called her to set up a personal meeting. She left the monastery within the week to visit Ava as we waited with anticipation behind our cloister walls. "What will happen?" we all wondered. "How do you ask one person for a large sum of money?" This was all foreign to us. So, we waited. None of us had ever met her and I am not sure she ever came to our liturgies or public services, so a mystique surrounded the idea of who she was. *Was she easy to talk to? Reserved? Enthusiastic? Skeptical? Curious?*

It was such a mysterious project, with an internal order that required continued surrender. The download of it to my mind and heart was instantaneous and provided its own direction and strategy, but traditional methods with budgets and strategic plans were entirely beholden to the non-traditional ways of Spirit.

As I reflected upon our community supporting us it occurred to me that they were supporting us in moving away from them. *What a generous selfless act to care for our needs over having us close to them. Their travel time would go from minutes to a solid hour for most if they wanted to join us for Mass or any other celebrations.*

As dinner approached, the doorbell rang. In silence we scurried to the door to greet her. Flinging the door open Mother Gemma unabashedly shouted, "She gave us $100,000!" The large check flailed back and forth, bending as she waved it above her head. We all started jumping up and down, rejoicing, rejoicing. Decorative plates whizzed out upon our serving table and upon them Sister Catherine put her homemade chocolate cake from the freezer.

Prayers were bypassed as we loaded our plates with food, plopped ourselves down, and waited only seconds for Mother Gemma to ring the bell signaling that talking was now allowed.

We sat captivated as she recounted every detail. Ava encouraged our community to turn to her again, keep her abreast of our needs, and remember that we could look to her for another donation.

On top of her money, the large mailing brought us $40,000. By the time those donations came in, I had a realistic grasp on the costs to come which would be quite high; so, my joy was anchored less in the growing bank account and more in the inner knowing this project was meant to be and the adventure that would be mine to see how it would come into form.

From the start, I loved the project. Unconsciously it was an answer to a personal prayer. *Ah, the chance to build something! To envision it without limits, to see it happen as a sacred unfolding!* My heart swelled; it was the perfect combination to satisfy my senses. All was orchestrated by God. All would be a channel of this beneficence, and I was blessed to be part of the flow.

As I continued to share the project with the local businesses and contractors, donations were channeled our way. Some of them were offered at less-than-optimal moments and required immediate pickup challenging our willingness and flexibility.

More times than can be counted, a close friend and heart-rich volunteer, Dolores Contreras, dropped what she was doing to help. We would rush to get the goods, so to speak. One time the donation was massively heavy for the two of us. On the loading side, men abounded and easily filled her vehicle. But we were on our own once we got to the storage shed on the site. We knew it would all work out. Laughing our way in her tiny car over the uncultivated road to the jobsite, we arrived when dusk was melting the land, making distinctions harder by the moment. We pulled up to the newly built metal shed and attempted to unload the heavy items. Tears in our eyes from laughing so hard, and unable to lift anything, we dragged and pushed and pulled piece by piece while darkness descended upon us. Half an hour later we rejoiced, hugged, and sang. We did it! *Now, if only we can make our way out of here in the dark.* Moments passed like slow churned butter as we inched our way over the rough two-mile road; slowly navigating boulders, we felt a bit like we were pioneers, or teenagers, plowing through the unknown.

The time came for us to visit Frank again with Pedro and Carmen driving us in the wee hours of morning. We skipped the soft drinks that time around.

Like last time, we were quickly and respectfully ushered into his conference room.

What would he design? How would he incorporate all the ideas and needs? How would it reflect the missions? We knew it would be beautiful, knowing his style and grace, but we eagerly wondered what to expect.

The unveiling of the conceptual prints was a moment so new, yet so familiar. Just like a beautiful sunset that captures your breath and carries it into the horizon, our new home took us deep into the beauty of our own call to be contemplatives, and to occupy ourselves with the one thing necessary. The monastery was grand and simple at the same time with its sweeping lines set in stone evoking the recollection of both the changing and unchanging nature of life.

The structure would be composed of fieldstone, with the chapel hosting traditionally thick walls of stone inside and out, and the remaining buildings framed in wood and covered in exterior stone. The entryway to the public chapel was an intricately woven series of arches angled gently into a set of super large wooden doors with iron hardware. My breath was taken away, *Yes, it will be made of stone, but with movement as though it were put there with a paintbrush.* One of the details we talked about with Frank, which he incorporated elegantly, was the design of breezeways between buildings. With temperatures boasting 100 degrees and higher in desert Texas we wanted to take advantage of the slight breezes alighting our hilltop construction site. The breezeways both channeled air around the buildings and enabled us to use more stone to increase insulation. While the up-front cost would be a bit more, the long-term savings would be greater; it was also quite romantic. Frank was quite attuned to using form in symbolic ways and even turned one of the buildings askew to represent that nothing in life is perfect.

We left the office grateful and overwhelmed. At home we studied the prints. We saw the chapel walls were set as high as twenty-eight feet, with the gable running higher, a detail we had not noticed. It felt unusual to be a small community of nuns living a simple life in a chapel that large. Mother Gemma and I were torn. After talking a while, we called Frank and expressed our concern. Sensitive to his charity we hoped not to offend him, but also wanted to honor our desire and concerns. We asked if the chapel walls could be about fourteen feet instead, and the wings of our cloister connecting to the chapel wall at a lower level. He explained to us that the lowest the walls could go would be twenty-two feet. By the structural nature of the design, going lower would change the roofline like a domino effect, and the lower ceilinged buildings would be too low for us to stand comfortably. Essentially the roof design was the defining piece to the interwoven levels of the monastery buildings. Our discomfort was great; the walls were high, and the floor plan was large. Without years of experience in monastery construction, we felt ourselves uncertain about the best course of action. North Dakota seemed so small compared to our plans, yet was it? I had designed rooms a bit larger than normal, since the cost was very low to add space so long as plumbing was not involved. In our discussion the overall size was easier to justify, but we found ourselves mulling and wrestling over the chapel.

By this time, I had researched the missions enough to know his dimensions were fairly standard. Most of the buildings in San Antonio, Texas ran about twenty feet wide by twenty feet tall at the wall height. They were also about as long as ours, thirty or so feet, enough to seat about one hundred people. It seemed from our discussion with Frank only two choices were before us, accept the design as is, lowering the walls to twenty-two feet, or start completely over. Starting over felt so wrong; perhaps it was the guilt of the work he had done, or perhaps it was an intuitive hit. I was rapidly learning that this project taught me we do not need great skill, great learning, or great knowledge, we only need unshakable belief, which shows itself as an awareness of the door of synchronicity when it opens, and the confidence to walk through it, knowing all we need is being supplied us.

We accepted the design with twenty-two-foot chapel walls. I had a copy printed and sent to the bishop immediately.

Approval of the conceptual prints from the bishop happened seamlessly and without a formal meeting, setting everything into motion. The flurry of events for the next three years was like navigating a snowstorm and enjoying the whirl and ever-shifting drifts moment by moment. Slow motion and full speed collided to coexist, taking me beyond boundaries and keeping me fully present.

Gemma obtained books on Mexican symbology and mission architecture in both Texas and California from which we could learn. As a natural writer and artist, she was fascinated with

Mexican art, enjoying the highly expressive and exaggerated styles and vibrant colors. She opened my eyes to the beauty that hid itself from me. She also introduced me to the beauty of icons, which I believe was being passed on from what she learned from Father Tomas. At first, I was disinterested in the flat images until Gemma explained the deep meaning and the sacred way they were created. My indifference turned to passionate appreciation. Her interest gravitated to the individual pieces of art and expression, which I loved as well. Here our conversations were rich. In addition, I found myself fascinated with the broad sense of how styles work, harmonize, and create meaning, fitting into the surroundings, creating beauty at a full glance, and using indigenous materials, for which she expressed little interest.

Research excursions were planned once we obtained permission from the bishop to leave the monastery for the project. He graciously gave us a blanket permission, rather than requiring us to keep logs of our comings and goings. In the months to come, that saved us much time and allowed us the liberty to embrace the project in a dynamic way.

The first excursion was to our beloved hermits, Father Tomas and the brothers. The men visited us often since their friendship had grown strong with the leaders, first Angelica, then Gemma. It seems to me they were a bit more relaxed than us, or perhaps their version of the Carmelite rule allowed them greater latitudes of their time on or off property; it could have been the fact they were men.

Along this line of reflection, one of my graduate courses revealed an influential historic moment around the institution of cloister. When I entered monastic life, the understanding given to me explained the custom as a fundamental aspect of being monastic. It was a level of commitment to solitude for the sake of the woman pouring herself out in prayer for the world; it was a lived symbol preserving the sacred nature of the call.

Cloister started as a law to keep women from freely going about, and for a while, all women's religious orders were cloistered, with permissions given if they had active services to perform.

This news was sadly shocking, but perhaps what we were living was a remnant of that old way of looking at things, thus explaining the difference between the men and the women's liberalities there in Texas.

The visit this day was filled with the same levity they brought during their visits to us. I loved hearing Gemma's laughter ringing through the halls as they took us on a detailed tour of the place. I also relished the connection we had with these men who seemed to truly be brothers.

Our infectiously generous friend set aside hours for this tour. He explained the roofing, the measurements of each building, the flooring, the woodwork and iron work, and icons. He went into details around storage, and ideas around sacristy needs. We walked. I took notes, and like a sponge, learned and learned. While discussing the chapel architecture an inspiration came to us, "We are right near San Antonio, why not go to the missions there to get ideas?"

And we did. But before that excursion could be planned, we had another joyful duty to attend. Another woman sought to join us. Gemma had been writing back and forth with a young woman from Rhode Island who was in vows already in an active order. This woman was hungering for the contemplative life and had chosen to explore the possibility with us. Christine was her lay name and her initial visit happened just after New Year's Day. What a magnificent soul. She was kind and deliberate. As she described her desires and experiences, it seemed she would flourish in the cloistered life with ease.

Gemma suggested she join us that month, and she did. Her order had already been prepared and supportive of her change, so the requisite papers needed to end her commitment to one community and begin her commitment as part of our community required only a couple signatures.

We were correct; she stepped into our community like a nun in solemn vows. Even though Christine did not need much adaptation to the life she started at postulancy, she had the freedom to go back to her original order if she felt inclined.

Gemma loved being with the novices. While she spent time crafting classes and holding private meetings for instruction, I got ready for our trip to the missions. Even though my plate was piling high with no relief with the monastery project, I was also the liturgist, preparing all the music for our rituals, and the assistant to Catherine in the kitchen, helping with food management in our cooler and the preparation of meals.

Before going to the missions, I spent hours researching each mission in our book, learning about the culture and influence of the time, trying to get an idea of the symbolism so we could know what we were looking at. Our dear friend, Manuel Rangel donated his time to drive us for our first trip to San Antonio. We went down that way a few times. Another time Debbie Hansen took us, and yet another friend took us as well. Friendships grew beyond the shared times of prayer and Mass, gaining great depth. At length our friends talked about family and career, mingling conversation in between our prayers.

Our choice was to craft our trip to fit in a visit to four missions, all in one day, and go to the Alamo if we had time. With my official architect ruler, a gift from Frank (still in my possession today), my notebook was filled with scrawled images, measurements, and dimensions. We were like kids in a candy shop. "Oh, look at this," Gemma would point to a sconce with ornate limbs.

"And look at this!" I would run my hands on the decorative iron hardware of the wood hewn door. Walls, windows, floor tiles, murals, trusses, ledges, steps, pews, sanctuary designs, wall patterns, and paintings were just a few of the accents noted in this little book of paper.

I was not trying to nail anything down, but rather be open to possibilities. Our plan was to get an idea, create a draft from which to get estimates or donations and see what came back to us. We unconsciously prepared ourselves for magic to happen.

"What are you doing?" people asked us over and again as they stood curiously looking at nuns in full habit. Sometimes we were too short to accomplish our goal to measure high doors so these observers would be employed into participation, which they enjoyed thoroughly, holding one end of a measuring tape, as we held the other, and scaling up sides balancing the metal tape against walls. More than once we recounted our story, and the miracles set in motion for our construction. Mission Espada held the most charm for me with its shorter walls, smaller dimensions, warm tones, interesting Spanish and Muslim influence for the entrance, and its facade bell tower. Mission San Jose was the mother of them all, developed like a fortress with full potential to be a self-sustaining compound. With its aqueduct system, sample living quarters, historical placards, and miniature model of the place giving a narrative of daily life, San Jose gave us the best sense of the motives behind the architecture. The mystery of these places—some walls only partially built, leaving it feel like ruins—was alluring, pulling me into conjecture of lives and events long past.

San Juan Cupertino and Immaculate Concepcion had elements of interest which were captured quickly as the sun was ebbing toward early evening and our day trip was coming to a gracious close.

We did work in a quick visit to the Alamo. While hundreds of visitors milled around like a sea of ants uncertain of which way to go, I stood riveted on one of the pairs of doors. They were dark and about six inches thick. The hardware was hand hewn with emblems in the riveted nails; the handles matched in the remarkable artisanship. Pulling the measuring tape out I kept trying to get it hooked onto the top edge of the left wooden door, but it was so high the tape kept falling back on my head. The second attempt I tried to scale it up the face of the door, but the metal edge kept getting caught on the iron holding the panels of wood together. After a number of attempts a few of the passersby helped us, and it became a visible community effort with others standing by and cheering us on.

As I scrawled the measurements into my notebook a soft, yet firm voice came from behind. "Excuse me," he cleared his throat and said again, this time more forcefully, "Excuse me sisters, could you tell me what you are doing?" We turned around to see one of the employees standing there with arms crossed and stern gaze. My heart started beating, I didn't realize we were doing something wrong but then it occurred to me that we never asked either.

We were taken into a large office where people were coming and going. They asked us a series of questions to which I responded with sincere detail, "We are Carmelite monastic nuns, and we were given permission to come here to learn how to build a mission style monastery," I started with hesitant enthusiasm. "Our friend here donated his time and so many in our community are all donating supplies, contracting work, volunteer time, and even fundraising support," my own voice filled with humble excitement as the recounting built momentum. "It is really an amazing miracle and we thought if we could measure things like doors and walls and windows, we would know the best way to go about our project."

After disclosing our motive and a few examples of the kinds of miracles happening we were told to take a seat. They left us sitting there for quite a long time. Since we were not alone, we couldn't talk about what was happening, so I found myself holding my breath and wondering, *Did we do something illegal? Could we get arrested?*

Finally, after what felt like an hour but was probably only about fifteen minutes, a man we had not met but seemed to be a manager came to meet us. "Hello," he said in such a friendly tone, "you probably did not realize, but visitors are not allowed to do what you were doing. We wish you had come to us first." I wondered what was going to happen next, which he satisfied quickly. "Your project sounds amazing," and unnoticed until then, he pulled out an architectural floor plan with a few elevations of the Alamo. He rolled the prints out and began explaining the details with the same kind of enthusiasm that I had about our project.

After his explanation, he handed me the prints, "Here you go," he said. "I hope this helps you in your project." And we were released.

Relief washed through us as we exited the property. Even though we were exonerated, I still felt a little bit like a criminal and was happy to get into Manuel's car to head to our next destination. We had started at 4:30 in the morning, and the day flew by as a timeless encounter fitting in all we had planned. The whirlwind visit included two extra stops. First, we visited Texas Timber Frames to discuss trusses for the chapel, and the second spontaneous visit was a suggestion from a local for an artisan to create our Stations of the Cross.

Texas Timber Frames was the epitome of professionalism, latest technology, creativity, and enthusiasm. With patience they taught us about their work. By choice their trusses were all mortise and tenon design using red oak from an Amish supplier in Ohio. "The oak is cut down at a precise time based on construction needs," one of the men began, "letting it dry only as much as the specifications required."

Another team member went on, "Our research has shown us how to time the process. Following these calculations, we allow the pegs to be completely dry, and the trusses to remain green enough to dry around the pegs. This increases the strength of the trusses over time."

The process seemed ingenious. We ran our rough plans by them. At this point we only had the base measurements of the chapel and our tentative open truss approach. My one concern was that the trusses over time would shrink too much, creating tension on the stone walls, to which their assurance was solidified by a kind of warranty system.

They pulled their computer out to enter our information and create a design for us with them in the office. We had very little expo-sure to computers and no familiarity with the rate of technology growing in society. I was mesmerized by the three-dimensional rotating truss floating on the screen before me. Quickly our specs were entered into the program and *boom!* There was an A-frame truss looking back at us, sitting upon imaginary flagstone walls. At this point they asked us a few questions, and we went out on a limb, suggesting sizes, and adding an *M* in the center of each truss to honor Mary. Not long after the words left our mouths, they had it sketched on the yellow pad before us accurately. We nodded in approval and one of the designers quickly hit a few keys. *Boom*! There was our truss, personally designed with symbolism. To give us a sense of the overall look, they hit a few more keys and, *Boom!* a mock chapel spread before us, showing the number of trusses lined one after the other. Since it was movable and three-dimensional, one of them began moving the mouse to have the design move into different angles before us. We could see exactly what they would look like from the ground, standing a few feet away, looking upward, or even at eye level.

While we were very conscious of the basic costs, which were not present in our bank account, this was clearly one of those meant-to-be moments. Asking for a moment alone, Mother Gemma and I met eye to eye, "Yes, they are perfect for us," we concurred. The news went to them, and with no idea how we were going to pay it, we reserved their services. Fortunately, this was a construction detail that, while needing to be ordered now to begin the process would not come to completion until much later in the actual project. Mark was the name of our personal contact. He was an energetic man on fire with enthusiasm to be the lead for the trusses for our monastery.

Our last meeting would be a short one, though we were a little unsure how to find the artisan. Locals gave us ideas where to look, and we found him. His storefront was his studio. A dust-covered man, simple and straightforward, quickly came from a room hidden by a back wall. "Hello," he waved a rag.

We threw our sketches out onto his table, eyeing his work as we did to get ideas. He seemed perfect for our desire. Immediately he called us to follow him, "Let's take a look at this," moving as he spoke. Just around the corner he revealed partially completed stations of the cross. Wouldn't you know that Spirit would provide exact samples for us to see. "See here," he gestured, "I hand carved those templates, so they are unique to me, then created the mold." He sensed our wondering if they were copies or works of art. "Then, I hand paint each one with the colors you want." The size was perfect and the colors of the ones we saw were very close to what we wanted.

"We want to let you know up front that we do not have much money and are building our monastery through donations, would you be willing to help us out?"

"No. What I do is art, and it is worth the price I charge. So if you have someone to donate the cost, you can have my services," he clearly responded.

"We would love to be able to hire you," Mother Gemma jumped in, knowing I felt the same way. "Will it be okay for us to let you know?"

"Sure, of course," he added, searching for a business card or paper. We did obtain a donor, and before the completion of the monastery construction, the finished stations were in our hands. They were breathtaking pieces of art. The body of the relief was an elegant cream, almost fleshy pink, and the border was a deep iridescent copper.

At this point we were exhausted. Manuel sweetly held the door open for us to climb into his forest green truck, so we could begin the three-and-a-half-hour trip home. The return was bittersweet, with physical weariness from the day mixed with a desire to be home standing in contrast to a certain sadness the adventure was over. Mother Gemma dozed while I enjoyed looking back at all the notes taken, remembering each place fondly.

Outside the monastery, Gemma felt like a close friend. However, the moment we drove up to the doors of our home her entire body would tense, and her countenance would shift to shades of gray. She would become silent, and though she never disclosed to me what was happening, it felt like she was re-entering a prison. *Soon we will be in a normal monastery and all will be well,* I would inwardly counter.

The next day the doorbell rang during our work hours. Mother Gemma quickly let me know it was for me. It was our close friend Danny Seidel. "Well, hello, Sr. Annunciata, how are you doing with this building project?"

"Danny, it is going great. So many people are giving so much, and your suggestion to use SK Engineering for the land testing gave us all the information we needed. They didn't even charge us for the time and analysis they rendered. Thank you," I confidently told him.

SK Engineering provided me with topographical maps of the entire region, affirmed we were making the best choice of where to build, analyzed the layers of earth, and found that the solid bed of limestone could be reached seven feet deep. This information would influence every part of the project and enable me to build the strongest monastery possible for my community. Miracle after miracle abounded.

He shuffled his feet a little bit and looked downward briefly, brushing his forehead, and adjusting his ball cap. "It's my pleasure Sister Annunciata," he responded with heart. "The project is why I am here, what else can I do? I want to be a bigger part."

I knew without a moment's reflection, "Danny we need a road. It is two miles from the main road to our building site and it is too rough for all the contractors that will need to drive it. We are building at the very end of that property so we can take advantage of the high point and the well that is already there."

"Of course! I would be honored," he said. Not long after, he visited the site and designed a few options for us. The land was riddled with large plates of limestone and jutting boulders. I had already gathered three other quotes that considered the challenge and the cost of materials.

Once he decided on a final proposal, we met there at the entrance to the property. A true Texan man of chivalry he jumped out of his white pickup truck when he saw me and opened the side door, lending a hand to help me up into the cab. "So, most of the way," he began, "I can run a blade and level things but here and there we will need to crush the stone. This is all doable." We slowly drove the fence line close to the final ascent to the tiny hill. "I think at this point we should wind inward," he began to motion with his hand and take the truck slowly around trees so I could feel how the road would go. His face shifted to pure joy, "This way we can preserve the trees."

How blessed were we to be cared for by this gentle man!

Danny began the road shortly after the conversation, donating his time between jobs. We followed his lead to begin with a caliche road. Even though it was less durable and would need more replacing, it was super affordable, and could easily be the pad upon which a stronger road could be built when we had more money.

About that time, I began to look into power for the new home. The closest pole in the hundreds of rolling acres of farmland was about ten miles away, run by the Texas Southwest Electric Co-Op. Fortunately I had already made friends at the SK Engineering firm who surveyed land. In addition to the report of the land which included soil tests, water, and well assessment and a sliced view of the layers going down ten feet, they donated a topographical map for our 640 acres, including coordinates and any other information our various contractors might need. This map made the phone conversation about power very easy.

"Hello, may I help you?" the gentle voice of Jim Martin came on the line. He was the general manager of many years for this co-op, and the moment I heard his voice, Spirit rushed through me.

"Hello," I began awkwardly. *What do I say to this man?* I thought since I had never needed to talk about power requirements. I just jumped in. "My name is Sister Mary Annunciata, and I am a Carmelite nun here in San Angelo."

"Well hello Sister Mary," he said, like we were old friends. And it felt like we were old friends.

"Hello," I said again, liking him instantly.

"What can I do for you, Sister Mary?" he encouraged.

"Well, we were given land by Pierce and Deanna Holt," my voice moved into free excitement, "and it is in Schleicher County. We are very excited to be planning to build our permanent monastery out there."

"Well, I'll be," he said with a Texas twang. "How are we so blessed to have you join us?"

"It is a complete miracle, Mr. Martin." I went on.

"Please, call me Jim," he interrupted.

"Okay, Jim, well we prayed to God and asked that if it was time for us to finally build, to show us the way," my words began to gush, "and right after the prayer we were given this land, and everyone here is helping us. We even have an architect already."

"Ah, I see," he warmly acknowledged more with tone than words. Our conversation ensued for a good hour. By the end we had it all worked out. After giving him the coordinates of our new site from my topographical map, he stepped forward with his proposal.

"As I see it, Sister Mary, we are so blessed to have you in our county, and we would be honored to provide your power. We need to have poles out that way anyway for other farms that will come down the road, so as I see it, this is simply an investment in our future," he drew silence from me. I was overwhelmed with the level of gift we just received. One simple phone conversation turned into three-phase power running for ten miles to the exact spot needed on our property.

I sat stunned when I hung up the phone. I didn't even have the desire to run to Mother Gemma to tell her right away. Within the gift was the bigger gift of his friendship which, like others, would last for years. Jim Martin retired about a year or two later. Who knows what would have happened if he had not been manager. Until then, he stepped forward more than once to our assistance, insistent that we were giving him much more than he could possibly give to us. Many times, we spoke on the phone to work out some or another little detail like old friends, though we did not meet in person until quite a while later.

You may be wondering if participating in prayer was even possible for me, it was. Somehow these early years, aside from any outside supply trips, the project fit itself neatly into community life. The initial inspiration when I stood in the sea of Texas goldenrods opened me to a download of understanding and skill to grasp the project scope and produce the organization and flow effortlessly. It was Spirit moving through me. Chanting and meditation kept me in the current of Infinite Intelligence and reinforced how I was a participating witness to what Spirit was creating.

In addition to my role with the project and my other duties, Gemma asked me to start helping her with the novices. Her fatigue was growing and her desire to lighten her load was great. At first it was teaching a class or two, but soon after, she asked me to be the one to meet with them one on one for questions each day. She remained the formal novice mistress, so I was required to bring all questions to her, then be the one to give Nicole and Christine the answers from her. I remembered how much Gemma disliked the position of being the messenger of the prioress in North Dakota. The recollection sparked sadness in me that she was choosing the same pattern, giving me responsibility with no freedom. I felt like she did, a puppet. The only difference was that I did not want to be in the position to be a guide to the novices.

Timidly I said one day, "This feels like too much for me, Mother Gemma, could I be released from being the point person for the novices?" The timidity was a cultivated reserve I had developed in my earnest desire to be faithful to God.

Sister Gemma's response silenced any conversation, "God is asking this of you, Sister Annunciata, so do it." And I did, and I could feel the support of grace. I shared with them what I knew of Carmelite living, patterned on my novitiate in North Dakota. They inspired me, which offered strength when I felt weak.

Christine's deep and natural devotion brought out all my rich stories of our northern community; the recollection of all the senses ignited by the liturgical seasons came forward through her interest in what our life would be like once we had a monastery.

We were getting close to the start of Lent so I shared with them all about the changes that would happen. "The evening before Ash Wednesday all the flowers and decorations in the chapel will be taken away. Everything will be stripped of embellishment, even our chant will become very simple. This will open our senses to enter a time of inward reflection. We fast all days but Sunday. It is amazing how we are plunged into a path of walking with Jesus during his last days before the crucifixion. And what I always find is that Jesus, Mary, the angels, and the saints are walking with me in all the places within that are in need of healing. It can be a time of great transformation if you open your heart to it."

Nicole and Christine were quite similar in the ways of deep reflection. They took their spiritual paths very seriously and were with us because they wanted to give their all and grow in love. They were also very different in their desires of how to live into this growth. Nicole struggled with observance and austerity while

Christine struggled because she wanted to do penance and live more strictly.

Christine drank up all the stories of North Dakota, with the intense ritual and rigorous schedule. Her contemplative nature exuded peace and steadiness. However, our Texas observance and customs were light in compared to her desires. She asked me more than once if she could stay up all night to deprive herself of sleep and keep vigil in prayer for the love of Christ. I talked with her about the path of the Divine being one of gentle love, and that we don't need to seek out suffering to further our union because suffering is already a natural part of life. This did not set her at ease. My heart sank, but eventually we let her stay up an hour. "Christine this permission is not to stay up for penance's sake but for love's sake," I had no idea if she shifted her intention.

Nicole, on the other hand, was a deeply mystical soul as well, but whose desires leaned in the opposite direction. She hoped we would be interested in massage oils and flower essences and elements that pleased the senses, not practices that deprived the senses like fasting and custody of the eyes. Our steady daily structure, which was relaxed compared to the monastery from which we came, felt constraining to her, she wanted time to do what she felt like doing.

"Why do we all have to fast and why do we need to fast? My body doesn't like it and I do not believe in self-denial. Why do we all have to work in the afternoons if I wish to be doing something different? Why can't I choose how I am spending my time?" she would ask in a variety of ways.

"I appreciate your desires and they should be considered as you discern your vocation, but our community has chosen this observance. Both ways hold truth, it is more a matter of what is right for you," I would respond. But my heart still went out to her, I didn't want her to have to feel so much tension.

Where Donna, the woman who joined us and left the year before taught me about poverty, Nicole taught me about obedience.

Most exceptions I asked for from Mother Gemma were denied, except for one. I was able to obtain freedom for her to play music in the afternoons. We had recently obtained two books of Greek Orthodox chant from The Monastery of the Holy Transfiguration in Boston, Massachusetts. The hymns and tones, utilizing their ancient modal system, were exquisite and gave her something into which she could put her whole heart. We would hear her angelic voice chanting one chant for hours at a time.

When she asked again about being exempt from our fast during Lent, I asked Gemma again.

"If she doesn't want to do our practices, she shouldn't be here," she firmly replied.

There I was in the position that Gemma found herself when she was novice mistress up north. She felt such tension to be a messenger about something she did not believe in, yet she was now choosing to keep the same pattern. I reflected deeply on this with sadness, *Here we are in a new foundation, free to make our choices and create new paths, but I am now bound to continue the same path.*

Nicole mentioned she had a spiritual director, so we arranged for her to have a call with him. She also asked that one of us talk to him as well, so Gemma put me in charge to have the conversation. He was a well-respected Benedictine priest residing in California. As Nicole said his name, goosebumps ran up my arms as my mind skipped to another memory.

Was this him? My mind skipped to a memory, *Could this be the same Benedictine priest who offered Mass on that fateful day in 1988 when my friend Janet and I attended a Mass before we went on our hike outside of Carmel, California?*

Many years ago, a Benedictine priest, renowned for his contemplative gifts, had spoken words that penetrated my heart to the core during Liturgy. I was taken in by the ecstasy of his words during the service. The end of the Liturgy came, and Janet and I remained in deep absorption, kneeling in the front row of the chapel.

We hoped to slip out quietly and start our long weekend hike. The chapel steps were filled with joyful familiar conversation by all the lay Carmelites who had attended Mass. It was slow moving through them, but we were stopped in our tracks as we saw this priest pushing his way through the crowd to us. Janet and I stood speechless as he stopped right in front of me. With sincere determination he looked me in the eyes and said, "Please, promise me you will pray for me."

I rang the number, wondering if I would be able to tell if it was him. We had not kept in touch beyond that fleeting encounter on the steps of Carmel-by-the-Sea monastery.

"Hello, this is Father Tom," the tone of his words felt familiar to my soul. Our conversation flowed slowly. He invited me to speak freely about Nicole. Since she had requested this conversation, I trusted it was okay.

"We are not sure what to do," I began. "We love having her, she is a wonderful addition to our community. She has asked to be released from many of the observances of our lifestyle, and we are not sure if having so many exceptions is a sign that our lifestyle is not meant for her. She feels like the observance is too severe."

Once again, I wondered, *What is essential to our Carmelite Rule and charism?* Nicole inspired me with her penetrating reflections.

I began reflecting more deeply, *The unchangeable part of our life was preserving the charism, to learn how to live and walk in God's Presence as hermits in community. The observance is the way each community chooses to live out that charism, hopefully keeping the observance alive so that it is a living symbol wherein the woman finds herself in God. Since Carmelite monastic nuns are autonomous, each group is free to discern their community observance. In addition to the Rule with its eighteen chapters, there are Constitutions prepared by meetings of nuns to give extra support in discernment. Though they were detailed and lengthy, they offered insights more than proposing obligations. So was this observance foundational to being Carmelite?*

The priest did not offer any suggestion, so I wasn't sure where to go. "Nicole doesn't believe in our fasting; it is normal for us during Lent to fast for breakfast and eat a light dinner, but she wants to be excluded from this, so we are not sure how to work with her on that difference," my words were hesitant, I didn't want to sound judgmental.

"Hmmm, to ask for exclusions such as that does seem a divide," he commented but nothing beyond that. Our conversation ended there. I thanked him for his time and refrained from asking him if he ever offered Mass in Carmel, it seemed wrong to turn the attention away from Nicole.

My internal conflict with no resolve led me to disassociate from it and ignore my inner guide. While I told myself it was an act of trust, I could tell that my inner freedom was disappearing. It was so much easier being anonymous in the community, scrubbing floors, and cooking meals. My playful disposition was being slowly replaced by a solemn face that could hide how I really felt. There was a certain feeling of being trapped but I couldn't quite put my finger on it.

These instances evoked deep reflection, *In my formative years (the first four and half years in monastic life), I was taught that Christ was always coming to me, speaking to me, and guiding me through all leaders and structures. At first, I questioned if this level of surrender of will and intelligent inquiry was healthy. Ultimately, I felt inspired to assent and jump into the observance to learn its path of union with God. And I did. Once this internal step was taken, I let everything else go and looked at Carmelite life through this lens. It was a tremendous source of grace and healing. Yet, it was also a cause of confusion now that I was called into leadership. This surrender wasn't leading me into freedom, instead it left me tenuous to use my voice, to ask for guidance when needed.*

At times my head would roll around trying to understand how it is ego driven to admit your workload is too heavy, or that you need guidance. As I sat wondering how to navigate this conflict, I flashed back to a conversation I had with Mother Anna years before. My spiritual director said that a contemplative, a true contemplative, "Doesn't need anything." She gave me an example of what she meant. "A woman entered our monastery as a postulant in the seventies and asked to take her meditation outside instead of in the chapel with everyone else. The woman confided that nature connected her to God due to her Native American background," Mother Anna began. "The woman said she needed the land and needed to be connected to the nature around her, but I told her that if she were a true contemplative, she wouldn't need an exception to our custom." The woman left.

Mother Anna's conclusion was not that the life was not right for her, but rather that she was not truly a contemplative. I silently disagreed with my superior, but I also wanted to be the kind of contemplative that my inner state would be unaffected by my outer circumstance. The entire perspective felt like a trap, eliminating the ability to look at it differently. Perhaps the woman who needed to be in nature was having difficulties practicing meditation inside because she wasn't called to *our* way of doing things.

The only answer that made sense for me in the moment followed this line of logic, *I am called to be Carmelite, Mary inspired me to join this Texas community. The superior asked me out of obedience to act and communicate in ways that are contrary to what is right in my heart, but God sees my obedience, and in this God is pleased.*

Lent came and went, and the glory and bliss of Easter infected us all. Easter unleashed new levels of joy as it usually did. The chant wove a golden tapestry of exultation every day and night. We feasted for days and had the leisure of table recreation. Nicole found new joy in our life. It seemed to soften the hard edges in her mind around community life. She loved two of my own favorite Easter chants, the Haec Dies and the Victimae Paschales, The first contains

153 notes for just one phrase. It builds and builds, like a wild wave rising with momentum and then cresting. The second is the traditional story of Mary Magdalene at the tomb. The time came for Mother Gemma to choose whether to invite her to become a novice or not. In the end all the nuns voted to accept her into novitiate if she wished to take the next step as well.

She did.

Her ceremony day was set for some time in May, keeping it in the Easter season which seemed a fit for her spirituality, so inclined to the Via Positiva. This ceremony is simple yet powerful. It happens just like an entrance, at the end of the Mass in the morning before the final blessing. Nicole, the nuns, and the priest all had parts in the ritual which stemmed from early Christian times. The long history of these traditions and rituals, which includes ceremonies of vows of poverty, chastity, and obedience as well, nestle within a longer human history, taking inspired elements from various rituals of Judaism and paganism.

Once Nicole recited her intention as the ceremony had it worded, the nuns recited their intention in welcoming her to Carmelite monastic life. The priest then offered blessings and consecration leading to the dramatic proclamation, "You will no longer be known as Nicole, but rather are clothed in a new name, Sister Magdalena of the Holy Eucharist." Her face beamed, every cell in her body beamed in that moment. For months she gushed with sentiments of how amazing and perfect her name was. *Were her reservations resolved? Maybe she was called given how much she could feel the gift of the Divine in her name.*

Adding to the joy that prevailed for the next month was my announcement to her and Christine that our yearly retreat was about to commence. As Sister Magdalena listened to all the details, her excitement was undeniable: "You mean I will have all this time to do whatever I want?" She was as bright as a lightbulb. We suspended the normal rhythm and hired a retreat leader who would give us talks, so the schedule was completely different. Inwardly I was aware of the unspoken community expectation that you would throw yourself into service by offering to cover duties such as cooking meals to relieve Sister Catherine, but I stopped before saying anything. Her thoughts felt fresh against the old messages from North Dakota emphasizing self-deprecation to the exclusion of self-care. "Yes," I said, "you can decide to do whatever feels uplifting to do."

Thank you, Magdalena, I silently expressed, *thank you for reminding me of my own longings when I had entered, and the trust that following your heart would lead to goodness.* Answers to my own questions were coming to me in unexpected ways.

Shortly after, Mother Gemma confided in me how much she disliked her own religious name. She told the story of how Mother Anna put it on the list of names, and how she submitted a name that had much more meaning for her heart. Once her ceremony came, and she knelt there with open heart, the name given her, Sister Gemma of the Angels, caused only sadness. All these years later she bore it like a sacrifice. It was so contrary to my own experience of hearing wedding bells when I heard, "You will no longer be known as Kimberly Braun, but rather, Sister Mary Annunciata of Jesus."

Gemma rustled with a thought, "I wonder if I could change it."

"Gemma, you should totally change it to what makes your heart sing," I supported.

"You know I love Therese so much," she ventured, "what about Mother Therese of Divine Mercy?"

"That is awesome," I responded. "And your feast day could move from September 30th, Feast of the Angels, to October 1st, the Feast of Therese!" My words excited us both. "Also," I went on thinking out loud, "your next feast day is your twenty-fifth anniversary of vows, how special would that be?"

She looked into the logistics of changing her name and found it was very easy to do.

At our next chapter meeting she told everyone about the change and gave us permission to start meeting to create her feast day which would take place in six months. The joy of the project was matching the joy in our community.

There was something about the permission to plan her feast day that felt like we were being a little deviant, a little like walking in the road instead of on the sidewalk. Outside this occasion we were never allowed to speak informally or create together.

Even though Sister Elisha still buckled at my assignment to lead, we found a way through it all.

Once again, I asked Gemma to assign Elisha the lead, but she refused. "You know," I tried to open discussion, "she really wants to have the chance to use her own gifts of leadership. She really wants to be your right-hand person," I thought it was worthy to address her need and concern.

We met the week following to decide what to do for her big day. Just before the meeting I learned that Saint Therese was also being proclaimed as a doctor of the church that year, 1997. What a synchronistic series of events. Over and again, I was sweetly surprised at how the Divine orchestrated a layered symphony of small things, like monastic dates lining up with big things, like Therese's well-deserved distinction. This happened for us in correlation with world events, individual prayer requests, cycles of nature, and every imaginable happening in life. Yes, the Divine orchestration was reflected in the microcosm and the macrocosm in perfect harmony.

We quickly decided on a feast day quote and card design which was tradition in our community to do when a woman professes her vows and for those anniversaries. This was a piece of art in the form of a card about the size of a bookmark. Manuel, our faithful printer and faithful deliverer of homemade tamales, gave us sample card stock, colored pens, and scissors to cut artistic edges. We chose a silver embossed font printed upon subtle pink paper boasting a quote of

Therese. It was a quote that Gemma loved; it was a quote we all loved.

During this time, I was researching music to see if there were any songs using the poems of Therese. One of our long-distance friends, a lay Carmelite musician in Pennsylvania who was also an organist and composer, wrote back.

"There is this woman in Philadelphia," I brought up eagerly at our next meeting, "who is willing to gift us eight songs she composed in honor of Therese, using her writings," my voice raised a little from the hopeful excitement. "What do you think about getting copies for Sister Gemma's feast day?"

Everyone nodded without hesitation. "Wow! That would be beautiful!" Sister Elizabeth exclaimed in her gregarious tones. Quickly I sent off communication in the now old-fashioned way, snail mail. The world was changing around us in 1997 but we did not have a computer. Even using the regular phone was a rarity. Handwritten letters, Palmer Method influenced I might add, were our primary form of connection with our friends and family.

The letter reached her and just two weeks later an envelope returned stamped from Pennsylvania. Excitedly opening the large envelope, the sheet music popped into my hands, and the words of my dear friend Therese's poems shined before me. Accompanying the copies was a heartfelt note from the composer, expressing her excitement to contribute to such a special day. The composition had a range that spanned the staff. *This is going to be hard for the sisters to learn,* I thought. Before introducing it, I played all of it through a couple times, shifting any notes or intervals that would make it easier to learn.

We had been given permission to practice for about half an hour after compline almost every night. Compline would conclude our day with a Marian chant. "Vir-goooo Mari----i---i-iaaaaaa," the last words would gently move us into grand silence, except this time. We had permission to practice for our surprise, so each of us would put our Liber Usualis on the shelf and remain kneeling as Mother Gemma took her leave.

Once the door closed behind her, we smiled and opened binders containing the ten songs from Pennsylvania. Everyone held their copies, and we went over each phrase many times. Sweet memories were being made, lingering even into this moment. A stream always moves, and we move on the faithful current of Divine Love carrying us on.

If we flow with our lives, the sense of destruction is minimized; only resistance creates a tension we call violence or destruction.

Sister Elizabeth worked on Gemma's personal feast day card. She had a terrific gift of drawing and loved crafts so we just left her to it. In addition to the artwork on the front, Elizabeth would craft a poem that would celebrate Gemma in her life of devotion drawing upon words of Therese or mentioning Therese's love for her, and of course rhyming from beginning to end.

Sister Catherine spent hours preparing her menu. My role was to craft a fun song to play on the guitar at table recreation.

Gemma loved—and I mean *loved*—John of the Cross. Her own choice of quotes would often be lines from his works. So Elisha and I came up with an idea to create small hand-sewn booklets containing excerpts of all his work. We called them, Sayings of Light and Love, taken from something he himself titled. The book was about three inches squared with approximately sixty pages. It was a miracle we were able to typeset and produce an original creative composition accurately laid out using only an old-fashioned typewriter from which we made copies on our old copy machine.

Sad news came our way during this time. We had noticed that after the initial fundraising mail-out months prior, new ideas were not coming forward. Our plate was full, so we put off calling a committee meeting. We were surprised, yet grateful to receive a letter from the committee lead, Claire. Gemma opened it eagerly, looking forward to reading about their ideas for raising more money. Claire began with a few kind words then line after line outlined the opinion of the committee around our choices, since we had shown them the rough draft sketches from Frank.

The body of the letter was a criticism of what we were doing and how we were doing it, presented as advice. We read on as each element of the project was broken down and commented upon. Since their role was fundraising and did not include being advisers, we were not confiding in them the layers of research and dialogue going into the project. The letter stung. Sister Gemma's brow stitched, and her face became flushed with a mild anger. She pushed the letter across the table. My heart just sank, realizing they were spending their time this way. In the end, Claire suggested that we turn to them for advice on how to build it and what to use for materials. The letter was signed in the name of them all.

We decided to meet with Claire and a few others to see what was going on. The meeting was uneventful as we did not know how best to approach the conflict, and found ourselves explaining the project progress, instead of inspiring their focus upon their role. A few committee members gave us other ideas of what they thought we should be doing, for which we thanked them out of politeness.

Sister Gemma wanted them disbanded and told me she would not meet with Claire again, that I would need to do it. Not long after that, Casey Williams came to us in secret. "I am going to step off the committee," she said, "I did not approve the letter even though it says it is from us all. The meeting is consumed with Claire going on about the building project, and what you all are doing wrong, and we never get to any fundraising ideas."

Two days later, another committee member stopped in. "Sister Gemma, Sister Mary, I am going to step off the committee, I am so sorry," she went on. "There is only discord when we get together, and it seems like I am wasting my time. I want to support you in what you are creating and not criticize you."

This was the final straw. We were upset, but again, not sure what to do, so we decided to disband the committee through a letter. Our decision was a poor one. Regardless of the difficulty of getting everyone together, doing so would have been the way for us to disband the committee from a place where they could hear our gratitude for all they had done up to that point.

Once this was decided, I turned my attention back to the project. There were many key pieces that needed to be planned, even before groundbreaking. Estimates needed to be secured, key contractors decided upon, and quotes needed to be obtained, especially in light of the mission style we were aspiring to build and even more imperative since we no longer had a fundraising committee.

Lighting was a common accent in each mission and one we wanted to imitate. Most had chandeliers hanging from the beams running the length of the chapel as the main light source for celebrations. An alternate daily source of lighting for visitors were sconces that could be turned on individually.

I sketched up examples to show as talking points. The first was a three-tiered chandelier with the bottom tier being a three-foot diameter ring with individual lights placed about six inches apart. The lights were designed to look like candles. The middle and top rings would be slightly smaller, like a tiered birthday cake. An electrical junction extended upward a couple inches with a casing to hide the wires.

Someone gave us the name of a blacksmith, Bob, who gladly came to us to talk about our needs. Not wasting any time, I slid the small sketch of the chandelier under the grille into his waiting hand. His glance gave him certainty on cost, "You know I am completely out of your price range."

"Can you give me an idea so I can know what I am asking?" I hoped to get as much information as possible.

"Well, three thousand to thirty-three hundred dollars per chandelier; that's what it'll cost you."

"Really," I said in a bit of disbelief.

The meeting was short and sweet, and while I was grateful for his directness, the information was saddening. *If this is the general cost of iron work, we will not be able to afford the lighting we want,* I quickly tabulated all the lights, grilles, and hardware.

He saw my disappointment. "Iron work is very expensive. You should go to Mexico for everything. I have a dependable contact," he smiled.

"Really?" I said eagerly.

Pulling a small, crumpled piece of paper out of his pocket, about the size of a receipt, he wrote: *Fernando 018834592600.* "Go here. The Ramirez family lives just across the border in Nuevo Laredo, and they can do all you want for a fraction of the cost."

The idea of Mexico… *hmmmm…* I mused about the possibility playfully. Inwardly I had a sense that Mother Gemma would like the idea, but I couldn't be sure.

Knock, knock, I lightly tapped her door after bidding the blacksmith goodbye.

"Well, what did he say?" she hopefully looked at me.

"Good news and bad news; he said each chandelier would cost us anywhere between three thousand and thirty-three hundred. He said these would be the prices for just about anyone here in Texas," letting her receive the surprise. "But, I don't know what you are going to think of this," I stalled, "he said we could get everything in Mexico, and he even gave us a name and number." The space between us was pregnant as I stood before her in trust that whatever God's will was, would be done.

Her mouth moved into a smile, "Well, let's do it!" she said, giving me a chance to reveal the excitement brimming below my calm composure which was striving to be open in either direction.

That night our weekly rotation of duties took place. Each week one sister woke everyone up for matins, another for lauds, another led the opening for the chant, including the reading of all prayers, another would lead the opening line of the chant, etc. This week it was my turn to wake everyone up for matins.

Awaking first, around 11:30 p.m., knowing I was the initiator of these women awaking to praise the Beloved in the night, contained a certain joy that never abated. There was something quite special about all the world sleeping while we kept vigil. That night, I made my way to each dorm, lightly knocking on each sister's door until it opened to signal me they were up.

Then it took an unusual turn. Exiting the furthest door from the chapel, my eyes were taking in the night sky as I moved swiftly to the chapel door which we always kept unlocked. About four feet from the door, I jolted to see a skunk in the corner, at the hinges of the screen door! We both jumped in acknowledgment. Dumbfounded I stood there, leaving him unintentionally trapped. With a quick shift of his butt toward me and a lift of the tail I said in slow motion, "OOOOOOOhhhhhh, noooooooo," my feet tried to move away as the odor singed my nose. I was sprayed.

He disappeared completely while I stood there bewildered. *What should I do?* Going into the chapel was out of the question, going into the dorm to get Mother Gemma didn't seem to make sense either, so I moved to the grassy courtyard. One by one the sisters came out of their doors, and I could hear, "Eeeeeuuuuw," as they spontaneously pulled their hand to their nose and mouth. The odor had traveled down the whole corridor. I let Sister Elizabeth pass; she didn't see me standing there in the corridor. Then both Sister Catherine and Mother Gemma came out simultaneously.

"Psssssst, pssssssst," I whispered loudly. "Mother Gemma, Mother Gemma." They both looked out my direction, their hands vainly shielding their noses from the odor penetrating the night.

"I got sprayed by a skunk," I whispered loudly. She started laughing, then Sister Catherine started laughing! Which got me laughing in relief too. Mother Gemma came a little closer, deciding what to do as she moved.

"Hmmmmmm, follow me," she motioned. So the three of us went right into the chapel, walking as swiftly as we could, picking up a trail of the other sisters as all of us raced into the kitchen. "Get your clothes off and get into the bathtub," Gemma said. I gladly followed any direction; the pain of the odor was uncomfortable and embarrassing.

Sisters Elisha and Catherine went to the cooler, fortunately situated just near the bathroom that had a bathtub, bringing out every can of tomato juice we had. Openers in hand, they emptied all we had into the bathtub, and I jumped in. "Aaaagh," it was so gross sliding into the bathtub. The thick tomato juice was mealy and sticky, and I dreaded it touching my body. I lay there and swooshed the juice over myself while Sister Catherine gathered my habit into a garbage bag, storing it outside until the morning would shine a light upon better solutions.

In time the juice washed me of the smell, it took two full immersions. Our matins became the vigil of cleansing Annunciata! *How grateful I was not to be alone.* I looked at everyone quietly as we all went back to bed.

Fortunately, we each had a second habit to wear for work. They were lighter and cheaper in material, but sufficient. The years of wearing a formal habit for Mass left me feeling underdressed for Liturgy even if my white cloak covered the garment.

Breakfast came, "*Din-din-din-din-ding*" the small hand bell in Gemma's lightly fingered grasp rang us into a recreation at table. We all burst into laughter.

"Oh my gosh! That was terrible!" we all said overlapping our suppressed emotions of the night before. "What happened?" Gemma asked. So I retold the story in great detail.

Everyone added their own impressions. "I had no idea what happened," Christine chimed in.

"Skunk, came to my mind as soon as I opened the door, but I thought it was far away," Sister Elizabeth threw in.

"You were so funny out there in the courtyard saying, pssssst, pssssst," Gemma teased and Catherine nodded.

Elisha's eyes sparkled, "Thank goodness we had tomato juice saved up for the fast days."

That morning Catherine took care of my habit. At a certain point I saw it, saturated in tomato juice, hanging on the fence. My eyes and bows said, *thank you, thank you, thank you*, as I looked at her. She got the message, and her maternal lovingness moved her head downward in acceptance of the gratitude.

Another day in monastic life. And another day of our two novices moving in opposite directions.

The annual retreat had inspired Sister Magdalena to open her heart more to the life, but not long after her internal conflicts with our lifestyle resumed. She left that summer. At the same time, we all voted to invite Christine into novitiate where she would receive her religious name.

All endings are sad, but the custom we Carmelites had for a woman leaving was severe. They simply leave without a goodbye and the community is informed of what took place during the day. When Donna left the year prior, I was crushed to learn this custom, and it didn't hurt any less when Sister Magdalena left.

Gemma let me know, "This is what we do as Carmelites," which was code for, "there will be no discussion about this practice." No one had left while I was in North Dakota so having someone leave without getting to say goodbye was new for me.

Christine's entrance to novitiate was set for August 15th, the Feast of the Assumption of Mary. She received the name, Sister Mary Felicity of the Trinity. This next step for her deepened her contentment which in turn inspired each of us. Our joy and her joy were complete.

Soil of Creative Impulse Is Tilled

Coming on the tail of this joy was another joy. Pierce and Deanna had prepared all the paperwork giving us ownership of the land. The couple picked up Gemma and me, taking us to their lawyer's office. Slowly he explained the papers, showing us the plot of land and the pre-arranged agreement as it was articulated in the highly finessed language of the law. The Holts gave us 640 acres, allotting to us one-hundred acres of the section in full ownership immediately and the rest to come at their passing. Up front the contract stated they could use the well that was our water source too, and the remaining land for grazing, which felt right given our lack of need for 540 extra acres; after all we were a small community just learning to get onto its feet.

I sat there in love. They were so happy to know us, to have us building a monastery on their property, to feel in some way that we were their special friends. And we felt the same. They were dear to our hearts, on a very personal level.

Early retirement was possible, given his success in football, allowing them to make their way back to Texas to begin a life as ranchers. Deanna took time to share with me their own building project of restoring an 1893 home to be their permanent dwelling.

The plantation style home had a porch extending around the four walls. She showed us gunnysack secured to the walls. "Look at this," she said as she pulled the old material from the wall. "This was their only insulation; Ashley and I have been slowly pulling it all away to see what is below." As a woman of deep devotion to God, just like Pierce, they used their resources to give back to community. "Is it okay to spend so much money on our home?" Deanna asked one time, confiding her doubts.

"You give so much love Deanna, I believe you can trust, trust, it is fair to accept this gift of a comfortable home as being from God."

As we made our way back home, with ownership papers in hand, they walked in with us. I can still see them standing there as we turned to say goodbye. "We want to do something else," Pierce said clearly and quietly. "We want to give you $50,000 to help get you started; it is thrilling to have you on our land, and we know there will be extra costs involved in building on our undeveloped ranch land, so this will be a little help for you to feel confident in moving forward."

Shocked, Mother Gemma and I stood there, "Really?" This blew wind into the wings of our project. We said yes.

Quick preparation for the groundbreaking ceremony, happening September 15th, ensued. The bishop, always making time for us, arranged this day.

Word of mouth formed our invitations. Mother Gemma spray painted the two shovels we would use to dig into the ground signifying the beginning of construction, and the bishop contacted various priests and helpers. And it was very simple, the entire blessing of the land was initiated and concluded within thirty minutes, 25 percent of the time it took for us to travel to and from our new building site, soon to become our home.

The day was bright and sunny, not a cloud in the sky. As our car arrived at the site, my own soul felt as wide as the sky and land around me. Here, here we are my Love. I am here to create with you, thank you, I silently and wordlessly expressed. I felt like I was part of a poem being written by the hand of the Divine.

People flurried in every direction while we set up the small podium and stands for the ritual. All showed up in full joy, which was the only ingredient we really needed for this simple service. About 150 attended the groundbreaking. Frank came down, the Holts were front and center, and even a journalist for the local paper attended.

I had no idea where I fit. Even though I was clearly a powerful part of the project, I was the youngest in the community and not officially designated with any title for my role. Fortunately, Mother Gemma stepped up to the plate, and since she was the leader, all revolved according to her direction. She took my arm, pulling me to stand right beside her. The bishop started the prayers, songs were sung, both of us added intentions, and then the two shovels were given us to officially break land while the formal consecration of the project took place.

Pictures were snapped, and Mother Gemma made the front cover of the local paper that week. Our larger community was then aware of the official start of the monastery construction in their midst.

The simple ritual was over as soon as it started. We all stood around happily eating sweets and drinking punch.

We waited until after the groundbreaking to give the committee the disbanding letter. It seemed most fair to be able to celebrate all the hard work to date with them since they had been an integral part of the project up until this point. None of us wanted the relationship to end this early, but sometimes the time for ending comes. The letter attempted to express gratitude and express the reasons for our decision.

A couple days later we heard that Claire called a meeting, she was crushed and openly cried. One of our committee members privately came to us, hoping the complaint they had spoken had not caused such an abrupt decision on our part. It was over, and while we were relieved, we were also incredibly sorry we did not choose another way to go about it.

Every other part of the project flew forward. In just eighteen months since the moment in the Texas goldenrods and the vote of our community, we had a major building project in motion. We had secured many subcontractors and suppliers and even had a final approved design. We had a road and three-phase power, and a storage shed among countless other donations. I sat in suspension as all my being felt the movement of Spirit, as within, so without.

Matching the flow of the project, our community was in the final two weeks leading to Gemma's big feast day and twenty-fifth anniversary of her vows. She would be able at the end of this celebration to have the religious name that made her heart happy. We rose at matins to begin the celebration before the dawn could bring in the day.

The inspired reading was an accounting by Therese of a moment of great illumination.

"My desires caused me a veritable martyrdom," she wrote as she remembered her searching inquiry to find a name for her own vocation that could match her desires... She went on, "and the apostle Paul explains how all the most perfect gifts are nothing without love. That charity is the excellent way that leads most surely to God. I finally had rest," she went on, leading her to cry out, "O Jesus, my Love... my vocation, at last I have found it... my vocation is Love! Thus I will be everything and my dream will be realized." (*The Story of a Soul, The Autobiography of Therese of Lisieux*, Chapter 11.)

We all knelt there in the midnight hour in silence. Mother Gemma was now, officially, Mother Therese of Divine Mercy. The room was bright white with Therese's presence there with us. About thirty minutes, and numerous chants later, we concluded, and all kissed their kneelers and left to return to bed. All but me. I lingered. Once I knew everyone was in bed, I went to the organ to quietly play and sing to express my love to her for a little longer.

Whenever one of us was honored, we all were filled with joy. This disappearance of myself yielded the fruit of fullness that is impossible to put into words. I could feel myself vibrate with Divine Presence, and in the vibration was the cosmic painting that made up this special day: Jesus, Therese, Mary, saints, angels, loved ones, ancestors, Carmelites, unknown realms, newly named Mother Therese, and each of my sisters here. There was a Spirit river flowing through me while I also felt myself to be the river.

The entire feast day surprised Mother Therese at every turn. All the songs for Mass and at our party, the food, the gifts, the poems, and how much love we showed to her, our leader. Her feast day card was a highlight, along with the booklets Elisha and I had crafted. The day was made full as we held the door for her and hid inspirational notes in her prayer books. I even let our practice of custody of the eyes go to smile at her with as much love as I could.

It was inspiring to see her witness what it looks like when a leader is able to receive. We broke out in song over lunch, using one of Therese's poems, "Jesus, c'est toi, Jesus, c'est toi, l'agneu je t'aime Jesus, c'est toi...."

And she exclaimed, "Sing it again, sing it again!"

Like children who do not want Christmas to end, we pushed against the clock until the time for bed was undeniable. Once again monastic flow softened the lessons of impermanence for me. There would be another special day the next day. The moment of the day is eternal and contained in the moment of a tomorrow.

The next day a few project items took precedence. We were required to give the bishop a working set of prints before hiring anyone other than planning contractors and power installments. Using my trusted architect ruler, I tried to work out our own solutions before calling Frank hoping to save him time, which happened much to my surprise. Within the day, we had a working plan which he saved to his computer. With this done, we planned a third visit to Frank but first we would meet one man that would become one of the most important participants of the project.

I am not sure how we learned about him. He seemed to be carried like an angel into our lives.

A cloud of dust preceded the loud diesel rumbling approaching our home. Soon after, a large red pickup truck emerged, and the placid driver could be seen through the driver's seat window with his ball cap and sun-drenched skin.

It was Michael Box.

He stepped down from the cab in an air of noticeable integrity and hardworking nature worn upon his face and dusty jeans. With a respect that sent chills, he took off his hat and shook our hands. "Nice to meet you both," he began in a modest, somewhat shy gesture.

I liked him, immediately.

Finding a general contractor was of utmost importance, and it seems he was our first interviewee. The simple plans, just a couple pages, unrolled onto the front of his truck. I held one end, and he held the other. We let him look at it, which he did.

Silently and slowly his eyes moved through each print.

"I normally build small residential homes," he disclosed to us. "This would be a new level of work for me," he continued, clearly intrigued.

We openly shared our intentions. "Mr. Box, we are building this dependent upon donations and do not even have a budget, but we believe God will guide us and provide all we need," I began. "Many of these details will need to be decided as we go, even changed if a donation does not come in, so our hope is that we can manage the flow of supplies and time and in a way that works for you to manage the project."

Our need was so utterly unique, and I was quite glad he did not run away at that point; after all we had no idea how easy or hard it would be.

His eye saw clearly. "There is no way I could be the one to juggle the conversations around donations," he agreed. Looking at me, "You do it."

"Me???" I started laughing in disbelief.

"Yes, if you are the general contractor, you can hire me as project manager," thoughtfully assessing his idea as he put it out there.

His nod seemed to be the personal approval of the plan.

I could see it would be a delicately interwoven relationship involving deep trust and a lot of dialogue. This arrangement would put him dependent on me for having supplies and contractors in place as we needed them.

It felt right. In fact, the thought of having a right-hand person excited me, but the reality hit me clearly, I am not seeking this role, my Love, my God, but if you wish it, I will trust You will help me do what I have never done before, I reflected inwardly. The level of management that was implied flashed before my eyes along with the need to seek supplies months and months in advance, store as items came in until they were used, the need to know who our contractors would be and who could donate when, along with organizing all the daily crews and activities, all displayed themselves before me like a life-size mural. Trust, I thought, is the only response that will meet the magnitude of the gift laid before us.

His YES was another sign of Spirit bringing confirmation, and his YES propelled my yes, into an unforeseen direction that would change my life.

Within the week we drew up the contract with the help of a friend. In the agreement we hired Michael as the project manager, we accepted the role of general contractor, and we secured his crew as our main carpentry subcontractors (which would include more spontaneous needs than either of us realized at the time).

Mother Therese signed on the line and asked me to sign below her since she was the superior.

As my fingers held the pen, I was aware that it was me in the lead role, that the project was falling into my hands increasingly each day, and that Spirit was moving through me. It was as though I was unappointed by the community even though I was in the role, while simultaneously being appointed by God because it was in actuality happening with grace having me in the lead.

It wasn't about credit, as I paused a bit longer holding the pen. It was about authenticity. A realization came to me, this means I cannot lean into support or understanding of my sisters for assuming the immense responsibility since my gift of service will take place without being named.

On another level, the signatures completed that day gave me even more freedom to accomplish the work, for it counted me as insignificant. And in this way God could pour forth blessings. Each time I spoke, support abounded for the construction. My words moved the community, the people of various faiths, the men of many trades, the suppliers who did not even know they had a monastery in their town, and even fewer understood what we did here. These exchanges moved me as well, deeply.

Frank was incredibly excited to have us come to him, saying he had a surprise for us.

Days later we anxiously bolted out the door after Mass, getting to Dallas a little after the lunch hour. Frank made it out of his door to greet us before we had a chance to get to him. He wanted to personally escort us. Opening the door, he gestured to the middle of the room where a scaled monastery crafted from thin balsam wood laid before us. It was for our speakroom so people could see it and donate to the project. And it was a breathtaking piece of art.

During our meeting, Frank realized the public chapel fell under the requirements of the law to have handicap facilities for every bathroom and entrance. In applying this code, the floor plan would not work because of all the intersections of roof to the varied wall heights. What should we do? Do we start over? We had worked so many hours on the floor plan.

He and I decided to work this out by phone, instead of using our precious appointment time, and turned to other details for the working prints. I spent hours and hours flipping rooms, and spaces, trying to make it work.

I flashed back to 1975 in my room on 8474 Smallwood Lane. Mom and Dad let my sister Kelly and me create our bedrooms. We were allowed to decide wall color and furniture and everything. Kelly went with her favorite color blue and paste-on animals on the walls. I decided to try to make it like being outside, even going as far as to ask for AstroTurf so the floor could be imitation grass. They convinced me to go with an indoor/outdoor green carpet.

Once completed I would occasionally feel like rearranging my room. When the urge would arise, my entire waking moments were devoted to measuring and creating ideas. White paper would be marked up with my pencil, first creating a box that had the dimensions of my room. I would figure out the legend of what an inch equivalated, and the size of every piece of furniture. Sometimes the furniture would be measured and cut out of colored construction paper so I could move the pieces around on the paper creating new ideas. Eventually what felt right came about and I would move all my belongings, by myself, to the new look.

Here I was again, twenty years later doing the same thing on a larger scale but with the same glee. Everything seems to be a preparation for the next moment of our lives, I mused.

Since an easy solution was not presenting itself, I proposed to Frank, "Let's see if we can get an exemption from the handicap requirement throughout the complex."

He and his associate called the contact for this permitting only to receive the disinterested mandate that the public chapel required us to apply the handicap law to the entire structure.

Hmmm. He and I spoke and wondered, since most of it was private residence, why wouldn't we be allowed exemption in the private areas, but follow the guidelines in the public areas? This was too much to ask Frank to work out, so I obtained the number from him.

I called that same day.

They required us to fax them information so we could discuss the construction project in detail. I pointed out that 13,000 square feet of the facility was private, for our cloistered community. I also noted that our infirmary, which would house our older sisters needing an extra hand was not only handicap-equipped but was designed to help them be as self-sufficient as possible. I showed them the entrances to our community spaces were all designed wide enough for wheelchairs.

The last point I made was that I was the general contractor.

Bingo!!!! This was it! As our own contractors, we were building our own private home which exempted us from the handicap law as it was written.

We couldn't have known it at the time, but this one decision saved us tens of thousands of dollars. If we had been obliged to the local laws governing public structures, we would have been required to complete a long list of permits issued upon inspections at various points of the construction project. This would have required the project to stop and wait for each stage of inspection, halting the flow of labor which I orchestrated like an ongoing symphony of paid and donated labor. The cost would be cumbersome.

Bubbling with joy, my fingers raced to dial Frank's number. I got his assistant and held my breath hoping we would be connected to him.

"We did it! They gave us approval I shouted!" Cheers pealed on the other end, "Way to go Sister Annunciata! Whooo-hoooooo!!!!"

"Roger, Sister Annunciata got an exemption from the handicap requirement!" he shouted to the room next door, "Whoooo-hooo!"

The exemption was quickly faxed to his office for our file. Another hurdle cleared. My acceptance of the role of general contractor as the owner, coupled with our building location, freed us from all permitting. It was a grace that made the project possible.

Our weekly chapter meetings burst with project details. Each week I prepared the long list of development to disclose to the sisters, outlining supplies, contractors, and development. Some items we voted upon, many we did not since there was nothing to decide, only news to report. Catherine, Elizabeth, and Felicity jumped on the joy train, seeing the fascinating speed with which progress happened. Elisha still put her hand up to vote with everyone else so she did not stand apart, but her face revealed sadness. There was an area that could be entirely entrusted to her, that is, the sewing building. This building was freestanding and structurally could be designed how she saw fit, so I jumped on the opportunity and invited her to reveal to me what she wanted and needed.

By October 15th, only four weeks after the groundbreaking, power came to our site. The day was windy and cold, and Casey Williams drove me out early in the morning to await the large truck bringing the thick wooden poles to be dropped for lines to reach us. Our jackets shielded us from the wind and the skies boasting thick white clouds threatened light rain, but the brightness of our smiles could not be hidden.

Plans in hand, clear on the final pole site from Frank, we waited near the well. The autumn wind evoked feelings of change, and this was the first actual change to the land we were creating.

That day, the ground would be drilled for posts that would rise about thirty feet into the air. Once power was there, we would have the ability to give electricity to all.

About half an hour later the truck could be heard moving over rocks and weaving its way to our hill. Primed by Jim Martin, the men were notably enthusiastic as they rolled out of the cabs and met Casey and me.

Prints unrolled across the hood of their trucks, and we ran through details. Moments later a drill so large it was anchored to a truck that needed to electrically maneuver it while a man controlled it from his place in the cab rose into the air.

Once again, I felt the monastery fully there as I looked at the open land before me. It was coming and would not be far away. Arriving home that day our little homemade monastery looked different. Our time here is coming to an end, I could feel the same change in the air coming through screen doors as I joined everyone for vespers. What am I feeling? I tried to find words, Gratitude for being a Carmelite, gratitude for being there, gratitude for being an instrument for our permanent monastery, gratitude for feeling my heart and body and mind being used in service.

It was there in Texas that the Carmelite book of Chant (I am not sure that is the official name) came into my hands. A large heavy book requiring two hands to hold it, the binding measured about sixteen-by-sixteen inches, the pages were thick, and the notation was large, old style with perhaps four staves per page. It felt like a connection to the many generations of Carmelites. Imagining Teresa of Avila or John of the Cross holding a book just like this back in the 1400s, my fingers slowly moved across the Latin words, chanting with ease the unfamiliar tones.

Like a swirling vortex my body moved up and up.

How can everyone be included in leading this beautiful chant, how can everyone feel valued, and still preserve pitch and resonance that is sweet to the ear? Sister Elisha deeply desired to lead the long chants and when Mother Therese would choose her, they would be off key, and we could not chime in. Yet, it made her so happy.

Mother Therese decided she did not want anyone who struggled with pitch to lead chanting from the ancient book of Carmelite chant. While Catherine did not care, Elisha had such sadness in not being chosen. Even though I had no influence, I wondered about it. I could understand it from both sides. Should everyone be allowed to lead regardless of skill? Should we only use chants that everyone could sing?

While these were my thoughts, they remained alone echoing in my head, longing to lay themselves out and be met with other's thoughts. This to me, was what it meant to create community, to discern together our observance.

About this time, we decided to have our new altar and podium crafted. As Spirit would have it, an orthodox company that crafted liturgical items to order came to our attention and I called them. The owners were two Greek brothers. During the lengthy conversation where I explained the design we wanted they vacillated, "Yes, Sister Mary, we can do what you want, but we are not sure we want to take you on. Our carver is our cousin and honestly, he is not always dependable. Plus, he is self-willed and doesn't like to follow orders all the time," they openly confided. "What if he doesn't follow the design? We don't want you to be mad at us."

We were not going to be let down, I could feel it. So I followed the intuition. "How about I fax you the design we want, and you let me know what it would cost?" They consented.

It did not take long before they returned a fax to us with a polished rendition to scale and with full detail and measurements. I called them immediately, "If Sebastian will do it, we want to contract you." He said yes.

Sebastian used hard wood for the body of the altar and some beautiful soft wood for the ornately carved columns and an iconic intricately carved scene for the front of the altar. We took the image from the book of Revelation. The podium was a simpler piece, keeping with the same tones. It seemed only weeks when they let us know they were ready to ship. Eagerly we followed the delivery by calling (yes, making a phone call on our land line) the UPS number each day to keep track.

The sun was casting golden tones upon our land when our new sanctuary pieces arrived. All of us went out the front door to receive the shipment. With the help of the delivery men, packing boards were unhinged revealing a breathtaking altar that brought tears to our eyes. We drank in the contours; the warm golden stain giving perfect accent to the scene of Christ in the image of a Lamb sitting upon the throne, and the various beings exulting, all framed, held captive by the mesmerizing columns of rotating carved detail, almost drawing the image out and up as it sat solid before us. The scene could not have filled me and each of us with more joy.

That very night our steady workforce of men showed up, gloves and carpets in hand, ready to step up their service and reconsecrate our sanctuary with these sacred items. The space was transformed, the old traditional items, bland next to the new ones, were quickly skirted down the steps and the new pieces, like chariots riding the sun, moved into the space lifting it, warming it, and creating a spirit of joy.

The rhythm of the chant, meditation, and prayer still held me in its arms as the project birthed day by day. Matins would come and go with sleep catching us into its light grasp, and ever so quickly rolling us into our stalls for morning prayer, lauds. Some days I went outside into the dawn to bring in another day with an hour of meditation. The fall and winter months bestowed a crisp air upon the arid land, feeling a bit like a firm cheesecake sitting upon a crumbly crust.

The moments flew by and the bright white sun just peaking its hello above the horizon signaled the time for Mass. If my eyes from meditation were not open by then, it would seem to tap me on my shoulder as if to say, "It's time, it's time." The sun looked like a sky-sized Eucharist brightening my heart with anticipation to receive Christ.

Mass was filled with joyous songs, many written by our sisters in North Dakota and accompanied by my moderately stable organ playing. Breakfast led to terce and sometimes after that I would teach one of the classes for the novices. While Mother Therese taught most of the classes, I was entrusted with teaching classes on Gregorian chant and the study of Mary, the Mother of God. Most days the project would consume me for the two hours leading to sext which was filled with phone calls for supplies, quotes, and possible contractors along with sketches for or from Frank, conversations with Michael, and appointments for potential companies to work with us.

The plans were rolled back up when it was time for sext, followed by our main meal, dishes, and then recreation with the novices. Lines of beginning and ending dissolved over and over, becoming more like gateways. Spirit used life like a tool, sculpting my personal life into one living act of love.

In the afternoons, I had three more hours of working on the project before our hour and a half in chapel for vespers and meditation, and then the final relaxation of the day where all of us could recreate together. The closing was both a climax and a relaxing with compline, our night prayer, entrusting the night and ending with a Marian anthem, every night. At this time, we were chanting the "Alma Redemptoris Mater."

"A-a-a-ahhhhh-a-aa-a-a-a-a-aal-ma-a-aaaah, redemptori-is ma-a-a-ater, quae pe-ervi-i-a-ah caeli po-o-o-orta ma-a-a-a-nes. Et ste-e-eeee-e-la ma-a-a-ris su-ccu-u-re ca de-e-e-enti surgere quicu-u-ura-at po-pu-lo. Tu-u-u quae genu-u-i-isti-I na-a-tu-u-ura mi-ra-a-an-te, tu-u-um sanctu-um Ge-e-ni-i-torem: Vi-i-ir-go prii-i-ius ac po-o-ste-er-i-ius Gabrie-e-lis a-ab-o-or-re-e su-me-ens il-lu-us a-ave peccatoru-um Miserere." (Written phonetically from our Liber Usualis.)

Silence flooded us upon the final syllable as the sound merged into the night.

There were always funny stories that came to recreation that added dimension to our days in silence. One day I had seen Sister Catherine crawling through the grass in the afternoon, under the clothesline. What?! I wondered, so curious was the sight. We all peered out from our respective windows, at least those of us who could see her. Just a moment before, she had been hanging white tunics (our undergarments) until her eye caught something about ten feet away from her. Catherine riveted her gaze without flinching, then she got down at the level of whatever this was. Then like a lightning bolt she grabbed a rake—mind you, this is my seventy-two-year-old friend doing this! And she started swinging the rake on whatever was there.

Her body shifted from tense action to relief. A shovel was used to move the object that had just lost its life; I couldn't see what it was and knew since the whole thing was over as quickly as it had begun there was no need to run out to help her.

That night we sat captivated as she recounted the excitement of hanging laundry during the day. "Well," she began, holding us captive with the drawn-out word, "I was just hanging the laundry and then I heard it, ch-ch-ch-ch-ch-ch-chchchchchchchcch, and only a couple feet away I could see a rattle shaking above the grass!"

Her voice began to escalate as we moved forward on our seats. "Oh my goshhhh," we all chimed in, waiting for more.

"So I jumped down to get on his level," her shoulders and face shrugging forward taking us through her motions. Her hands moved off her lap, as she described, "Then I slowly crawled through the grass to see the rattlesnake's face, and out of nowhere, he raised his head slowly at me!" One of her hands shaped now like the head of a snake raising slowly as our eyes followed her gesture; Catherine had us hanging, "Then I jumped! Oh my gosh," the reality hit her and in recounting she jumped out of her seat, acting out her surprise and motioning how she grabbed the rake leaning against the pole. "Then I grabbed the rake and started pounding," her arms full out above her head now, motioning like she was swinging an invisible rake while our mouths hung wide open.

"And I killed him," she laughed and sat down with a matter of fact. We joined her laughter which seemed to continue reverberating into the silence once recreation was over. Our time of sharing always led directly to compline, which was for me a perfect segue from one embrace of friendship to another embrace of the Beloved into the silence of the night.

After compline that night I returned to my office to work until matins. I assessed the scope of our wrought iron needs, which included inside and outside lights throughout the complex. It was clear that it was a pressing matter for us to get to Mexico as soon as we could.

Our final design was going to hinge on whether or not the blacksmith's advice to use Mexico artisans worked out. If he was right, we could keep the mission-style design through all the accents. If the man, Fernando, and his family were not right for us, we would have to either rethink the theme or put raising money before construction to ensure we could pay the local contractors needed for such a demanding project.

We had no way to talk with Fernando, our phone would not call that number, but we could set up a trip. In Spirit-filled fashion the details were all worked out, and a larger plan than expected fell in place before us.

Asking big favors of our friends like this was new for us and we were hesitant to impose. There were just a few we knew well enough to know they would be honest with saying yes or no.

We decided to ask Pierce if he would make this big trip with us. As a cattle rancher he had seasons that were packed and times that were slow. This was one of the slow times. He was thrilled to be asked. Our trip would include suppliers in Monterey, prompted by a few construction workers there, and end with finding our Nuevo Laredo contact. There was a Carmelite monastery in Monterey willing to host us and a good friend of one of our friends who wanted to treat us to dinner and a tour of the city.

Just a week later we headed out before sunrise on a Friday morning. With only our prayer books, a change of underwear, and my own contracting notebook, we headed out. Having Pierce with us made supply stops fun, for he and I could talk about the specifics, like tile and grout, colors, and durability of materials.

After a stop or two we did it, we crossed the border into Mexico.

It felt weird, driving into another country as a nun. The border was chaotic. We were motioned to pull into a holding area, like everyone else, and get out of the car. That was my first experience of the advantage of being a nun; we were not only treated with respect, as though we were the Virgin Mary herself, but also quickly given permission to go.

We headed immediately to Monterey, about three hours into Mexico. The cloister was in the center of town, easy to spot because of its bright salmon color and high walls. It was very hard to find the door, however. We walked down one block, no door. Turned the corner, walked down the next block, no door, then turned a corner and walked about halfway down until, Bammm! There was the large wooden door with iron hardware.

We trusted their graciousness given we ran hours late and had no way to call them while on the road. They embraced us warmly and once the door shut behind us, an oasis opened to a courtyard. They had a courtyard filled with bougainvillea and other trees and flowers, framed by arches and stone. It was magnificent even though we could only see it by the light reflected by the moon. They gave us cheese and bread and talked in broken English, as I spoke for us in broken Spanish. Not long after, we were in bed.

We rose slowly to the melodic Spanish cadence of the large community chanting lauds. After a quick breakfast with them we left for the day's adventures amid more hugs and warm embraces. We were invited to come back anytime we wished.

One of our San Angelo friends had arranged for us to be hosted in Monterey. This gregarious couple met us excited and proud to share their town. All the people we met spoke English, so it was easy for me to lay out plans. Quickly I saw these suppliers were too expensive for us. The last stop was a bell manufacturer. They took us on a tour of their casting system where we learned the ratio of metals they used and how they cast them, including the ability to choose what note would be its tonic ring. They were the logical choice for our bell tower, so I ordered three bells according to our plans, choosing one to ring D, one to ring A, and one to ring A above middle C. The experience bore fruit because it let us know what would not work for us.

As the sun began to set, which it did early behind the looming mountain range, we finished with a tour at the main cathedral of the city. The wife, a bubbly intelligent woman, told us she had a special dinner prepared, a perfect end to a perfect day.

We made it to their home about 7:30 p.m., thinking we would have dinner right away. It was already much later than we ever ate. Instead, they sat down on couches and invited us to join them, proceeding to tell us all about their family. Eight-thirty rolled around, and we were still sitting there; my stomach was growling by this time but did not want to impose on their hospitality. I thought, *Maybe I misunderstood, and we are not having dinner.* The night waned on as I struggled to listen and contribute to the conversation. Nine-thirty came and went, and we continued to visit. The clock struck ten and our hostess stood up, "Well it's time for dinner, are you hungry?"

I chuckled inside. "That would be wonderful, can I help you?"

She had a feast prepared and upon feast day plates we ate. Her lemonade was put into a decorative pitcher before being served, along with matching glasses. I laughed inwardly at my rigidity around food.

Not long after, we rolled into bed and rose with our inner clocks around 6:30, so we prayed as the rest of the house slept. Our last stop was to find Fernando.

Nuevo Laredo, the city on the border, was busy with pedestrians and cars, and while absent of high rises, it had the bustle of people moving about like a big city. We began our slow inquiry to find Fernando. Choosing lighting and hardware shops, I posed the question, "Quieren hablar tu familia que muchos supplies para totas Mexico, una persona llamo est Fernando… Conoscen Fernando?" Through sheer patience from them and perseverance from me, each person sent us to another person until one shop owner figured out who it was we wanted.

We obtained directions and quickly moved through the boisterous streets that felt like a Mardi Gras party back to the car.

Fernando's shop was off the main street a few blocks into a more residential area. The houses were splashed with vibrant color and Fernando's was one of them, converted into a store. The residence was huge and magically draped with bougainvillea in full bloom. We walked through the iron gate into a world of Mexican goods from all over the country.

Approaching the main desk, a kind, thin, older man with bright blue eyes set off by his dark skin met us. Mateo was his name. His esteem for us as nuns was immediately evident. "Sisters" he took our hands in his own, "we are honored to have you enter our shop." We were lucky that he spoke English.

Asking for Fernando, we were told he was in a meeting at one of his other stores and would be unable to meet with us that day. We explained how far we had come, what our mission was about, and the great need we had to speak with him. Mateo took us very seriously, but this I learned only after getting to know the Hispanic culture, because his response was relaxed in ways that could easily be interpreted as not caring too much. "No, it's okay, just come back tomorrow," he said. We persisted, mostly out of concern for Pierce who needed to get home.

Mateo liked our modest audacity. He jumped onto the phone, and for about five minutes they spoke animatedly in Spanish as we looked around curiously. "He can meet you at the other store in a couple hours; here let me draw you a map," pulling out a piece of paper he scrawled a couple streets and drew arrows so we would not get lost, landing us moments away from another location. Nervousness that the meeting would not happen was replaced by relaxation.

With a certain pride for his country's artisans Mateo gave us a tour of the store, talking about the various places from which their goods came. There were many rooms, all painted different colors, and upon the colored backdrop tapestries, wall planters, sconces, and more hung like individual art pieces in a gallery.

Lights of all sizes and shapes hung from the ceilings, some low and some high. Hand-carved dining tables with matching chairs held full dining sets of authentic tella vera, candlesticks, and handmade table runners. Delicately painted boxes, shrines carved to honor some saint or Our Lady of Guadalupe, iron wrought table bases and stone planters inhabited every corner, yet there was not a sense of overcrowding. I suppose with all the colors and styles, the sheer chaos made the store feel like a huge field filled with all sorts of different wildflowers. Everything to create a house bursting with the flavor of Mexico could be found here.

My heart and mind were flooded spontaneously with a line of Scripture playing out before me, "Eye has not seen, nor ear heard, the great things prepared for those who believe." (1 Cor. 2:9)

After a few hours, we took off to meet Fernando. His mother was the first to greet us. She quickly skirted from behind the counter and took us in her arms; Ana was her name. Not long after our meeting with her, and thank goodness she too spoke English, her son

Fernando arrived. He was close to the same age as me. What a pleasant surprise.

Fernando was very kind, respectful, and a little shy. Even though he was a quiet person he spoke with the intelligence and assertiveness befitting a businessman. We made our way through the store into the courtyard. We sat at a wooden table painted white, with an umbrella shielding the bright sun from our eyes. Bougainvillea draped close by, the sky was bright and clear, and we began our dialogue.

I rolled out the conceptual drawings from Frank and began to speak. At this moment, like sheer grace, Mother Therese looked at me to take the lead, and I launched forward with tremendous enthusiasm and ease. First, I laid out our vision, then went into our needs, both materially and logistically regarding timing of construction flow. I tried to be as clear as possible about our limited budget, saying like I normally did, "We are doing this for the love of Jesus and Mary and depending almost entirely upon donations."

Since chandeliers were the motivating factor in coming to Nuevo Laredo to meet Fernando, I began there. Together we looked at the overall dimensions of the chapel which had a wing for the public and a wing for the sisters, forming an L-shape that kept the cloister hidden from view. We would need twelve large central light fixtures. In detail I explained the lighting needs and the exposed beams we had contracted with Texas Timber Frames from which they would hang.

Fernando and I discussed the electrical component since this would require the most thought. We tackled questions such as how the wires would run through the chandelier, where they would go into the wall, if they would run through the beam, or alongside on an unseen part, and where the switches would be. All these details needed to be decided up front since we were choosing solid stone walls. Once the stone facing was laid, a forgotten wire could not be run.

In community, living in silence, we cooperate, but rarely do we plan together or improvise, or create; I never even noticed up to this point the transition from leaving behind this quality of my life because of my dramatic love of the entire Carmelite charism. Now two loves were merged, being a contemplative and being a creator.

As we nailed down the details of the chandeliers, I asked how much they would cost. Fernando paused, looked at the sketch, reflected on time for labor and cost of materials, and said "Three-hundred dollars per light; would that be okay?" That meant that all twelve lights would cost only thirty-six hundred. This was comparable to the cost of one light in the states, and the world opened the possibility of accomplishing our dream.

I pulled out my list and we touched briefly on a full range of items. He let me know if he had them in stock, if they could be made, and what would be the general costs. His prices were a source of great hope. In addition, they donated many items to us each time we made the trip, which built our alliance even stronger. It was much easier to legitimize the time and cost to us of making the trip when we compared it to all we saved. I could see immediately the savings would easily be more than two-hundred-thousand dollars.

Timing was the most critical part of our project, as it is to any construction project. If you understand the flow, you can organize the various suppliers and subcontractors in a way that keeps things moving smoothly. This not only saves the project money, but also assures you will have what you need, when you need it. Michael Box and I brought this gift to the project. With his understanding of construction for years as a general contractor, with my ability to envision with ease, along with the work orchestrating donations and working out details, we were a great team.

Working with Fernando also saved an immense amount of time. It freed me up from the need to shop around for quotes on every single item. While we would not order everything from him, we could turn to him first. After a long meeting he showed us a well-loved Mexican restaurant close by.

When was the last time I had been to a Mexican restaurant? I thought. The restaurant in Nuevo Laredo was bright orange with multicolored murals on the walls, festive music piped through speakers played in our ears, and the aroma of peppers, tortillas, and beef floating through the rooms, sparking appetites larger than the stomach could match. We ate just like my family used to eat at El Adobe our favorite Mexican restaurant in an era when it was new in America.

We wobbled our way back to the store to say goodbye. Before leaving he gave us the information of a retreat house (the Holy Spirit Retreat House) in Laredo, Texas that was run by The Brothers and Sisters of St. John. It could be a place for us to stay on return trips, which we did. Fernando also turned us on to a man from Guadalajara, named Blue Eyes because of his light skin and bright blue eyes. In the timeless realm we seemed to inhabit in those days, we fit in a quick visit since he was close by. His stone captured attention with its varied colors formed by the volcanic ash in Guadalajara. He was able to custom design anything, so we ordered the columns for our inner courtyard.

Contact information in hand, we headed out. Another long fruitful day left us fully satisfied with this first visit to Mexico. We set out to have another first: crossing the border to our home country. What a striking difference to pull up to the large, highly organized lines of cars to be checked, all motioned to separate stalls comfortably sheltered from potential rain. All the officials were dressed like police officers, maybe they were, and held themselves with great seriousness.

We were liked immediately by our officer. He kindly ran through the requisite questions, up to the last one. "Do you have a gun?" as he looked down to check the no box. I started laughing, his eyes darted up with grave concern, which caused me to choke down the outburst.

"I am so sorry, it just felt like such a funny idea since we are nuns." He understood and smiled.

We decided to drive home that night, a nine-hour sojourn from Monterey. By about midnight Mother Therese was asleep but I decided to stay up and keep Pierce company. I am not sure how it happened, but we started a quizzing game of Spanish words, with the little flashlight out of his glove compartment and the handheld book of English to Spanish and vice versa. I began to pick out really obscure words which Pierce would translate in either direction. We probably laughed more through silliness and tiredness than from the game. Before we knew it the truck pulled up to our home. "Thank you so much, Pierce; I am sorry you still have to drive home," I whispered even though we were all awake.

Not one ounce of tiredness existed within my body as I arose for lauds two and a half hours later. As the project grew, my own energy increased while my need for food and sleep decreased. Any minor physical discomforts disappeared too.

The project keeps unfolding in the universe around me, informing my own sense of self without conscious reflection, through new insight and new creation. *It seems to be happening in one way, love,* I thought before going to bed. Love is the gateway to the exchange that happened, and the building is simply its expression, the people were its expression, the moments became vehicles holding the expression in consistent place.

The modal tones of our chant caressed my heart the next morning at lauds. We would alternate sides as we chanted, which felt like we were throwing love notes, or a beach ball, across the choir.

Michael, as our project manager, was one of the greatest gifts we could have been given. One of the benefits is the immediate access we had to the best contractors for each area of need. I followed his suggestions exclusively. The largest area of discernment and trust I needed to exercise was around who we chose for things like plumbing, air conditioning, septic, masonry, electrical, and all key structural disciplines.

Simultaneously, our families stepped in to donate funds toward important liturgical items like icons and statues.

Part of any flow is the ability to let go. As people were stepping forward, one of our main anchors was stepping out. Not that he desired to do so, but up front we knew Frank, our generous architect, would be unlikely to be free for the entire project.

As the universe would have it, we were under a very tight deadline to give working prints to our bishop. Even as Michael and I were discerning crews, we couldn't begin any construction until the bishop approved the working prints.

Both Frank and I knew what needed to happen and both of us dragged our feet. His time was beginning to be taken up for a few paid clients with their own deadlines. Finally, I initiated the conversation. "You know Frank, I think we are going to need to find someone local to do the working prints, I wish we had the money to hire you, I am so sorry." My heart sank as I said it.

"Yes, I knew this day would come," he said, sad yet relieved.

"We could not be doing this without you; you have taught us about architecture in ways I will never forget, and the day will come when our very own monastery, inspired by you, will sit in harmony with the land.

Signs Align

We had to find an architect very quickly. Two men were interviewed, both had strong qualities that would serve the project well. In the end we chose to work with Alfonso Torres. Alfonso was approachable and kind. He expressed so much gratitude and humility to be a part of the project. His relaxed personality coupled with his expertise made him the perfect man to become our anchor architect. Time would show our choice to be one of invaluable blessing; yes, he was a blessing.

The first visit to his office he showed me the computer program that would generate our plans. Just like at Texas Timber Frames, Alfonso put in a few specs and turned it into a three-dimensional rotating image where he could add a window, take away an outlet, or make any alterations in minutes.

Up front I admitted, "Alfonso, the entire design is in my head, aside from the beautifully hand drawn pages from Frank and the floor plan. In addition, the final creation will depend upon the flow of donations."

He was still eager to work with us given the parameters: "Sister Mary, we can put see owner or see g.c. [(see general contractor) both of which pointed to me], everywhere you need flexibility."

One week later Alfonso called me, "We have the first set of prints ready for you Sr. Annunciata!" I was there the next day. After warm handshakes and even warmer words he ushered me into the print room, "Here, come here." The sound of the printer warming up riveted my gaze and only seconds after, he stood beside me. The first sheet slowly rolled through the wire guides as unexpected emotion welled up within me. The second sheet, and the third and the fourth, and on they went. My heart beat a bit stronger as the presence of this miracle, our monastery, was showing up on these large pages. We had divided the sets of architectural prints into four sets, the chapel, the novitiate, the admin (which included kitchen, refectory, infirmary, and sewing), and the hermitages. Each had a separate sheet for every angle and a floor plan overlaying. Finally, there was a complete floor plan for the entire 17,000-square-foot structure.

He printed several full-set copies, one of which I took immediately to the bishop's office.

Our bishop, ever supportive of us, approved them without a question, seeing we were proceeding responsibly. He didn't ask for budget projections, strategic plans, or any further detail.

It was another big YES from Spirit.

From this point forward the meetings for the project multiplied. I had to go to the locations of possible subcontractors, since few were willing to come to us, and really it was impractical to ask it of them. If they needed to show us something of their work, or bring up something on their computers, it would not have been possible in our little speakroom.

One of the first men we hired was Mike Lane of Lane Weather Mart Michael Box and I went together. With a wide smile and bright clear eyes, he stretched his hand to shake mine, something we did every time we met. He understood the demands of the project, the dependence upon donations, and subsequent challenges that could impose upon timing for his part. Mike was willing and eager, and it did not hurt that Michael was my right-hand project manager, a man of integrity and great reputation. I knew he was our man. Mike even participated in the aesthetic aspects of the project when it came to the placement of units.

Not once did he keep us waiting, and every time he arrived just as promised. Each meeting was a ray of sunshine.

The next team member came through Alfonso Torres. It was Paul Wilkerson, an MPE engineer. Paul and Alfonso showed up for our first meeting quite differently. Alfonso brimmed with a broad smile and Paul stood quietly, arms crossed against his long black trench coat. He looked reserved to meet a nun for the first time and sat somewhat sideways in his chair. We sat in the speakroom looking at the plans. As effortless conversation ensued, his coat came off and he began leaning enthusiastically over the prints pointing out how amazing the project was.

Paul was innovative, smart, and resourceful. It was going to be a pleasure to work with him. Since he oversaw the mechanical, plumbing, and electrical engineering, we would be talking every week.

Michael and I realized a critical supplier would be the one from whom we obtained rental equipment, which included everything from scaffolding to Skytrax to front-end loaders. They would have to be incredibly flexible for a project of our size and with all the unexpected needs that would arise. Michael and I talked. "Sister Mary, I really like Roberson Rent-All; do you want to give them a call?"

Michael picked me up so he could support me in the conversation with them. The moment we walked in the door more than one employee shouted out, "Hello Michael," to which he smiled broadly and tipped his ball cap.

"This is Sister Mary, and we are building a monastery," Michael started in with pride and humility all wrapped up in one. Everyone gathered around to see the curious woman in the long brown garments. I liked them immensely.

The manager summoned the owner on the company phone, "Mr. Roberson, she is here with Michael."

A tall man with graying hair appeared and put his hand out to take mine. "Sister Mary it is a pleasure," his voice was warmer than the handshake. "Michael," he nodded as he motioned for us to enter the private conference room.

Wasting no time, I rolled out the prints and fleshed out the scope of our needs. Mr. Roberson sat there nodding and smiling. I confided in him, "We can predict some of our needs, but not all of them. We are completing this dependent upon donations, which means we could run into instances where we need a piece of equipment at the last minute, does that seem okay to you?"

"Absolutely," he responded without hesitation and then he took a further step. "Sister Mary, we would be so honored to be your supplier and I will give you at least 40 percent off all orders. Let us support you, Sister Mary; you will not be disappointed."

Leaving Mr. Roberson, I reflected how running this project connected me even more deeply to the hearts of others. The years of silence and prayer, turning a gaze to all the world and allowing the joys and sorrows of the world to move through the cavity of my heart prepared me for these relationships. Each of them had a story; each of them came into our lives for a reason, so I held an honored place of being, not only the general contractor in close working relationship, but also the woman of prayer that held space for their sharing and took it back to my community. It was moments like these that led me to long for more money, so that I was not dependent on so many donations. I made it a habit to pay contractors immediately and write lots of thank you notes.

Michael and I entrusted the pad to Danny Seidel, who was the best possible choice. Using crushed limestone, he created the canvas floor, twenty feet larger than the plans all around, providing a level surface upon which we could build. The highest point of the hill was the chosen center of the pad. Even though it was in our private courtyard, bereft of buildings, it was the natural choice giving septic and plumbing a natural grade away from the structure. At the same time, we decided the septic tank placement and gray water field would go to Danny Webb. The exuberant Danny Webb: I wondered at our first meeting, *could Michael's subcontractors get any happier?* With chest wide open and big hugs for a greeting, this man was a walking smile.

The planning of the underground became one of my favorite parts of the project. Orchestrating everything that would lead toward the structure operating smoothly was fascinating.

Randy of American Plumbing stepped on board too. Michael said he was worth his weight in gold.

During our project it was not uncommon for Michael to call me over to show me the quality of his soldering.

Parts of myself began to unravel; places within me untouched up until that point came forward like brilliant sunshine that had been sitting patiently. These rays of sunshine were multifaceted, all ever-present in my silence and observance, but not experienced in this way.

Laughter was a steady hallmark of our work. Michael and I became especially close, taking every measure to create a monastery that would last for my community. Our exchanges were like breezes lifting everyone else high. Most of my team members became my friends, openly sharing their private lives with me, which subsequently were shared with my community for prayer. They took our project deeply into their own hearts, like they were building for a beloved family member. They would even bring leftover supplies from other jobs and donate extra time whenever they had it.

As the pad was being built during the winter we ran into a series of strong storms, causing about a three-month delay. At first, I felt a little impatient but soon realized it was a gift. The long winter months let me focus on the larger timeline of the project and all its needs. We were even more solidly set up for our concreate pours to happen at the best time of the year, and more and more supplies were secured and stored at our site.

During this time Mother Therese began educating the community about icons. She ordered inspiring videos for our nighttime recreation. We learned that icons were considered sacred windows into the Divine, they were held by most traditions to be the Word of God. I had already reached out to an orthodox iconographer in Ohio who had been recommended to us and we were in the process to contract him. He continued my education during our long calls.

In early Christian communities, a style of praying an image into art came forward the resulting image was called an icon. Taking a line of Scripture, the creator would meditate for hours, fasting oftentimes to open his or her soul to the experience of the Spirit through the image held only in the heart until it would come forward onto the canvas. The canvas would be prepared for hours and sometimes days. When we began to work with our iconographer for the building project, he explained that three-quarters of his time would be given to preparing the materials. Even the colors to be used would be hand mixed to the perfect consistency and tone.

The colors had meaning, the gestures had meaning, the combination of persons had direct meaning, and all was passed on through tradition. For instance, Jesus would be prayed/painted with one eye a little different from the other to emphasize his humanity. Blue and red were used to show Divinity and humanity with one closer to the skin and one further away depending upon which part of their being was foremost on earth.

Our first icon to be ordered was an image of Mary as the Mother of the universe with Jesus in the center of her being. We had a similar image in a book called *Mary of the Advent*. Each icon we ordered had to be approved by our iconographer's bishop. The creation of an icon was deemed a sacred venture and it was also seen as writing theology. This meant their church needed to put its stamp on the icon as being a true message of Spirit. Four of our ideas were approved but the requests we made for Carmelite saints could not be since they were part of our tradition and not theirs.

The other images ended up being of Jesus the Compassionate, an image of him crowned with thorns, Joseph, husband of Mary who was the protector of our Order, and Elijah, who was the co-founder, with Mary of our Order. This iconographer became a friend as well and talked with me for more than an hour each meeting to teach me about icons.

We also had the need for three large, stone-carved items. First, we wanted to have the Carmelite shield carved for the face of the entrance to the speakroom and guest room. The road leading up the hill would end with this stone facade facing the approaching cars and the chapel entrance to the right. Second, we wanted to have an original statue of Mary carved for a niche that would sit above the arches framing the doorway into the main chapel. And last, the most complex need would be the carving of the arches around the mentioned door. Our doors would be very large like typical missions, with a small inset door for everyday use. The arches were a masterpiece, concentrically nestled, growing larger with each new arch from the doorway outward, until they protruded from the stone facing by about ten inches, sitting upon cut stone pillars that were halved. We were planning to have a different design on each arch.

The first direction I took was to ask around for local carvers who could be available or who were within our price range. Unable to find one, I turned my attention to thinking outside the box to a wider range of possibilities. *What magic could happen, if not local then perhaps national*, I mused. Somewhere along this initial inquiry some literature for the Basilica of the National Shrine of the Immaculate Conception in Washington, DC fell into my hands.

The modern design of the statues on the outside of the building did not attract us. However, I noticed there were statues only partway along. It looked like a work in progress. I researched and called to find it was one man, a renowned Antonio Lombardi who was the lead carver, a well-reputed veteran of the craft. I decided to try to get a hold of him with a subsequent phone call.

After a few rings a kind, older man with a heavy Italian accent answered, "Antonio here."

Surprised for a moment I paused, then jumped in, "Mr. Lombardi my name is Sr. Mary Annunciata and I am a Carmelite nun in Texas." In a few exchanges I laid out our project, the miracle of how it was coming together, and our desire for a specially carved statue of Mary to sit above the entrance.

"I would be honored to carve the statue for your niche my dear Sister Mary," he easily offered. "It seems a miracle that you would call me today. My wife is very ill, and I am leaving to be with her during these final weeks. Will you and your sisters pray for her, Sister Mary?" he softly confided in me.

"Yes, of course, Antonio. We would be honored to include her in our devotions," I responded.

"Yes, the basilica has chosen a modern style, but I have been carving all my life and can create anything you wish," he assured me. So we set a time to speak the following week, and I had Alfonso send him working prints of the chapel so he could understand the scope of the project.

The following week I sat down at my desk to call him. "Ah my dear sister," his tone was like honey to my ears, "your project is magnificent. It will cost about thirty-thousand dollars for the stone and carving for your three-to-three-and-a-half-foot statue of Mary," he quickly stated.

He knew, and I knew, he was out of our price range. "Yes, dear Sister Annunciata, you need to work with someone other than me," Antonio must have felt my heart sink, I really wanted his kindness to be a part of this monastery.

"I have an idea for you. There is a man in Brady, Texas who worked a short while with me creating mosaic floors. His name is Paul Vricella. Would you like his number?"

"Really? This is amazing!" Unknown to the public, we would still have Antonio as part of the project after all through his generous referral.

I dialed the number immediately. A gregarious deep-toned voice answered, "Paul Vricella."

Beside myself with joy, I said, "Hello Paul, I am a nun in San Angelo and Antonio Lombardi gave me your name…" My words trailed easily toward him, immediately feeling the rightness of this contact. Quickly a meeting was set up for the following week.

This time Michael drove, showing up right after Mass. We laughed and talked the whole way as heavy winter clouds hung around us, creating mist and attempting somberness in vain upon the joy inhabiting the truck. Even though Brady was only two hours away, it took us three because he liked to drive slowly. How funny to be driving with a true Texan in a big red truck going a little under the speed limit. "I don't see any need to hurry," Michael said. I liked him. His speed spoke to me of his steady nature. Along the way he told us about how Brady was rich with granite. Strewn on the side of the road were rocks and boulders not made of limestone, but of granite. We arrived to see an unhung sign revealing their rapid expansion, Corner Stone Company, which was named after the Scripture that refers to Christ as the cornerstone.

Ah, this is going to be golden, I thought. Given how spiritual we were, anyone who also merged the words of two worlds was a person with whom we probably wished to work. Driving up after us, he bolted out of the car, even more gregarious than the picture formed from the phone call. His wife was outgoing as well and very kind; Kathryn was her name. He took us all around his place where projects in process abounded. Along with carving granite, he carved stone, created iron art, and sand blasted.

Paul bubbled with ideas matching my level of creative vision and within an hour we had arranged to work piece by piece, agreeing to agree as we went along.

Leaving there by noon Michael took us to lunch. He pulled up to a medium sized breakfast and lunch place bustling with customers and lively in conversation. It was so foreign to Mother Therese and me that we failed to notice the stares that must have been following our every move. Waitresses balancing three plates on an arm, weaving through chairs, holding their bodies in every direction as their side glance let us know we had been seen. "Sit anywhere," one waitress shouted out as she pulled more plates from under the heating lamp. So we did. We all ordered three egg omelets with hash browns and buttered toast. Michael got coffee as well.

How odd it feels, I thought. I noticed how out of place it felt to get coffee at noon. I chuckled inside, *What is wrong with me that my own formation has led me to feel this way?* It wasn't a judgment as much as an observation of how accustomed I had become to the monastic norm of having coffee only once, in the morning after meditation. A little joy moved through me with the disruption to my routine.

Arriving home in time for vespers we rang the bell. "Welcome home," Sister Elisha greeted happily. And immediately we entered the chapel to pray. My soul poured itself into the silence. Like a dam that had to be plugged up so the water could be used for electricity, my soul, by the sheer power of desire, broke the dam and the water of my inner being poured itself into the ocean. It wasn't dualism as though being out of the monastery was less spiritual, the boundary-less way of communing in our protected silence revealed to me I was being given different ways of being in Spirit.

That night another Paul, our newly secured MPE engineer, took time to have a late-night meeting with me after compline around 9 p.m. He had been reflecting on our project ever since we had first met, and I could see he wanted to meet as soon as possible. First, he went through his many ideas for the project. Then he went on,

"Sister Mary Annunciata," his tones revealing his swift move from the uncertainty of our first visit to warm desire to now be friends, "I want to make this offer to you." A single sheet contract was placed before me, breaking his work into three or four payments. The cost was strikingly low.

"Oh my gosh," I uttered, "really Paul? You would take us on for so little?"

"It would be a joy for me, but I need to have you sign this as a confirmation as soon as possible so I have you on my calendar and do not over book my time," he asked with sincerity.

"Of course, I will give this to Mother Therese right away and we will let you know in just a couple days."

"Perfect," he said with a certain glee, packing up his things into a soft leather case and making his way to the door. We shook hands letting our big smiles travel into the gesture.

That night I shared the offer with her; she acknowledged it but expressed no evident recognition of how great a gift this was to us. I tried to convey to her the magnitude of his offer and the effect his reputable work would have upon our venture. He would be one of the foundational relationships. "Okay," she said tiredly, "give it to me, and I will sign it and mail it off."

Dimly trusting hands gave the paper to her. I walked out with a feeling in my gut that it wasn't going to get signed. I was hoping we would sign it immediately and send it off.

The niggling did not leave me and about four days later I had a feeling she had forgotten. When talking with her, she shuffled the papers around on her piled desk, moving the glitter glue from a project, pulling out some bills, and right before my eyes sat the unsigned contract.

Frustration, sadness, and worry all ran through me. "Mother Therese," I started trying hard to guard my words from emotion which would trigger her, "Paul is waiting on this contract, it is really important. We could lose him as our MPE engineer, and I promised him we would choose immediately so he would know, especially given the level of donation he is making."

She took it badly, reproaching me for my words instead of joining with me to recognize our failure. I had given him my word. I asked to call him to apologize, "Absolutely not," she refused me to be honest with him.

This compromise she asked of me caused me to hit a wall of confusion. The requirement to compromise and the resulting confusion came up regularly for me with Mother Therese but most of the time it would be within the workings of the cloister; I was generally able to maintain the level of my own personal integrity in the outside relationships. I took my call to lead the project very seriously, willing to shoulder all that was involved in leadership that was in relationship with so many. I did apologize at my next meeting with Paul, without making any reference beyond that.

One day Mother Therese called me into her office. "Here, can you take this call?" she asked. "This woman wants to donate something to us, maybe you can talk with her about the details?"

Beverly Grenda began, "Hello sister, each year I choose a charity to donate a stained-glass window to in gratitude for another year of doing work I love." *Did she know we were building?* I wondered, holding back the desire to interrupt her.

"Would you like to receive a gift from me this year? You are the recipient that came to my mind this year," she confided with no idea what was coming next.

"Did you know we are building our permanent monastery?" I jumped forward with the pause.

"No! That is amazing," she acknowledged. Immediately the window we wanted came to mind. "I normally create a piece that is about twelve inches by twelve inches."

This caused me to pause in my response. Her gift was small compared to what we were holding intention to have; I wondered if it was too audacious to reveal what we would like. The words to say to her made my chest pound, always a sign that the words were of Spirit, so I went forward. "Please, do not feel any obligation. What we are really wanting is a large five-foot by three-foot oval stained-glass window for our sanctuary, a replica of the Holy Spirit window in Rome." Once the words were out my heart went back to its normal rate.

A gasp happened on the other line followed by a long pause. We sat there, then I could hear her speak amidst tears. "The Holy Spirit window is the reason I left my old work and became a stained-glass artist. It all happened when I was in Rome," she began. Recounting the story of her radical change took me into the sheer grace doing stained glass was for her. At the end she said, "I knew someday I would be asked to do this window and now is that day, YES, I will donate this window."

Beverly's gift was a pure labor of love. She did not stop there either for she also created a window of our Carmelite shield for our chapter room and a leaded glass piece for our bell tower. From her first yes, I placed the creation completely in her hands, wanting her to feel freedom in how she did it, what glass she chose, and the final design. Meeting at her studio did not even happen until she had spent months gathering glass where she revealed the copious hours that had been spent choosing colors for each segment.

One by one other subcontractors and suppliers began to seek us out as the word of our project flooded the community. There was a sense of local pride in the idea that a mission-style monastery would be in their own community. To my surprise one of the largest roofing companies called me—in fact the very owner called. "Ah, this is Mr. Harrison of Harrison Roofing," he said hesitantly. Mother Therese passed me the phone.

"Could I come by to talk about your project?" he asked.

"Sure," I invited. Even though we had secured the roofs for our hermitages, I knew we might need to go with a larger company for the larger structures.

That night Mr. Harrison, still in work clothes, walked into our speakroom. By this point we had stopped trying to converse from behind the grille. I was given the freedom to meet with any construction workers around a common table. Mother Therese opened the door between her office and the visitor space into which I walked with plans under my arms. His kind round face exuded respect as he humbly took his hat off, stuffing it under his arm.

The plans flew open without much ado, I was curious to hear what he had to say.

"Magnificent, this building is just beautiful," he started. "A structure like this needs to have a copper roof. My team can put one on that is standing seam," he said with firmness of conviction.

"What does that mean, *standing seam*, I mean?" My interest piqued.

"Well, you take sheets of copper, and using a machine to help, fold the edges up and over, creating a kind of curb on both sides. Each sheet interlocks and once we put them in place, we hand crimp them. They form a helmet that is impenetrable, like a metal helmet," he explained.

Continuing, his voice moved a little more quickly with excitement, "It is so much better than metal roofs with fasteners, even when the fasteners are hidden the metal is pierced and has a chance to develop a leak over time, whereas this type of roofing has no chance of leaks due to punctures."

Immediately I hoped we could take him up on this idea. "You know we do not have much money. If you can get the copper, I will let you put it on!" The words came out of my mouth like we had been friends for years.

Normally that would have been uncharacteristically forward, but something felt okay about the playful challenge. "Yes, I can!" he went on. "We are just finishing a big project of creating a roof in the shape of a saddle for a large building downtown," he pulled out a picture, "so I have access to lots of copper for only fifty-two cents per feet, would that be okay?"

Having already done an incredible amount of research, prices were fresh in my mind and this price was incredibly inexpensive. "Absolutely," I said. We talked about the cost of labor next. He knew we would need as much donation as possible and also that we would be time sensitive at key moments to his men coming to finish the roof. In the end we named a general number for labor and left the final quote entirely open. Our instant trust was this great.

It was clear just months into the actual construction that we needed more consistent help.

The normal course of action for a monastery is to turn to family for support. In North Dakota the caretaker was the uncle of Sister Angelica (the first prioress of the Texas foundation). Reflecting upon who among our families could help, we realized quickly that most of the nuns' relatives were too old, or not with us anymore. I was younger by twenty to thirty years and all of my family were possible candidates. Amazingly my sister, my dad, and my mom were all interested and thrilled to even be invited. In the end it was my mom who was able to say yes.

Over the next couple years, she, and sometimes Lewis, her second husband, would come eighteen times for two to three weeks at a time during which they would devote all their energy to the building project. This was a great gift to my role for it gave me the ability to organize the larger supply driving needs into the times they would be with us. Knowing how dependable my mom was to her word it was a source of comfort to rely upon the help. I had not revealed to anyone the number of hours that oftentimes went into the night, spent in coordinating the supplies for the project. It would be a massive undertaking for a project this size to organize even if everything was paid out so the fact that we were creating largely through donations, the organizational demands were exponentially greater.

The weather cleared up, giving us the thumbs-up from nature to set our contractors into motion. Michael moved his trailer there so his crew would have a place out of the sun, and his wife, Polly, would sometimes come out for the day and cook us all lunch too. The first day he moved his trailer I made sure to be on site to meet, for the first time, the core crew of men that would work every day with me. Harry, Michael's brother-in-law, was the right-hand lead and Michael's two sons, Chad and Craig, filled out the team. Their respect in meeting me showed itself mainly through their quiet hellos and handshakes as they looked me in the eye. I looked forward to the journey ahead with these men.

It was so exciting! We had a fence donated to surround the building project, leaving the remaining acres open for Pierce's sheep to graze freely without bothering construction and we brought in large barrels of oil so machinery could refill as needed during the job. Anticipating the challenges of building an hour from town we wanted to have as much support as we could on site; this would allow workmen to save precious time. The choice also felt like kindness and good planning, to take care of our many crews in the long hours they would give to us.

It was time to build the pads for the hermitages. Michael and I had decided to build these first as we worked on the underground and footings of the main buildings. This way we would finish the buildings that sat at the far edge (saving us the time it would take to move around the large buildings if we built them first), and they could also serve as storage places for the many donations that came our way.

When the morning came, I remember waking up so brightly, like it was Easter. *Today, today we plan the place for each of my sister's cells. Today each of them will have their very own place to dwell. Who am I that I get to participate in this moment?* I smiled while lingering on my thin mattress before rising.

After morning meditation and Mass, I packed the working prints under my arm and glided to Mother Therese's door. "Knock, knock," I lightly tapped.

"Who is it?" an irritated voice responded. Shivers went down my spine and fear rose. I entered trying to bring my joy in an unaffected way, but I failed, and my faltering made things worse. She yelled at me.

Holding tears back I stood there not knowing what to do.

"Just go, I don't want to go," the words pulled strings leaving me feeling guilty, but I couldn't see for what reason the feelings arose. It felt like being punished for having joy.

The moment invited me to look within and lean into God for my happiness, alone. I could feel that God was present within me as the joy in my being.

Mother Therese relented, "Sister Elizabeth can go; let her know to get ready."

I felt sad she didn't want to be a part of such a big day; love and worry and all sorts of feelings mingled like a sea within me.

Let go. Accept what is. Accept you don't understand what to do. Ask for guidance. Trust.

A common mantra within sounded again.

Sister Elizabeth was not privy to the exchange, so she met me at the door with tremendous energy. Her joy was the grace that brought me back to my own joy. We met all the key players at the jobsite: SK Engineering who would provide the measurements and leveling needs for each hermitage once we chose its placement; Michael, of course; Alfonso, our architect; and Danny, who would build the pads.

They were all willing to pray with us, so we stood in a circle and did just that. We asked for guidance; we offered gratitude, and we trusted that each hermitage would be placed according to God's

Will and yield endless years of bliss and happiness for the ones who resided there.

Once complete, we got to it. Elizabeth and I let the view be our determining criteria. The back side of each hermitage would be a double three-by-five window so the sister could have a wide view of the open land. We stood facing that direction and assessing the best views for each dwelling. Once the position was decided, our work partners staked corners, measured, and took notes to create the working prints.

"What is it going to be like to provide such beauty for our sisters?" Sister Elizabeth and I were like two schoolgirls giggling as we talked and chose each spot.

About this time, we received a surprising letter from our mother house. Mother Therese had printed and sent pictures of our trip to Monterey, recounting the amazing miracles happening in the project. "Well…We were quite surprised to see white feet flashing in your picture!" the words of Mother Maria Teresa seared. Not one word about all the amazing blessings happening. She went on, "What are you doing down there? The council is appalled at your lack of modesty. If you are going without socks now, what is going to happen next?"

We may have put our socks back on but decided not to tell them about our choice to build hermitages. *What kind of response would we get to move from the poverty-driven choice of nuns from past ages to live in dormitories to the beauty of every nun having her own dwelling*, I thought. Since they had not asked us to confide any details of the building project, we kept our plans to ourselves.

At the end of the day Alfonso asked to talk with me privately. "Sister Mary, we are going to need a structural engineer. My colleagues and I were talking, and we think Charles Fowler would be perfect. Could I set up a meeting for us?"

"Absolutely," I was curious to see exactly what a structural engineer does. Mother Therese and I went to meet him the next day since she was feeling better. He stood before us, solid as an anchor. *No wonder he is a structural engineer*, I thought. Charles was serious, quiet, and precise.

"We want our monastery to last five hundred years," I said while rolling out the plans.

"We can do that," he responded as he took in the scope of the project.

Seeing my own curiosity, he set in to explain what he does. "You see, we take into account the height, the relationship of the structures, the land on which it sits, the predictions of wind and weather and…" he went on, quickly revealing to me how intense and detailed his contribution would be.

"I can have my prints ready for you by next week," he assured me, seeing our need to move quickly. And he did.

My monastic observance still flowed easily with my growing responsibilities on the site. It felt like Divine Presence was interpenetrating me each moment, through each phone call, in each contact, through each decision, even as I did mundane things like write a check or create a shop drawing. My hand would move, and it was more like my hand was being moved by Spirit. My love for Jesus was morphing into an experience of Christ in all. Praising the project was praising Source.

During this time the grace overflowed into all metal in my possession turning to gold. One morning while dressing for Mass, without reflection I dressed as I did for years. This day my profession crucifix (the item bequeathed to you on the day of your profession of solemn vows) seemed to pull my gaze, *look at me!* and I did. My heart started beating rapidly; it had turned gold. The cross sat over my clothing, close to my heart, not touching anything that could have physically oxidized it, and it had turned to gold. The same had happened for other metal objects such as the wire of my rosary.

It remained gold.

Charles, our new structural engineer, faithfully delivered his plans the next week, which meant I had all our working prints, including the architectural detail and MPE prints for every building. I could now follow Michael's advice to secure our major lumber contract. I had hoped to choose Bowman Lumber because its owner Mike was such a great person, but he humbly encouraged me to choose City Lumber, equally great, but much larger. "They will be able to give you a larger discount and keep with your time schedule," Mike Bowman told me. I still leaned into him, along with Lowe's and many others, for smaller needs. The same week, I walked into City Lumber. All around me, dusty, jean laden, seasoned men who were builders bustled around me with their large flatbed carts loaded with wood, nails, rebar, joiners, and the like, some looking at me quizzically, some modestly side glancing to see the young woman clad in a full brown habit and veil with construction plans under her arm. Setting up the contract was easy. They gave me the general contractor discount. It would be another powerful supplier, delivering trusses and drywall right when I needed them, and right where I needed them.

The next stop was to decide where to get the plumbing and electrical supplies, and San Angelo Plumbing eagerly set up a meeting with me. "We are building this monastery for the love of Jesus and Mary," my common introduction came out of my mouth with enthusiasm and confidence.

"So," Roger, the manager, began, "you will want fans in these rooms," quickly tallying up our private space. "That is twenty-three, and you will need fourteen toilets, twelve sinks, nine shower heads, two bathtubs, faucets for the kitchen and sacristy, am I missing anything?"

I was impressed at how quickly he could size things up. I added a few extra needs. "Oh yes, I missed those," he said.

"That looks like it," I said. "Will you be able to help us?" I assumed he would offer a discount.

"Okay, we will be happy to donate all of this to your project," he smiled.

"Really??! Really?" I gasped. "Thank you, thank you, may God reward you. I cannot tell you what this donation does for us." He gave as though it were but a couple pennies from his pocket, "Sr. Mary, we are happy to be a small part."

Elated, I left. An entire plumbing supply was given to us with one short conversation, and then I could mark it off my list. They arranged to have them in stock closer to the time, about a year away. Many arrangements were made like this, and all—well, almost all—were true to their word.

While small supplies were being secured, Michael's mason was finishing his stone facade upon the shed. He had just completed the stone facade around the well and the power shed sitting two feet from it. His workmanship was so impressive that I tried to get him to agree to the entire project. He clearly refused, telling me that I really needed an entire crew for such an endeavor. He was right, so I hired two more masonry crews.

Michael and I decided to divide the project into four stages. Since the chapel would take the longest to build, we would hire crews to work there immediately. The pads for the hermitages were ready to go so this portion began at the same time. Michael was insistent that a professional concrete finishing company be hired for the main buildings, but the small ten-by-fifteen-foot dwellings could be tended by his men.

The Concho Concrete Company had generously given us a certain number of free loads of concrete, then a steady discount after that for each additional truck. They knew the drive would be an hour each way and were happy to provide early morning deliveries to help avoid overheating. This donation as well came through a simple conversation. I can still remember Casey Williams, my driver for the day, waiting in the front as I met with the men and laid out the plans. Just an hour later, with my steps barely touching the ground, she saw me emerge and knew.

"They are giving us all of this!" I said, explaining to her the details of it all.

With the underground for hermitages completed, footings and floors poured, we turned our attention to Charles's specs for the chapel. He required thirty-six pillars to be dug, three feet in diameter, seven feet deep until they hit the solid bed of limestone onto which our sweet sacred monastery would be built. When the pillars were dug, within the same day, a round rebar cage needed to be dropped into the hole, and the hole filled before day's end with concrete. "How are we going to do this?" Michael and I scratched our heads.

Instructions asked that not even a tablespoon of dirt was to be found in the deep holes. In addition, every batch of concrete was to be tested as it arrived at the site before any pour was made. If it did not pass the test, we were supposed to send it back.

Quickly I realized the challenge was going to be to keep flow with requirements this meticulous. It was really not his fault, I had told him five-hundred years, but expected the request to be taken as a general way to say we wanted things to last a long time, balanced within our financial capabilities. I asked Alfonso if there was anything we could do. My largest concern was to make sure my sisters were protected under the ten-year warranty that comes with stamped working prints. "Sister Mary, our firm can absorb the structural design under our architectural insurance; we can let Charles go."

That day I let Charles go, paying him for the quality design he gave to us, making the commitment to use his brilliant design.

Anchoring Deep

Charles taught me so much. He spoke with ease and confidence about wind variance and velocity upon the physical dimensions and the materials we had chosen to use. He also taught me the importance of the earth to ground the building. The pillars are his genius, and in his own way he anchored us, giving us invincible support.

This had spiritual implications for me as I sat at the jobsite and reflected, *As beings of many dimensions we have as a support system, the earth, from which we have come. This is true in many ways. The earth is one with us on the level of matter, so there is a bond that strengthens us in our physical being. The earth provides us ground on which to stand, giving us a sense of confidence to be tall and spread our light to the world. The earth also supports our movement, for as we walk, we have ground on which to move. Our dreams and our desires are encouraged by the earth. It is one aspect of an incarnational spirituality.*

The auger for our pillars was donated by Roberson Rent-All for the day. This day was our first major orchestration, requiring Michael's men for the rebar cages, the auger men, the concrete company, and a few others to work together. Magic was in the air.

This was one of the only days I left the monastery at sunrise to be at the building site. It was one of the weeks Mom was there to help, so she sat outside having arrived early, and I was able to slip out without notice. The dew was still in the air when we arrived at the site; the morning sun reflected upon the pad as though it were a pond of calm water.

Michael and his crew arrived at the same time the auger was hauled up the small hill. Even though we had marked the pillar locations the day before, we double checked them. This was such a leap of faith. We did our best, over and again, then jumped forward in surrender. That day, it seemed that time existed and disappeared as we worked under the clock to finish before sunset.

The auger was set up at the first hole as Chad and Craig worked on the cages to be used. The drill bit began its descent into the earth and the first soil was moved. The plans instructed us to drill until we hit solid limestone and could go no further. Charles believed it would be between six and eight feet deep.

Soil was tossed up on every side, splaying like splashes of water as the drill descended. Three feet in diameter is over half the height of most women, so this was quite large against the white pad. Abruptly the drill stopped moving and we knew we had reached our goal. At least on this first one. "Only thirty-five more to go," Michael shouted.

It took a few minutes to back the drill out of the hole and reposition the auger over the second location. Since the machine was so big, it had braces that were dropped to the ground on each side to hold it still as it vibrated into the earth. We began the second hole and the other crew members worked on cleaning the first one. Even though much of the dirt was sprayed to the side as the drill worked, there was still a surprising amount of dirt that had settled into the bottom. Shovels were used and turns were taken by Harry and Craig to thoroughly clean out the dirt. Even though we thought one tablespoon of dirt left would not make a difference, we did strive to clean out even that one tablespoon.

The rhythm continued through the day. Some digging, some cleaning, some building cages, some helping the concrete pour. I helped by making sure the locations were accurately marked and setting up the subsequent days' schedules with crews since we were confident we would finish this step that day. Since we had the auger for *one* day, and the concrete set up also for *one* day, we figured Spirit would make it possible to complete everything in the *one* day.

By late morning I realized we were behind schedule. Some of the holes were very slow to drill. "Let's pray," I asked. So the men stopped probably more out of respect than desire to pray. "St. Joseph, we entrust everything into your hands. We know you are the protector of our Order and a carpenter yourself, help us complete what we have set out today." Everyone snapped back into action.

I decided to jump in and start cleaning as well, much to the chagrin of Michael, who didn't think I should have to do the manual labor part of the project. He felt this because I was a woman and a nun, and he had a deep sense of respect. At this point, I had taken care of all the other details for the following days and wanted to contribute to the hard work being done.

It was very difficult work. At first my hands attempted to yield the shovel by leaning into the hole, but my arms were too short, and the blade only swished the dirt around. So, I decided to jump down in the hole. It worked. It was easy to scoop up the dirt with my hands, but the hole was too deep for me to get it out of the hole. I tried to toss it. "Sister Mary," Craig laughed, "I don't think that is going to work," and he handed me a larger scoop. He stood over me to receive my shipments of dusty remains, so we did it together.

At about noon, the trucks of concrete made their solemn trek like migrating elephants bringing deliveries for the first ten holes. They dropped their chute and poured away; if they had been elephants, it would have been like they were pooping and moving on.

As quickly as one arrived and left, another would show up. It was my first experience of being responsible for ordering live products in a timely way. A bit nervous, my calls went out for each shipment, knowing they were going to do as I asked—me, little nun, only thirty years old.

Five p.m. came and we were still digging, with sunlight waning in the distance. We all gathered around the auger, pulling dirt away as it dug deeper and deeper. We were on hole thirty-one with five more to go. The heat was on, and the smiles were still on our faces; we were going to make it, by golly. I began to throw holy metals into the pillars being excavated, trusting these saints and angels to come to our aid and move us from a space of time to timelessness as we finished the job.

Daylight faded and we moved on to the last hole. It was the last hole and the last concrete truck waited about twenty feet away. Effortlessly the drill descended into the earth until we hit our mark. "We did it! We did it!" Everyone started cheering and patting each other on the back.

We arranged one of our longer stone inquiry runs for the same week. The first stop was a second visit to Paul Vricella who mentioned he had a surprise for us. "Can you set aside a few hours?" he asked over the phone in a slightly mischievous tone.

"Of course," I said. "We will leave the entire day open."

In keeping with our vow of poverty we used every part of a piece of paper, that is, when we needed paper. When I was in formation, I remember rarely using scrap paper except to write notes from my spiritual reading into a notebook, or to scribble a quick phrase to communicate with my fellow cook in the kitchen as we prepared the meals.

At first, I held all the details of the project in my head, but at a certain point realized I needed to start keeping records of phone numbers and notes. This gave me the opportunity to collect scrap paper, and it is upon scrap paper that the major designs of our monastery were sketched and given to our contractors and artisans. One of those sketches was the design for our Carmelite shield to give to Paul. The shield would be placed in the facade of the visitor side of the entrance and would be the first image people would see as they drove up to the monastery.

We arrived at Paul's by eleven. He had a sparkle in his eye as he took the sketch from my hand. "This is remarkable, and I can easily carve this for you if you could secure the stone. Now, we'll need to take my truck for my surprises, are you ready?" He looked at me and then at my mom. She was generally silent out of respect for being the driver.

"Let's do it!" I said.

We drove down his driveway. "Did you know that granite is the primary stone of Brady?" He pointed to large reddish stones riddling the country road.

"I had no idea," I said.

Up to this point, I didn't like granite very much; the pattern looked so busy. Fortunately, I didn't say anything for moments later we pulled into a massive granite quarry where I fell in love with the stone.

Paul parked and ran to open the door for us. "Rhonda, I want you to meet Sister Mary," he introduced us with a certain pride to know each of us. After short greetings, Rhonda was curious to see the plans under my arm. I kept them with me always, under my arm or in a canvas bag, for the entire project, ever ready to lay out the miracle to all who held interest.

We were given a tour where I learned what happened within the earth that produced the stone. They had numerous types of granite and uncountable forms in which they sold it. "Sister Mary," she turned to me, "would you like to use granite for your floors and counters? It would last forever, and I would give you all you need from our remnant piles for just five cents a pound. You can also have any pieces from our stockyard you want for free if you can haul them away."

I was speechless for a moment. Effortlessly I tabulated the amount of money we would save if we accepted her offer since I had already priced out many options for our floors and counters alone. She was willing to tailor the shipments to our exact floor measurements for every area.

"Could I run this by our architect to see if he can work up shipment orders for me?"

She nodded, and we hugged. Paul was beaming with ideas of what he could carve for us as we moved through the stockyard.

As we left, I quietly reflected, *How much I have to learn. Looking superficially, I didn't like granite and even had an opinion. But once I learned how the earth produced the stone, I cannot help but be in awe of its beauty. Isn't it like this for everything in life?*

"Sister Mary, I have two more surprises for you. There are two men you must meet. My friend, Lou Beretta, is new to carving but is quite good. He could be a perfect choice to help you stay within your budget. And Rob Teel owns a stone quarry outside Austin in Florence. Everyone knows him to be a very generous man. I really think you should try to visit them," Paul said.

And we did. One grace leading to another. One voice leading to another. All joining for one great purpose which we served.

Lou was easy to get ahold of and eager to have us drive to him. We were not able to reach Rob. "Rob has the softest heart I have ever seen. He will be very generous. He is generous to a fault," his employee encouraged us when we left a message.

So we made our way to Lou. He and his wife lived in a mobile home sitting on a wide-open plot of land.

"Sister Mary, it is so nice to meet you," he shook my hand warmly with his eyes glazing slightly, revealing how moved he was to meet a nun. He greeted my mom warmly as well. Not long after his wife, Bernadette, joined us with the same warmth and a tray of tea and cookies.

"You see, Sister Mary, at one point I learned that my family back in Italy were well esteemed stone carvers. The yearning to carve stone rose within me, but I feared leaving the security of my job. Bernadette and I prayed and decided to sell our house and move here, where stone abounded, and I could learn how to do what my family did. Once we started the journey, we knew we would never look back." Bernadette nodded and took his hand in her own.

I showed him the drawings and he showed me his shop. He loved carving so much that he started teaching me how he carved using point perspective. What an endearing man, and the perfect man to carve the arches and statue for the public church entrance.

"Lou, will you carve the statue of Mary for the niche above the entrance to the church? And would you be willing to carve the relief for the five arches that create the entrance and lead to the mahogany doors?" I could see tears in his eyes.

"Sister Mary, I would be honored. I will do each of them for six-hundred dollars."

It was my turn to be moved. *How could it be that two of the most important carved elements, worthy of at least twenty-thousand dollars, would be carved with dedication and love for so little?* I bowed. We shook hands to make the deal. I would provide detailed sketches; he would provide the exact measurements and dimensions of the stone he would need, and I would bring him each piece of stone.

We were not going to be able to meet with Rob on the same day, and it was too late to make it home for vespers. Getting into the car the phone rang. "Sister Mary?" a kind voice inquired.

"Yes, this is Sister Mary," I responded.

"This is Rob Teel from Continental Cut Stone. I am so sorry I missed your call. Would you be able to come to see me in a couple days? I just got back from a project where we are building according to ancient Mayan architecture and need tomorrow to follow up on the details."

"Of course!" I was glad for the delay as it seemed good to see if Michael could go.

Coming home that day, I debriefed with Mother Therese; she looked so tired. A heavy weight was upon my heart. "Would you like to go to meet Rob? I have been told he is an amazing person and will probably be a big part of our project."

"No," she despondently said, "I have too much work, I don't want to travel." She skipped vespers and dinner that night, feeling too tired to want to be with her community.

What lonely moments these were for me. Because of our life in silence, she was the one person with whom I could speak about the project.

Once again, I began to silently reflect, *Years prior, early on in my healing journey, I learned about my deep gifts of empathy. It was an uprooting experience to discover the permeable way I lived in the world. I embraced the need and invitation to learn what it means that we are interconnected in a field of energy, and I am sensitive to it in ways I didn't understand. I thought my monastic life would have prepared me for the inevitable challenges that arise in life.* I felt for myself, but more so I felt for my community and my leader. I also felt powerless.

A few days later we headed out to Rob's place. Michael relished the time to tell us about growing up in East Texas with its rolling hills and grassy lands. We even passed an exit where he had wrecked his car as a young man.

We drove up the road leading to the entrance of Continental Cut Stone with large pieces of limestone strewn out upon the grassy land. It looked like they were sunbathing under the blue sky. The work building was bustling with happy people going in and out of their offices. We were greeted with true Texan warmth, offered a drink, and then encouraged to give Rob a few minutes. The offices were set up around a large open space with tables pulled together in the center. Someone cleared off the space so it could be used for our discussion.

As we waited, I had a quick sweet recollection, *There is nothing to lose. Just like there was nothing to lose when I cast myself into my call as a Carmelite, so there is nothing to lose casting myself in the service of this project. All in all, there is nothing to lose in living life to the fullest.*

Rob emerged and swiftly moved right to me, "Sister Mary," he greeted me so kindly taking both hands into his own, "what an honor it is to meet you." I reciprocated and rolled out the plans without a moment's delay.

"Rob, we believe this project is meant to be; we are doing it for the love of Jesus and Mary." Rob was not Catholic, few of my contractors were, but it didn't seem to matter. All could feel the inspiration oozing from the project and my enthusiasm. I ran through the largest cut stone needs such as the bell tower, oculus windows, and the entrances.

He had been in the business for so long it did not take him long to size things up.

"Sister Mary, we can do this job and don't worry about cost, I will never charge you more than what is possible. I can even donate all your windowsills and capstones for walls," he added.

We had a long conversation about various details of many of the pieces. It was one of those conversations where everyone contributed and was valued. Admittedly, I did not want the meeting to end. Rob would prove to be one of my closest friends through the project. He was the one who celebrated the shop drawings drawn on scrap paper that I faxed him. He was the one who would make sure to tell me each time we spoke, "Sister Mary, remember you are doing an amazing job." Supportive words were not the norm in our monastic life, so hearing a little encouragement from time to time truly uplifted me.

"Sister Mary, do not worry about deliveries either. I have a driver running across the state almost every single day. Whenever you need anything, you just let me know and he can fit you in on his way out or back in."

It was easy for me to plan ahead so my needs around last-minute help were rare, but on the occasion it was needed, Rob's driver was there. We ended up accepting 198,000 pounds of remnant granite from Paul's connection that was faithfully delivered by Rob.

Numerous times I was able to return to meet with him personally, especially when it came to ordering the bell tower pieces, or one of the cut stone windows, so we could pore over the plans together. Some of these pieces weighed over a ton, so being accurate with measurements was imperative. On the visits, Sister Elizabeth or Sister Catherine often accompanied me. On one of these trips, he confided his desire to meet a life partner. Our community added him to our novenas and prayers and before the project was over, Katherine came into his life.

When he met her, I found myself reflecting, *What a mysterious gift it is to be a part of blessing and Spirit in each other's lives. In North Dakota I would witness over and again how any prayer request given to us resulted in something grace-filled happening. But I believed it was not so much that we prayed for the request, but that the faith of the one asking was the agency that opened to the uncreated agency, and we were just supporting that connection. It seems it is more sophisticated than that, however. It seems to me we are all just participating in the good that is not so much this for that but is rather a movement of the Beloved coming to fullness. In the process we are all uplifted, all celebrated, and all affected.*

Concurrent with all of this was the hermitages popping up before my eyes. Michael's crew was our main on-site crew. They were expert carpenters but were also capable of building small homes from start to finish. This made them perfect to be on site in service to whatever part of the project was staged out by Michael and me. They had the dwellings framed so quickly that the other contractors could sweep through like waves from one building to the next completing all the attenuating details.

Our new masonry crew willingly agreed to four dollars per square foot for completing the hermitages, including gathering the stone from our land. Together we calculated the total number of square feet, giving a budget for the job from which the lead man could make draws as he wished just so long as the project was completed.

Bobby Castillo came into the job at this time. He was a double recommendation. Michael thought very highly of his artisan quality work in laying stone floors, and he and his wife were close friends of our community, very strong devotional Catholics. We had hoped to hire him to lay our floors, and what we had as material was granite. Far off to the left, placed along the fence line, the palettes sat until we needed them. We had our own granite remnant field into which we could walk and choose which types for each part of the monastery. The most beautiful to me was the vibrant red, which was saved for the refectory floor, the kitchen counters, and the infirmary.

Bobby started with the hermitages, using the granite most common, a kind of pink. While stone was being laid on the outside, starting at cell one, floors were being laid on the inside starting at cell eight. Paul Wilkerson finalized the vents, and Clay Crooks blew in the insulation. Metal roofs were completed with hidden fasteners. This point of the construction bore its own magnificence through its culmination of all the planning.

Another culmination came around my reflection on the word *sin*. It was a word that wove through almost every prayer we said and a word that I felt a unique relationship with as it came out of my mouth. In its varied uses it holds a spectrum of meaning pointing to a separation from God. On its most extreme edges would be the way Luther is recorded to use it, that we are, in our essential nature, dark and displeasing to God. He uses the words *cow dung*; He believed and held the faith that Christ stood like a cloak in front of us, so God only saw Christ. But *sin* expresses a multitude of meanings. In some cases, it points to the way we came into the human condition; in other cases, it points only to our actions. What seems to be common is that sin has to do with separation—permanent or passing—between us and union with the Divine.

My own mystical experiences crafted a path of confidence. I found myself praying the prayers with all my heart and writing poems that claimed my status as sinner while having undaunted confidence that my Beloved saw me only with eyes of unconditional, eternal love. My path was not one of reparation through penance but an utter abandon into the arms of the Beloved. From that place my fear of facing any part of myself was dissolved, for this love cast it out. From this embrace I took full responsibility for my life without shame, blame, or guilt.

Not all in our community felt that way, which left me oftentimes reflecting on the use of the word. It also gave me tremendous respect for the uniqueness of every path. Mother Therese, when she was my novice mistress, shared with us during a class a vision she had where sin set her on land with an uncrossable chasm between her and God. The image struck me so deeply that fear gripped my heart. *Could this be so?* I thought. *Could a mistake be punished forever like that?* While I couldn't feel the possibility of it being true, I also wanted to be open to my Beloved revealing that it *could* be true. It felt like this belief would perpetuate an attitude of self-judgment and overwhelming guilt. Yes, this punitive way of looking at God felt like it encouraged us to wield mallets on our heads at every mistake.

The God I was getting to know was not like that at all. I found with Teresa of Avila and all my other Carmelite mystic friends, the same all-encompassing unconditional love, but how can this understanding be so different from the construct of sin and set us free?

And my friend and fellow Carmelite of mine, Therese of Lisieux, spoke of her gradual growth in inner freedom which followed the lines I was feeling myself encouraged to follow through my own mystical experiences. At first it took effort for her to trust what is called her little way of confidence. She was a young nun, living in a monastery in France where Jansenism was a guiding belief. Jansenism was a movement emphasizing human unworthiness and the need for reparation. In addition, this time in French catholic culture was characterized by an extreme fidelity to the pope that through its effect, placed influential power in the hierarchy over power in the individual's experience of and relationship with God.

She opened herself to discover, as all mystics do, that *God is a God of love. God does not want sacrifice, and God does not punish. God sees us as worthy and the object of love. God is at her very core.*

Standing apart from the main beliefs of her community, she pioneered a new way, a way returning to the compassionate Christ as an example of the unseen Divinity.

I penned this poem while in Novitiate during a time of meditation with exposition of the Eucharist. Four years later my small notebook opened to the spot, and I took time to re-read the words.

> Why dost Thou come, Oh Lord
> And how dost Thou come?
> How dost Thou come to me who art
>   not only low but sinful
>   not only little but nothing because of my pride
> Why dost Thou come?
> Who art Thee Oh Lord
> Who art Thee that Thy power enable Thee to come-
> Yes, I know, know but little, but enough to confess
> that it is Thy Power of Love
> That which Thou Are that Thou mayest come…
>
> And if Thou spoke the Unspeakable Word, the Word that would rend my little ungrateful heart,
> that my sins could keep Thee from coming
> I know, know but little, but enough to confess
> that THAT would be weakness-

so then all powerful God
How manifest you are in that little White Host
How pure, innocent, loving
and how all mine you are
show me more,
surrender Thyself to me that I may surrender to Thee
and lose myself in the Infinite horizons of Love

For that is thy Loving Will, my Loving God.
Manifest Thyself for Thine Own Goodness
For thy Glory, Power, Wisdom, and Strength
For Thyself, Oh Love.

As I reflect upon these words again, all these years later, they strike an unpleasant chord. It has such archaic language, and points to an ultimate annihilation of self as the path to union. The placement of God as only outside of me, coming to a me that is bad, seems untrue.

But there seems to be traces of truth there too. For when we are only identified with a limited sense of our self, or a false self, coming from fear and ignorance, we create separation. Separation within ourselves, from the Divine, and from others. This to me is sin and when we surrender to the Power that encompasses everything, we open up to the place where connection and freedom are found. We are no longer separate, but we find ourselves intimately and mysteriously united to all in this Power. This helps us understand how to navigate the paradoxes of life, abiding in and as the Ineffable.

Over and again, when I poured myself out in this positioned attitude or belief, I would find a rushing of Spirit sometimes upon the crown of my head and sometimes arising within my heart. It seems, somehow, that way of opening to the Divine took me away from my limiting thoughts and opened me beyond boundaries and ideas into the outpouring of Source.

Looking back, I discovered that I held both, and it seemed to come from the experience found at my own center where God/Source IS and I Am, the place where the paradox of I and Thou dissolve in Beingness.

I was able to pray with even greater penetration, *I still feel unworthiness threaded subtly in me. How can mercy come even to these places?* In the wordless recognition, deep caverns of compassion opened inside me, mysteriously. These caverns seemed to be more spacious than the simplistic definitions of right and wrong or good and bad. Peace erupted in my thoughts.

Our dear Sister Felicity asked to see Mother Therese and me that morning.

She confided that her stomach seemed to be getting bigger in an uncomfortable way. With the large, multi-layered habits we could never see her stomach. She pulled up her scapular, revealing what looked like a football jutting out before us. "Haaaaauuuuh," we gasped. An appointment was set up immediately and I was told to go with her.

After tests were run, we were called into Dr. Stolsky's office. He sat there somberly, and a folder sat squarely upon the desk between us and him. "Sister Felicity, I am so sorry; you have fibroids." We both welled up, Sister Felicity held her breath as he continued. "This is good that it is not cancer, but they have grown immensely throughout the uterus and ovarian tract. I believe a complete hysterectomy is the only option to ensure that they will all be taken out, and that no more will continue to grow."

Even as religious and with vows in celibacy, there was a deep sense of loss that habited those moments including loss of the feminine and of maternal qualities. It felt like a ton of bricks was upon our hearts. Her eyes shared her emotion while her posture was calm and quiet. Surgery took place one week later. Mother Therese and I accompanied her, sitting in the waiting room until we heard the good news that she came through flawlessly.

Not long after, we were allowed to visit her in recovery. Her face was so open, so vulnerable. Her heart broke open before us and wordless acceptance flowed effortlessly into tears down her cheeks. I had never seen her so unguarded.

The time finally came for the attendants to usher us out of the building. Reluctantly we left, concocting a plan on our way down the corridor. "Tonight," I said, "how about we put together fun songs and gifts for her?" to which Sister Therese eagerly concurred. The five of us spent the night creating a card, songs, and decorations.

When the next morning came, it took overwhelming patience to get through Mass. My head was caught in thoughts about being with Sister Felicity. Skipping breakfast, all of us except Sister Catherine rushed to a friend's car so she could drive us and all the party favors to Felicity.

"Are we allowed to do this?" we wondered as we drove.

"Of course, we are," we discussed, but it felt like we were being deviant. At the front door of the hospital, we tumbled out with music, guitar, balloons, gifts, spiritual bouquets, and other random decorations. Being in full habit we felt a bit conspicuous and kept our eyes down to avoid the attention.

"Look at those nuns; what are they doing?" We overheard nurses and visitors curiously whisper to each other with eyes glued upon us. There were even a few who sauntered behind, not wanting to miss the show. Giggling, we stopped before her door so she wouldn't see us before we began singing. The strap flew over my shoulder, and clammy hands grasped the neck and the pick, while the others pulled music from the bag.

Strummmmmm, strum-strum-strum… Strummmmmmm, strum-strum-strum and we jumped into the doorway singing, "The jo-oy of the Lo-o-ord is my strength, the jo-o-o-oy of the Lo-o-ord is my strength, the jo-o-o-oy of the Lo-o-ord is my strength, the jo-oy of the Lo-ord is my strength."

Her eyes, like rivers changing course, swiftly flowed our way with utter amazement, releasing tears of joy to see us. It was owing to Mother Therese that we could create such fun. Therese brought a charism of humor that was contagious. She had a way of tickling your funny bone and in her role as prioress, she inspired spontaneity.

I admired her for taking risks and knew of her deep conflict around observance for years. In Texas she confided more than once, "What does it mean to have spiritual friends and be a leader?" She would ask as she pointed to the writings of Teresa of Avila. Teresa considered her monasteries to be gatherings of spiritual friends, something we were discouraged to consider in North Dakota. Mother Therese wrestled with these considerations for all the years I knew her.

Her innate creativity, general openness to new ideas, and her personability were the alchemical combination that Spirit used and would continue to use during all her years in that community. We left our sister and happily returned home for the night. I fell into bed, so happy; so very happy.

As within the monastery, so without at the building project; it was a time of great joy, perhaps it could be considered explosive for it was time to dynamite for the septic tank, which would sit not too far from the eighth hermitage. This was the expertise of Danny Webb, so we christened him with the name *Dynamite Danny Webb*, for his personality was as big as the job he did. It took him seven sticks of dynamite, reminding us of the deep bed of stone on which we were building. Alongside creating the septic system and fields, we completed the underground. It was a proud moment for Michael and me to have worked through all the plumbing, air, and electrical channels running from multiple breaker points and hubs to countless ending points. The next step was to move above ground, so his crew set in to build all the forms for the concrete pour. Overlapping this stage for most the project, the hermitages reached completion. They were our first example of what would emerge before our eyes over the next two years, beautiful and strong to behold.

The chapel required a two-foot footing, loaded with rebar and also tying into the thirty-six pillars poured. I hired a concrete finishing team who would take control of all the details for the pours. This was such a critical moment, so I confided in my sisters, asking directly for prayer. Once the concrete was poured, we lost access to the underground, so Michael and I pored over the details to see that we were ready. Everyone rose into prayer that night for perfect weather. The pour would start at sunrise, and I would arrive partway through the job. The night before, after compline, I went back to the office and suddenly realized we had forgotten something. I tensely but hopefully dialed Michael's cell phone number.

"Heee-llloooo," his natural easy voice answered.

Ah, relief I felt, "Michael, we forgot to run the PVC for the pipe organ power. What are we going to do?"

"Let me call Oliver, who is graciously working with us as our electrician at this time," he offered, his voice betraying a little tenseness alongside mine.

"Okay, I will wait here at the phone until I hear from you," I offered.

Moments went by and I distracted myself with other details. Surely it would be okay but to think that all those days of going over our work we missed this detail every time made me stumble. But also, it seemed guided that we found the mistake before the pour, even if that mistake revealed itself only hours before dawn.

Riiiii-iiiiiing,

"Hello??" I jumped on the phone.

"We're all set," Michael confided, "Thanks for catching that one, Sister Mary. Oliver will get out there at 6 a.m. It will only take him about fifteen minutes, so don't worry, we will have it covered. You do not need to get out there before your normal time."

"Thank you, Michael, thank you so much!" We said a quick good night and hung up.

By my arrival around nine the next morning, twenty plus men were already working, the morning sun casting a glow upon their diligent movement. "Sister Mary!" many of them called and I waved from the passenger seat.

The car had hardly stopped when I jumped out to see what was going on. The pour was sectioned into four parts and the largest section, the chapel, boasted pounds of concrete already, with men atop it with big flat metal shoes that looked like round cross-country skis. They had rakes to smooth and vibrators to release bubbles from the wet thick gray soup. The second section, the administrative wing, was surrounded by concrete trucks, looking a bit like fat elephants all clustering around a lake for a sip of water.

I couldn't contain myself from bustling from one to the other. Then it dawned on me, "Oh my gosh, I had wanted to put a medal of St. Michael in the chapel floor!"

"Robby [the team leader], can I put this medal in the chapel floor or… is it too late?"

"Oh, Sister Mary, sure you can put the medal; we have plenty of time," he happily said.

"Come here," he said. "You'll need to put on these shoes, and I will hold your hand as you walk atop the concrete. What you want to do is slightly lift your feet, and slightly slide, keeping yourself parallel with the loose floor beneath you."

"Okay!" I sat down to put on the shoes and naively thought, *This will be fun!*

The shoes were like heavy weights, and I could hardly move my legs. He guided me up from sitting and helped lift my legs the short distance from the pad to the edge of the form.

"Now, take this flat blade and let it help you balance," it looked a bit like a big spatula. The medal was grasped by my clammy left hand and the blade was in my right. Most of the men were so curious they stopped working to watch.

Moving just a few inches, the thick batter beneath my feet squeezed to the left and my feet began to lose balance, but it was easy to regain. Instead of going forward quickly, I spent a few minutes feeling the substance below me. All the muscles of my body flexed and relaxed at the same time. The palpable sensations were exhilarating. Memories of taking the compost upon the winter North Dakota drifts of snow came back… there were some similarities but more differences for the concrete below me responded like a slow wave to my movement whereas the snow drifts lightly bent into the rhythmic movement atop them.

It was impossible to move more than a foot at a time, bringing to life the metaphor of "moving like molasses" or even the phrase, "it felt like I was moving in slow-setting concrete."

Finally arriving at the center point, the designated spot for our medal of St. Michael, I slowly bent my knees until my hand could touch the movable floor beneath me. My left hand pushed the medal into the floor so it would be lodged deep.

"There, it's done," I joyfully asked St. Michael to be in the building in all his fullness, and I thought of doing this for my sisters while the men watching cheered.

At this point, everything stopped. I had moved about ten feet from the edge and was now unable to turn around. Robby realized I had no idea what to do, as I stood there feeling helpless and silly.

"Sister Mary, gently lift your left heel about an inch or so and pull your foot backward slightly. Good," he assured as the first step met with success. "Now continue to move this way, letting the entire weight be in your heel," he counseled. This was incredibly difficult.

Even more slowly than the trek to the center, the return to the edge steadily happened. It was a sacred moment of pause for us all, in a project that was moving at a lightning pace.

Medals, relics, and devotions were very important to us. It was not a rigid narrow need but a relationship with those they represented, those we believed were with us and cared for us. Angels, saints, holy ones, they were as much a part of what we were doing as we were. For me it was a celebration that gave support and joy. With the steadiness of my leadership on the project, I found those with whom I worked opened themselves to these devotions even if they were unaccustomed.

The first shipment of supplies was done in Mexico. Fernando had called to ask when we could pick things up. I wondered where we could store the chandeliers as they were too large to fit in our hermitages easily, not to mention the many other lights. I decided to call our new friends at The Holy Spirit Retreat Center and ask them about temporary storage.

"Hello, Brother John Raphael? This is Sister Mary Annunciata."

"Sister Mary Annunciata," he warmly responded, "our mutual friend Fernando said you would probably call us. May God be with you. What can I do for you?"

"It's so nice to meet you," I started. "We are coming down next week. We hired Fernando to craft many of the iron items. We are building our permanent monastery, praise God! And so many are helping us."

"Congratulations," he said. "You know we just finished creating working prints for a new chapel. Hopefully I can show you some time."

"Brother, could we stay with you? It would be awesome to meet you and learn about your project as well. Also, I know this is a lot to ask, but I wonder... do you have any storage space? We have so many donations it would help us to leave twelve chandeliers with you for a while."

"Of course! We have a thirty-foot-long storeroom completely empty," he said in characteristic monastic generosity.

"Thank you Brother, I can't wait to meet!"

"And we cannot wait to host you; just know you always have a home with us."

Our friend Manuel took us. We decided to break the trip into two days. Four-thirty in the morning our friend arrived to swoop us up into our mission. He quickly attached the flatbed I had secured for us, and we were off while the world was still enveloped in silence. Like other trips, we sat quietly meditating for a while, then pulled out our flashlights to see our books of chant. Looking to the side I could see Manuel with a smile of bliss upon his face.

By 1 p.m. we reached our destination monastery where young zealous full habited priests met us and ushered us into their space. Brother John Raphael took both my hands and looked into my eyes deeply.

We shared our construction plans with each other and then enjoyed a short meal. By 4 p.m. we took off to cross the border. "We'll be home at sunset," I promised.

Crossing over the border this second time felt so familiar and happened with such ease. We even knew exactly where we were going, so within minutes we parked in front of Fernando's store.

"Mateo!" I exuberantly exclaimed as we jumped out of the truck to meet him standing at the shop door.

Not far behind was Ana. "Sisters, Sisters, it is so good to see you," she took us into a big hug. "Fernando is with the welders right now; they are just putting the finishing coat on the lights."

We decided to look around as we waited. Mother Therese pointed out different carvings to me. The amount of detail on their chairs and tables and armoires filled the eye with delight.

On one of the front tables there were all these ornately painted wood figurines, but as I looked more closely, they were skeletons! Skeletons in painted cars, picking flowers, dancing, eating, or drinking; so many different positions but all of them were laughing.

"Do you know our custom with skeletons?" Ana asked, picking up on our odd looks. "We celebrate All Souls' Day here, from the evening of November 1st to November 2nd, by honoring all those who have gone before us. We process with candles into our graveyards and sing songs of love and longing. These skeletons are part of our celebration of the dead," she proudly conveyed. *It all made such sense, how I wish we could honor death the way they do*, I reflected.

About half an hour later, Fernando came in, "Sister Mary, Mother Therese, so good to see you," he said in his ever-calm voice. "Here, let me take you so you can see your chandeliers and lights."

We walked to one of the work studios. Turning the corner, a young man was spraying the finish on the administrative lights and not far behind him were all our chandeliers. They looked exactly like the rudimentary sketch I had faxed him only a couple months prior. He had done everything exactly as we asked.

"Look here, Sister Mary, do you like the way we put the wire through the main column and then at the top we put a movable piece," his hand moved the cylinder up and down, "so you can decide how much of this you want once you mount it to the truss," he finished.

"Yes!" was all I could say. They were so beautiful.

Thank goodness we had the flatbed. All the iron items fit easily, and once loaded I wrote him a check. They added two armoires, a decorative case, and a wood statue carved by an elder from San Miguel.

"Please, sisters, take these as gifts from us; it is for the church." Mateo said.

"Fernando, what do you think about building all our pews and kneelers? I could send you a sketch just like before."

"Sure, Sister Mary, but you will need to supply the material for the kneelers." He wrote down a supplier from the United States.

After we loaded everything, we headed for the border to get back to the monastery. We left Fernando and headed back for our first border check with a huge load of supplies.

As expected, we were asked to pull over for a detailed inspection. Everything felt like air, so I knew we were golden. We jumped out of Manuel's pickup to greet the police officer. He ran through a couple questions, curiously asked us about our religious order and where we lived and signed off on us to pass.

Dusk hit our backs as we unloaded the chandeliers, yet light was all around us. And my heart held so many insights, *We have the light of God in nature, giving us the confirmation of another day of loving. We have the light of God in our purchase, by the ease of being provided for as we placed our confidence in Him for our new home, and we have the light of God in our new friends, impressing upon us our unity as human beings in the world. We have the light of God in our hearts, filled in this moment with gratitude with words unspoken.*

Once again, the lens of my monastic years with concentrated hours of silence, chant, and meditation intensified the quality within me that could be touched by the grace of every person, event, and moment. I had become very penetrable. With the balance of being in the monastery to keep me rooted in divine presence and being with others as an extension of walking in this presence, my lightness and joy were almost untouchable, even amidst challenges.

That night, lying in my room, a memory flashed back to me. Mother Therese and I were standing in my cell in North Dakota. At that time she was my novice mistress, so it had to have been about 1992. Each morning the novice mistress would visit the novices one by one to answer questions about monastic life; it was the only time we could bring anything up ranging from practical details to spiritual meanings. After about half an hour she and I prayed together to open ourselves to further healing in Spirit. This had become a common practice since I went through a major breakthrough on January 2nd that year. The breakthrough caused me to be so drunk in Spirit that it rippled to those around me. *The beauty of living in community is how deeply we affect each other,* I thought with gratitude. Maybe I was the one with the breakthrough this time, but undoubtedly someone else would be next week, and we would all ride the train of grace that came through her and into the monastery.

Once we finished praying, I blurted out, "We are going to found a monastery in the desert and in ten years I am going to die." While I didn't feel any passion as it came out of my mouth, Mother Therese looked at me with surprise; I don't think either of us took any note.

Now, lying here, near the border of Mexico, we were doing just that, building a monastery in the desert. A phrase during that time in Novitiate came alive again. "We possess the prophetic message as an altogether reliable thing. You do well if you pay attention to this as you would to a light shining in a murky place, until the day dawns and the morning star rises in your hearts." (2 Peter 1:19) When the phrase first came alive, it was an opening to a channel of love between me and Mary through an icon I had of her and baby Jesus. Her very presence, the Divine Feminine, spoke without any words, the message exuding from the image and arising within me. Now that same arising was in each and in me as the building project came alive with magnitude as well.

Manifold Ways
of Spirit

The first abrupt end between our project and a hired crew was not long in coming. It was very hard for me. We had hired a well-known construction company, and the owner met with us personally and gave us an excellent quote on completing the block work for the chapel. According to our specs from Charles, which we followed even though Alfonso had taken on the role and liability, the first two feet of block was to be laid and poured solid with concrete before moving on, to establish a strong bond with the footings and pillars. Then about every four feet laid another pouring of concrete with rebar strategically run through the height which would bond that section and extend it into the next. *What fun to understand all of this*, I thought. *How is this happening so easily? Thank you my Beloved.*

This company had many crews, so after the contract was signed, he entrusted the project to one of them. This meant I had three masonry crews on site every day.

Arriving after Mass on their first day the block had just about been laid two feet up. I walked through, thanking them all and saying hello. Then my attention was caught. It looked like they were not putting the new rebar in for the next layer, nor pouring the block solid before moving on. I stopped the crew and asked to speak to the leader in private, feeling great discomfort, "It looks like the plans are not being followed."

The crew leader assured me that the requirement was not necessary and would take his men extra time if we did it that way. "We have been laying block for years and this is overkill," he went on, confident that I would follow his suggestion.

"No," I said. "We need to do it according to the specifications here. You signed a contract that these plans would be followed and if you do it differently then I will lose the ten-year warranty on the work if something were to happen."

"Sister Mary," he went on, a bit more forceful, "you can trust us. This step is really a waste of time and supplies. I am doing what my boss said to do." He not only was asserting his point, but also handing off the responsibility to the man with whom I first spoke.

"I am sorry. It is not a matter of opinion; I am going according to the contract to protect my community." My heart felt incredible pressure in needing to insist. "Could you stop your men while I call your boss to discuss with him, please? I am sorry to do this, but it is necessary." The conversation ended, and I retreated with Michael to call the man in charge.

"Hello, Mr. Bridgeton?"

"Yes, this is Mark," he responded.

"Sister Mary here."

"Well, hello, Sister Mary, we have a big day today, don't we? Are my men treating you well?"

"They are very nice, thank you, Mark. I am calling because they are not following the plans and when you and I spoke you agreed to the quote given to follow our plans which I presented," my mouth just put it out there quickly on a small wave of courage.

"Ah, Sister Mary, I can't believe that, really?" He responded. I outlined what was being skipped. "That step really isn't needed," he began the same spiel his crew leader had given me.

"You mean you signed the contract knowing you were going to do it a different way?" I went forward, still riding that very small wave within me. It was my care for the community that gave me the courage to have this conversation so bluntly, and Michael stood next to me for support.

"Sister Mary, that is why you hire professionals like us. You need to trust that the job we do will be good. Plans are meant to be guides to what we do. Believe me, I will stand behind my work, I have been in business for thirty years and my reputation is strong."

"I do not doubt that." I continued and said the same thing in different words.

He went on a bit longer, trying to convince me, but he had lost my trust. If he had told me his opinion up front before signing, I could have asked Alfonso if the step was needed, but if I just let it go now and something went wrong, it was not on them, it was on me, and the ones to suffer would be my community.

I fired my first crew. I felt my youth as I watched these seasoned construction men pack up and leave. It was a terrible feeling even if it had been the right choice.

"Sister Mary, you did a great job," Michael affirmed. "That was not easy to do, but I would have done the same thing."

Then our chapel sat without a crew to raise the block walls.

The next day I had the pleasure of Sister Catherine going with me and we had a special surprise for her. Mother Therese had given permission to have her or Sister Elizabeth accompany me regularly, much to my delight.

Pierce was giving us use of their jeep so we could drive ourselves from the road to our building site, to get around more quickly.

Pierce met us. "Good morning sisters," he smiled in his joyful yet modest way. "Here is where we keep the jeep," Sister Catherine's smile broadened across her face, and she looked at me with excitement. We dumped our lunch and my plans into the back, near some of the bags of food for the sheep.

"Now, Sister Mary, get into the driver's seat."

I had not driven since 1991. Sister Catherine needed no prompting. This seventy-two-year-old nun was spry and adventurous and like a faithful consort; she quickly buckled herself into the passenger seat. Not long after, once the clutch became more familiar under my foot, we set off for the site. Our veils were blowing in the wind. Her mouth was smiling broadly as the jeep bumped its way towards the construction site. We had the front glass down on this first ride until we learned about how to raise it, and light dust caused her eyes to blink, but she wouldn't have shielded her eyes even if mud was flying her way; her joy was intoxicating.

About halfway up our road we heard shuffling behind us, *What is THAT?* We wondered, so we both looked back. About a hundred sheep were running after the jeep, thinking we were going to feed them! Catherine and I laughed until our stomachs hurt. Just for the fun of it, I stopped. Instead of coming closer, they stopped too, standing still, their eyes glued on us. Then I started forward again for about a hundred yards, and they started up. Then we stopped, and they stopped. We played this game a few more times until knew we needed to get to the site.

"Ohhhhhh," Sr. Catherine gasped as we pulled up to the site for the first time. "Sister Annunciata, I had no idea; this is beautiful," her heart swelled. And in that moment, all my hard work felt rewarded. Finally, another sister could be part of the process; it was a healing balm.

My mom was there for another one of her own generous stints to help us for two or three weeks. Sister Catherine was given permission to go with us to a stone quarry I had discovered that specialized in sandstone, which had the hues we hoped to use for the chapel walls and floor. As we passed through Brady, not far from the granite quarry, we found another quarry that had strikingly white stone, all chinked into brick-sized and cornerstone pieces. This stone would fit a design Alfonso and I had worked on quite a long time. The facade of the monastery entrance has arch reliefs. We wondered if it would be possible to accent them, versus using the same-colored stone and this white stone was perfect. It didn't even cost more, so we secured half an eighteen-wheeler load.

Once we made it to the sandstone quarry, Sister Catherine and I looked through the different grades and colors while the manager explained what layers of the earth they came from. Together we chose five pieces that would be the color range for our floor and walls. On that day we signed the contract for two eighteen wheelers.

The next trip, Sister Elizabeth was allowed to go with us to pick up the artisan pieces Rob had finished for us and to visit a company that had a great price for concrete block. If they worked out, the cost would be about 30 percent of the normal price.

After Mass we exited as inconspicuously as possible, though Sister Elizabeth's exuberant smile attracted our friends to her without effort. Graciously greeting those who came to us, we only delayed a couple moments. *Even though this cloistered lifestyle is one defined for us, and into which we walked, it creates with me a certain uncertainty about who I was when I left the cloister. Walking the Carmelite path, is it about the custom or the charism? And what is the charism in the varying instance of life?* I wondered about the healthiness of this construct that created an identity that was relative and not absolute. I strove to choose charity in each instance, but it was not without a little hesitation or doubt.

Sister Elizabeth had a field day at Rob's, literally. She is a very intuitive person and immediately warmed to his generous soul. While he and I worked out some shop drawings, both my mom and she roamed in the grassy remnant yard, enjoying the sunny day. There were a few pieces Sister Elizabeth liked, so we chose those to be taken to the site on the next delivery. This day, we also picked up the two finely cut oculus windows for the sanctuary and the facade. The facade was a replica of one of the California mission facades.

"Sister Mary, you did a great job on this shop drawing, showing us how the window will sit in the wall, what dimensions it needs to be upon the stone, and then upon the concrete block. You should be very proud of yourself," he made me blush. *Why does it offer me respite to hear his kind words? It didn't feel like it came from insecurity even if it was not according to our Carmelite custom to express appreciation.* I reflected once again.

The block making plant was a flurry of activity. It felt like men were scurrying everywhere like working ants. Our meeting was brief but surprisingly comprehensive. They took our plans, crunched some numbers, told us how much block we would need, and what our price options were. While they did not offer us a discount on their normal block, they did offer to deliver it for free. They also offered us a great deal on their misfit block.

"You may not want this block; it ranges in thickness and in size by about half an inch, but, if you do, I can give it to you for pennies." He asked me to think about whether it was a good choice. I asked if I could defer to my new masonry crew to see what he thought and how it might affect his cost, which made sense to him as well.

Somewhere in the day we ate lunch. My mom pulled out a cloth, setting it on whatever was available, remnant stone, grass, the hood of our truck. Then the cheese, fruit, salad, and cold cuts would emerge from her cooler. Freshly made healthy salads, colorful with carrots, cucumbers, vine ripened tomatoes, various cheeses, and pecans, sometimes even peaches or watermelon. She purchased reusable plates, silverware, and even fun little glasses into which sparkling water was poured.

Mom got us home by vespers and Elizabeth, just like Sister Catherine a few days earlier, was given front and center at recreation to take the other nuns on the journey of the day.

The last appointment for this visit of my mom's was to Beverly Grenda who wanted to show us her progress on the stained-glass window. Beverly had been collecting glass and wanted to be sure she was on the right track for the Holy Spirit window. I completely trusted whatever she decided, but this visit gave us the opportunity to celebrate her process.

While at her house, Beverly shared more deeply about her visit to Rome many years prior where she found herself mesmerized as she stood before the powerful Holy Spirit window in the St. Peter's Basilica. This moment touched her heart so deeply she longed to bring that same gift to others, compelling her to change careers.

After telling her story, she took us into her studio to show us the various colors and sizes and pieces she had collected for the window. With such care she contemplated the shades that would work, the sizes, and the relationship for all the rays that extend outwards from the dove. Beverly then turned to talk about the dove itself. She talked about how the dove looked like it was landing on you from above even though the window was in a wall.

After Beverly shared in detail, I rolled out Rob's plans for the cut stone that would frame her creation.

There was only one problem to resolve. The window would not be open to natural light since the bell tower sat behind it. Inspired, Beverly spoke, "Sister Mary, I could create a second window that could sit in the bell tower; this would help."

"Oh yes, that is a perfect idea, Beverly. In addition, we could arrange for lighting to sit in the stone frame and illumine throughout." Another creative solution came through collaboration, and she donated this one as well.

We found our replacement crew, through Michael's recommendation. Glenn O'Brian was his name. His son, Greg, was going to be the crew leader, a man whose kindness was palpable.

"Glenn, we were offered mis-sized block. Would you want to work with it? I understand either way, even though it will save money, it could take too much time," I laid out the details specifically so he could choose which way we would go.

"Sister Mary, weeee'lllll be fine," he said in a strong Texas accent. "Go ahead and save the project some money." So I ordered the first load of block.

The workings of manifold Spirit continued to bring new friends into our lives. The next one was Don Otto. Mother Therese and I visited his supply office when I discovered them through some research. Magic filled the air once again as we entered the door. It was as though we had been expected. The front desk attendant ushered us into the office of Don who stopped everything and gazed at us. We were like a rush of grace as he himself attested.

"Sister Mary," he warmly began, "I will do anything I can to help you, anything. You can ask me for any need and if I can do it, I will."

The largest order we made through Don was for our doors. He worked with a company that handmade pine doors in New Mexico. The company supplied our doors and Don built all the jams, storing them for months until we had a place to protectively store them on the site.

San Angelo Glass designed our flower sunroom. Luca Ricci donated time to stucco the back side of a wall of the Novitiate and ended up joining us as our painters. Pella Windows sought us out and provided insulating windows giving us the highest quality for our home. Slowly I was able to create a long list of small crews from all disciplines to complete small, donated jobs in between their paid work saving us tens of thousands of dollars and allowing more and more of our community to participate. A local company even worked with me on designing and installing our walk-in fridge. The owner playfully said, "I have never donated so much until meeting Sr. Mary!"

Mother Therese asked Mrs. Decker for more support, and she readily gave another hundred thousand. And a grant I had written to the Kennedy Foundation chose us as their recipient for fifty thousand, too. Our mother house also gave support to our bank account. I could easily foresee what our main crews would require in order to finish their contract and it looked like we were going to make it.

We decided to lay the block for the chapel within one week so that the pours at each stage would meet each other. Greg O'Brian and his crew worked out their strategy while Michael and Harry created a plan with Chad and Craig to mix the concrete and lift the loads as the height rose. Roberson Rent-All offered to get the scaffolding in place and move it as was needed. The only part I needed to play was to order the second shipment of block after the first day. Something inside me still wondered if the misfit block we had would be too difficult for laying, and I was ready to change so my men would not be held up.

The draws O'Brian's crew was taking did not match the level of progress, so I decided to ask Glenn again about the block before I had the second order shipped.

"Hi Glenn, Sister Mary here. I wanted to let you know that you only have three more draws left but there is about two-thirds left to complete on this phase of the project. So that means at this rate your men will not have draws for about three weeks of work."

"Really?" he said with a bit of surprise.

"Yes, so I want to check before I order the last shipment of block. Do you want me to order the regular size so they can lay faster?" I asked, open to his response but also having a strong intuition that hoped he would concede to my changing the order.

"No, we said we would do it with this block and by golly we will," he insisted.

"Okay," going against my gut, I followed his direction.

The second order of block came, and the walls went up and up. There was this foreboding feeling within me, a feeling there was going to be tension around payment to Glenn even though I made the situation known to him in advance so we could adjust our decision.

Three weeks later I got an invoice from him for six thousand eight hundred, after all the draws had been taken. My heart sank. Unlike the masonry crew that had finished the hermitages who felt terrible to ask us for more payment than they originally agreed, Glenn approached me with aggression.

"Hi Glenn, Sister Mary here," I started.

"Well, hello Sister Mary! How are my men doing out there?" He asked.

"Amazing, their work is stellar. I have an invoice here for $6,800.00, but you have taken all your draws, so I do not have payment for you," a little bit of fear in my voice.

"Now, Sister Mary, my men need to be paid for their time. This project is a big one and to do it we need to be flexible," he probably sensed my fear of this confrontation.

I had no idea what to do, *How do I handle this for it could be a snowball effect?* And it also felt like he was pressuring me instead of having a dialogue with me.

Michael and I talked it over. "Sister Mary, absolutely do not give him money. He agreed to do the job for the contracted amount and so he is bound."

"But Michael maybe there is another way? His son is so responsible in his work I would hate to lose him."

We mulled over it for a day then Michael called him with a proposal for the inside of the chapel. We had outlined every part of the job and asked him for a quote. Our intention was to allow him, since he promised he would make up the draws once they got to the inside, to begin to take draws on this work.

We felt a possibility this would satisfy everyone involved. We really didn't have the money. Our bank account may have had a large balance, but all that money was tagged for labor and supplies ordered and work to be done.

This idea sufficed up front, but the pot had been stirred, and he began speaking to me in tones that felt dominant.

To raise more money Rob offered us endless supplies of paver stone, perfectly sized to be sandblasted with names and laid on our sidewalks. It was a brilliant idea to which Paul agreed to participate by sandblasting. For the feast of Our Lady of Mount Carmel, coming up in only a few months in July, we created and sent out order forms for the pavers to everyone we knew. For only one hundred dollars, a person or family could have their name paving our steps on all the walkways in the back part of the monastery for as long as we existed.

The orders flooded in at first, then continued with a steady trickle, adding to our funds weekly. I had no idea the final count. *How much we are loved, and what an inspiration it will be to see our family and friends' names every day as we live on our hill*, I thought.

Paul Vricella once again came with the connections needed. We were going to need a masonry crew to work solely on the outside of the chapel, while O'Brian's crew worked on the inside. He connected us with Juan Navarro. He even brought him out to the site to check out the job and meet us. To our joy, he even brought the external iron crosses he designed and welded that would go through the roof for the sanctuary center and facade; it felt like Christmas in May.

He looked at the job, "Hmmmm, see this mortar here? This is not very good. See how the mixes do not match? My work is much better than this, I can promise you that," he sold himself. I wasn't very comfortable with him dismissing other masons' work, but he did have a point.

"Would you be able to work for four dollars a square foot, including gathering the stone from our property?" I asked.

"Oh yes, of course. But what about travel for me and my men? We have nowhere close to stay; can we stay here?" I had not even thought of that for he lived in Brady which was about three hours away.

"Let me see what we can do and get back to you. Will that be okay?" I asked.

Paul and Juan left. Michael and I thought he would be a good fit. Looking over to the large storage shed I realized it could be converted into a home for the crew. The shed had a large garage door installed by Overhead Doors, with a smaller entrance door right beside it. This would provide easy access for a crew of six men, and even ventilation during the hot days. It was a little inconvenient since we had donated supplies staged there, but this could easily be worked out. The Salvation Army provided everything that would make it possible to sleep, cook, and enjoy their time. Dolores and I spent the day dragging the items and placing them in a room-like fashion around the shed.

The following week, Juan pulled up in his white pickup truck, all his workers piled in the vehicle like sardines, laughing and talking, with arms hanging out every window, happily enjoying the ride. It made my whole heart smile to see their joy. I was a bit nervous having men I did not know on our property. We had so many thousands of dollars of supplies strategically piled within the fence line. The first couple weeks I walked through taking mental note of everything. My memory was sharp and served me well as I perused the status of things each morning. All was well.

During this time Mother Therese spent more and more time in her private cell or in the speakroom, away from community. Her office was becoming messier by the day with random objects and piles growing. Her exhaustion grew, and she would not let any of us close to her.

I found myself feeling turmoil. I was worried about her and wanted to support her, and I was also feeling stressed. How do I care for her, and also stand by as she misled the community, telling them she was doing the work I was actually doing. It all left me feeling more and more alone. When this first started to happen, I was not concerned as I saw it as a chance for me to practice the hiddenness I had so enjoyed up to that point. When I felt a desire for her to reveal how much work I was shouldering, I judged myself to be motivated by my ego.

But certainly friendship and bonding mattered as well? Understanding and transparency in the community could have supported me and the project.

Irritation became her dominant mood each morning and it was leaving me more and more afraid to knock on her door to go over the project details. It was not uncommon for me to be yelled at for laying out simple decisions we needed to make for the project to move forward. While I had developed an endearing indifference to kissing the floor to acknowledge my faults in North Dakota, this continual correction was leaving me humiliated.

Before knocking I would pause and coach myself, *Breathe, Sister Annunciata, breathe. Grace will hold you and Spirit's presence within you will protect you.* But fear still increased. The project, so full of grace, tied me to the morning routine that evoked fear. *Where is the grace in this?*

One time, in the evening, she stood before the sisters and lied. I was surprised, anger arose within me. As she retreated to her office, I followed unsolicited. "Mother Therese, how could you say that to them? It's not true!"

"It doesn't matter," she despondently answered.

"Yes. It *does* matter." I found words, "It matters that we tell the truth."

In response to my standing before her challenging her, she turned red, her eyes blazing, then she shoved me, hitting my arm. Crushed and afraid, I ran out of the office, through the kitchen and as far into the back as I could to get away. I tried to calm down.

A few hours later she sought me out. She was the last person I wanted to see at that point. With a sincere heart and tears in her eyes she asked my forgiveness. My heart bent in easy forgiveness.

However, the incident did not create an opening for us to talk about the need for help or support.

I felt unsafe and trapped. While I was placing so much hope on us getting out of the matchbox house and into a monastery, I didn't know if things would level out for us once there. Since I was leading the project, I couldn't look at personal options to care for myself without letting hundreds of people down, foremost my sisters. Shortly after this exchange I stood out on the site as the crews arrived wordlessly praying to my Beloved, *I am losing hope for our community. Please give me hope.*

Hope stood before me in the form of the project. Every detail was a miracle in naked light. The manifold work of Spirit was undeniable, so I placed my trust in what my Beloved was showing me.

However, when this exchange happened and added onto the stressful mornings, it felt like my home became something of a chimera, a participation as one who was there and not there. I still held fast to acting in love as much as I could, but my gaze turned downward more than up, and my heart turned inward rather than shining out. I was slowly losing my sense of freedom in community.

The loneliness that was growing felt dreadful. Cloistered life is already extreme in its solitude. But normally, the solitude led me into presence, so how was it that I was feeling isolated? *Does anyone feel concerned? Or confused?*

I did not know that this process was the beginning of a dark night of my own soul. Along the way lights would shine, and my inner sense of self was growing in a mysterious way through the contrast and confusion. *My vocation led me here, and here I am for my Beloved and my Beloved for me.* That never changed. A flashback came to me.

It was nine years earlier, in the mission Santa Cruz. Most days I would find myself lost in some form of bliss as I fit in visits between work and school. This day, I was doing my own version of the Stations of the Cross. I came to the station when Jesus falls for the third time. Kneeling before the image, white light poured down into me from the crown of my head through my body. I felt illuminated in a love between Jesus and me. Tears streamed down my face as I experienced myself with him during this moment in his life, a moment that led to a painful death. *I long to be united with you in every way. Let my life be one with yours*, I ardently prayed into the ear of my Love.

Could what is happening now be what I prayed for?

Joy came to our home once again in the form of our new tabernacle. Mother Therese and I realized we would need a new one for the new space. Looking in a liturgical magazine, we both thought, *Why not see if they can make us one with our own design?*

I promptly called. "Of course, we can create anything you want. Why don't you send us a sketch and we will give you a quote." The design was the scene of Jesus on the cross with Mary and John standing on either side and angels on the side panels. It was approved by all in the community and after six months, our finished product, costing about thirteen thousand, arrived at our home.

The timing was perfect, for in a few months Sister Felicity would be making her simple vows. Her love of the Eucharist was tremendous, and if she had been allowed, she would stay in the chapel for days on end, kneeling before the tabernacle in happiness. It seemed a worthy house for Jesus Christ, drawing the gaze to contemplate the beauty of the eternal God.

Just as glorious, in a more earthy way, were the men at the Carpet Shop. They became my subcontractors for any flooring not granite. Every time I walked into the shop, all the men would yell out, "Welcome, Sister Mary! So great to see you!" and they would gather around to talk about our project and hear the latest news, just like Roberson Rent-All.

The Carpet Shop decided to donate the linoleum and the labor for the Novitiate floor. We chose to keep the Novitiate simple to help new potential sisters let go of the many sensory things the world had formed them to desire, like security and comfort. With the rest of the monastery so beautiful, it was a small deprivation to have simple walls and floors. It was refreshing to walk in there with its wide open, white space.

The Alvarez family replaced our first electrician who had donated his work for as long as he could. They were unbelievably dependable. So much so, I hardly remember them other than the three times we went over details. He would come in, sometimes bringing his young son, complete the work and quietly leave, sending his invoice in the mail. On the home front, friends like the Walshes brought meals to offer us support.

The Face of the Beloved Everywhere

The steady support of day drivers provided an unseen current of support that did not escape my notice. There was a generous list of women and men who would give up an entire day of their time to drive me. I spent time on weekends making phone calls to set a schedule. Almost always it would be leaving after Mass and returning before vespers. Once I had drivers in place, I could craft the appointments and jobsite work with freedom. It was a relief to know we had such a powerhouse driving team. At that time, as monastics, we had not even thought that getting a driver's license was a choice we could make.

Nancy Collins was one of our steady drivers who drove for me one day a week. This commitment offered her community and support considering the recent loss of her husband. She insisted on providing my main meal for the entire day, which ended up being quite a deviant treat of one seven-layer burrito from Taco Bell, two bottles of diet Pepsi, and a Butterfinger candy bar.

Jean Ann, one of our former fundraising committee members, would often drive me as well. These were precious moments of sharing as dear friends. During one trip, she talked the entire hour, revealing to me her life path and her happiness with her husband

and children. So great was her gratitude for her family she donated fifty thousand dollars to sponsor the bell tower. We committed to having a plaque with her children's names placed near the ropes so the sisters ringing the bells for prayer could see them and remember them in their hearts. People like Jean Ann took my heart in their hands and stretched it, making it like a matrix to hold presence for them, leaving me humbly bowed in gratitude day in and day out. *It was one gift to pray for those entrusted to us; it was another facet of love to hold their lives with sacred presence as an open, silent friend. Both ways resonate as calling in my being,* I reflected on one of our drives.

Every drive to the jobsite led me into a sea of staging work crews, solving problems, discussing details, and celebrating progress. It was invigorating. One particular day revealed a large problem we did not expect to have.

My main masonry crew, the ones sleeping in the storage shed, spent hours culling the field stone from the 640 acres of our property to use for the project. As I drove up, Juan Navarro walked straight toward me: "Sister Mary, could I talk with you for a minute?"

"Of course," I smiled, and we walked to a private spot.

"There is very little stone left to be excavated, Sister Mary. It looks like there is a lot because the land is so rocky, but as my men took picks to the protruding stone, we can see they are only the tips of large flat plates running deep. It would take dynamite to create usable facade stone from all this rock."

What are we going to do? I thought. We still had the entire chapel to stone, not to mention the facade for the entrance, the sewing room, and the infirmary.

Arriving home before vespers I told Mother Therese. She in turn brought it to the community and we prayed together for an answer. From there I forgot about it; after all, this project was really being run by Jesus and Mary and they were doing a fine job so far so I figured the answer would come soon.

And so it did.

About a week later we got a call from a man with a sweet long drawl offering us the field stone on his property. Michael and I whipped out there lickety-split to be greeted by a lean couple, clearly farmers all their lives. They reminded me of the famous pitchfork painting with their long angular faces and thin physiques.

We took time to get to know each other, wherein I learned they were Methodist and a bit curious about what it meant to be a nun. Once we had started a friendship and filled our bellies with tea and cookies, the husband suggested we look at the stone.

"Sister, I have been stockpiling this stone for years. It just gets in the way of my farming, but I don't have the money to have it hauled away, so I just have it all around the land in piles. You would be doing me a favor to haul it away. Yessirree, you can have it for free if you will just take it off my land," he said with eagerness.

This could not have been a better scenario! FREE stone for our building, already gathered for my masons?! How much more quickly they will be able to go if we put it close by in piles, I thought hopefully.

Invited into his worn-out pickup truck, a mainstay for Texas ranchers, we navigated around the perimeter of his land. He had numerous piles, and we visited every one of them. The stone was different from ours; it was slightly golden green while ours was more a gray blue, and theirs had glistening specks of crystal pieces in it.

The stone looked easy to work with, and all the pieces were about double the size needed or smaller. Michael and I were impressed; actually, we were more than impressed, we were overwhelmed. There was enough stone for two or three monasteries, probably about 3,000 tons, and all we needed to do was to find a way to haul it all away.

"We would love it," I told them. "Let me see if I can find a way to get it to our site. This will be the indicator we were meant to have it," I told them both. On this project we trust in God to orchestrate things for us. They appreciated the dependence upon God.

That night two phone calls put us in business. Danny Seidel and Danny Webb both eagerly agreed to take a day and haul what we needed. Michael and I crunched the numbers and decided we would have more than enough if we stockpiled 1,000 tons. Danny Seidel confirmed that should be an easy transfer.

Dynamite Danny Webb met us with a big smile, along with Danny, and we all headed to the farm. Michael and I led the way while two dump trucks, one front-end loader, and one pickup truck with an extra man followed us. The couple joyfully greeted us.

The men were all impressed with the game plan and did not need much conversation. Michael and I went to the site with the first load to show them where to stage the stone. Since this part of the project would happen over many months, we had to consider how to keep it close to the sanctuary while keeping the land open for equipment and supplies to move to other parts of the project.

Proudly we showed Navarro the stone, "You will not have to hunt for any more stone."

He smiled at my words. The next day his crew started using the stone.

"Sister Mary," he called to me as I drove up in the jeep with Sister Catherine beside me. "Can you come here?" he waved. Something was up.

Jumping out I bolted over, eager to hear how the first day went.

"Sister Mary," he rubbed his forehead and eyes, tossing his wavy dark brown hair in the process. "This stone is too hard, we can hardly break it." He took me over to one of his men swinging a huge mallet.

"Ooooohhhh," I watched.

He picked up a piece, "See this, it is hard crystal. The stone must be dolomitic, similar to stone used in Europe years ago," he admired and despaired at the same time.

"It is all we have. Is there a way we can work with it? After all, we are still paying you four dollars a square foot when before you were gathering it as well."

"Yes, that is true," he pondered. "Okay, I will put one man on breaking the stone all day, getting piles ready for us to lay." And he did. The young man wielded a heavy mallet, turning every pile of stone into pieces that could be picked up and used with a little chipping here and there. The stone luminously flashed when the sun shone upon it at unexpected angles. There was something thrilling about having ancient stone for our most sacred space, tying us to the saints, mystics, and ancestors that went before us.

We decided to finish the foundation pour the following week. The weather was perfect. Late spring still offered a chill in the morning air and the heavy heat would not descend for about another month. Harry, Chad, and Craig spent all their time framing the large spaces: the administrative wing with its attenuating sewing, storage, and infirmary buildings, for the concrete floor pours. Digging the footings, the wood framing went quickly. In but a day or two, we were ready. Like normal I would walk through to check all the measurements and see that all the PVC was run. The kitchen portion caught my eye. *Aren't we supposed to have a floating frame here?* It was the one room we decided to forgo flooring and try out stained concrete. The plans showed a raise needed of about three inches.

I went over it again, and again. Surely I do not see this correctly for these men have a lot more experience than me. But it irked me to say something, so by the end of the day my sense of duty overcame my personal doubt and embarrassment. Michael and I walked to a private point, close to the makeshift Marian shrine we had built with loose bricks and one of our small statues as the project had begun. Many of us started our workday with a quick intentional kneel here before launching around the place. She sat visible to our eyes from most angles, at least until the walls went up.

"Michael, I have been poring over the plans, I am probably wrong, but still figured you would want me to say something. It looks like we are missing a floating frame for the kitchen pour tomorrow, don't we need a three-inch rise here?" I pointed to the kitchen.

"Sister Mary, you have to tell us these things!" he said with a smiling firmness. *Why did I put myself through the agony of not speaking*, I wondered.

Michael pulled Chad over; they both sat down as Michael opened the plans. He looked so kind in that moment. The sun was moving over the horizon, casting a glow upon his face, though his eyes could not be seen under the hat. He had on two gifts from me, worn out of respect for our playful friendship. One was a scapular since he was working with Carmelites, and the other was a hat where I had cross stitched, *All for the love of Jesus and Mary*, on one of our road trips. Michael was not Catholic, but he sure was willing to play with me in my devotional propensities.

One of the qualities Michael prided himself on, and rightly so, was how he and his crew left each jobsite at the end of the day. Even if they had not finished a particular part they would tidy the entire area, sweeping the floors and stacking supplies for the end of the day. Each morning as we would begin, it would be like a fresh, blank canvas, creating a newness as our hands and hearts set to work.

As Michael and Chad fixed the framing, I reflected on the power doubt can yield: *It seems to me to be one of the chief veils that hides us from being in our flow. Doubt weaves its web into all areas. We can doubt our abilities, doubt our goodness, doubt the goodness of others, doubt new positive thoughts that stand in contrast to old ones that no longer serve. And every time doubt is embraced it takes us out of our flow, out of our YES. Doubt stops movement, creates tension or even pain, and can limit us from realizing who we are both individually and collectively.*

My own doubts followed a pattern. They came when my inner perception, intuition, or skill met with someone else holding a different stance. Doubt for me had its little threads in wanting connection that did not have difference or contrast. *This is utterly impossible to avoid*, I recognized.

Another one of my mom's visits gave us the pleasure of having Lewis come too. Mother Therese and I decided to work in a couple of short, in-state road trips for this time. My mom and Mother Therese had grown close over the past year of her coming to help, and the introduction of Lewis into the project added even more joy. Though my mom was the main helper, he came as frequently as he could.

Our first trip was packed, and Mother Therese and I slipped out after Mass into Lewis's green truck. They drove so far from Kentucky but were ready to drive some more. Mom pulled out seltzer and trail mix and we were off for the day. Lewis attested the day was packed with a schedule that was more than humanly possible, but we always seemed to fit everything in.

"Sister Mary, you expect us to warp time with all these appointtments," he would tease me and smile. This trip, we were in the middle of Texas after visiting a potential supplier that was too expensive for us. We only had an hour to make a two-hour drive through a hilly area. The sun was looming, not far from putting us into dusk, and Lewis was driving about ninety miles an hour! We were laughing so hard, a steady occurrence on these trips. How could the building be happening at all if we looked at it from a purely analytical perspective? This man who was a renowned researcher, esteeming the scientific method of investigation developed flexibility in relation to what was possible when it came to this project. *There always seemed to be an abundance of time*, I gratefully recognized.

Earlier that day we had passed a woman walking down the road. Her face was downcast, shoulders shrugged forward, sadness forming a wake at her moving feet. "Can you stop?" I asked quickly and the truck pulled over to the side.

I jumped out and ran back to see her. Wearing a religious habit gave many liberties and one of them was the social acceptance of doing non-traditional actions. Greeting her with a hug she sank into my arms. My broken Spanish, her only language, was unnecessary for us to speak. We looked into each other's eyes for a few moments, and I motioned to ask, "Can I give you this?" a medal of Mary Magdalene sat in my hand. Her smiling nod let me know it had been good to stop, because she was an angel in the form of a stranger, and I could be an angel for her as well.

Slowly the community bonded with Mom and Lewis through the constant help they offered. My mom would spend her entire day running errands, picking up Sr. Elisha's MS medication, fulfilling Sr. Catherine's grocery list, and fitting in a few surprises for us. They also seemed to cover many of our costs for things, considering it a joy to be close to us and rarely asking for reimbursement. At one point we discussed the possibility of them being our caretakers at our Chapter meeting. Everyone was happy about the idea. It seemed even Sr. Elisha enjoyed my mom, even if she was MY mom.

We formally invited them. They said yes, so long as the role began once my brother, Adam, was into college. What fun was this going to be to have family that was so caring take us all under their wing.

With the addition of caretakers decided, and the time for Sister Felicity's profession, our community was growing. She was going to use the same simple profession ceremony we used in North Dakota, which was an ancient service for the consecration of virgins. I couldn't imagine a woman better suited to join us; her innocence and intensity were singly devoted to the Divine.

Keeping with tradition, she took a private, in-home retreat for ten days before the big day. August 15th, the feast of the Assumption also felt a fitting choice for this zealous soul longing to be taken up into the embrace of Jesus Christ, the love of her life. As her retreat began, she knew she could talk with any of us but did not have to either; she was given complete freedom. Sister Catherine and I set up her tray with a plate, silverware, napkin, and all the little extras. She was allowed to dish up each meal before we got there and choose wherever she wished to eat by herself. I took full opportunity to put flowers and inspirational quotes on every tray for each day, just like we did in North Dakota. Inspired by Sister Teresita, with her swirling calligraphy, who would leave prayers and messages of love in hidden places for me and every sister on special days. I passed on the tradition.

Life was filled with such joys up north. Sister Felicity's retreat set me down memory lane. Sister Teresita and I seemed to gravitate to extra touches, and while she gave me notes, I started secretly vacuuming her dustmops each Friday. Some time in the morning, after a week of swishing the halls and chapel, the mops would find their way outside the cellar toilet. This toilet was mine to clean. We all had at least one that was ours alone. For about a year the thought had never crossed my mind, then one day I looked at those mops. *I could start cleaning them for her and she would never know!* The game began, and each week I would giggle through my secret charity, trying to clean them as quickly as I could and holding my breath she did not suddenly show up. She never did, but I always wondered if she ever figured it out.

She had no clue. Once I moved to Texas her first letter to us all had a surprising final paragraph: "So, it was just last week that I *finally* learned who my secret mop friend was, *Sister Mary Annunciata*," she playfully wrote.

Another note in this batch from our sisters up north was from Mother Anna: "Sister Mary Annunciata, we miss you. We miss your laughter, your presence in choir with an alto voice adding its harmony, and we especially miss your golden potatoes." *What??* I thought. *All those years I thought she saw me as a failure in making potatoes*. I started crying with relief. Every time I saw her red pen write my name by the potatoes, I assumed it was because I was a failure at doing them well. I was humbled by her and by my own pervading negative self-view.

Sister Felicity's profession day came, and it was absolutely beautiful, infusing our community with appreciation and joy for our life. We had flown some of her family in from Rhode Island, which caused our celebration to overflow from the inner cloister, sprawling into the speakroom and beyond. Debbie Hansen, my mom, Casey Williams, Deanna Holt, and all our other women friends pulled together a party for the front of the monastery to host the packed chapel after the service.

While the gatherings were wonderful, my real love was the Liturgy. We played songs she loved and sang chants that spoke of union with Christ. Our chaplain, a recently hired Dominican priest, gave a rich homily in the true charismatic fashion their order was founded upon.

Sister Felicity's look of love was indescribable.

Fortunately, her family stayed a while, giving us an excuse to extend the celebration for days. Our monastic life celebrated big feast days for eight days. Christmas and Easter both had octaves, repeating some of the same themed exultant chants each day, and introducing different aspects of the feast in new chants for each day. There is a gap in my heart living in a society that moves on so quickly instead of lingering in the good. How many people take down their tree the week after Christmas not knowing the season lasts another month?

The building project was going smoothly and there were always details to be done behind the scenes, so it was easy to stay close to home. There was plenty I could do from afar so that I could be there for Sister Felicity and her family. I had already developed the habit of staying up late to follow up on necessary details to keep the project running smoothly.

The following week travel resumed.

Lou was hoping we could come see him. He had received the large carvable stone from Rob of Continental Cut Stone and wanted to show us his measurements before proceeding. Mother Therese and I worked out a trip with Michael. We also chose to visit one more stone quarry on the way.

Michael's big red truck swooped us up and off we went. Mother Therese was tired that day, so she rested while he and I conversed about the project. We started brainstorming the best ways to proceed with the administrative wing. The hermitage floors, along with the tiled showers, were being completed by Bobby Castillo who was contracted from that time forward. It was perfect, for when we needed him in another place, he could let the hermitage go, without ill effect, jump to the other section, and then return once done.

We chatted all the way to Lou's workplace, which felt like only moments from when we started. "Sisters, it is so great to see you!" Lou boisterously approached us, opening the door for our exit. "Come here, come here," he motioned, walking about five feet ahead of us. In just moments we had entered his sheltered carving space to find our more than life-size stone, sitting in the center of the room.

The piece was brilliantly white and stood about eight feet tall and four feet wide. Untouched other than light pencil markings, it stood ready to become an image of Mary. She would be ours, made just for us. This was the longed-for work of his life, and the fulfilled desire of our community to have her sit in a niche above the entrance to the chapel. It was a match made in heaven.

"Now, Sister Mary [Mother Therese was looking at some of his other work], I am using this point process that my family uses in Italy," he eagerly stepped into teaching me. "What you do is define the place of the statue where the stone will protrude forward most and let this be the one point from which you map. See here, all my pencil marks? Those are my maps and other key points. Then you carve between the points, letting the statue come out at you," his voice raised excitedly.

He must have said, "the statue will come out of the stone," at least ten times. It was a project worthy of thousands of dollars that he angelically accomplished for hundreds. During this visit he also gave us the sketch he made of the design for the arches, along with exact stone specifications for us to order from Rob. The ideas we gave to him were perfectly portrayed in his use of Mexican style symbols. Wheat, grapes, and vines formed most of the images on the largest arch. The second largest arch would be the place for our Marian quote, and the third largest was a weaving of beautiful fat roses on a single vine.

By this time all the walls of the administrative had arisen, the copper roof was almost in place, and the facade stone was placed, eliminating our ability to sweep across the project. Then we had to turn corners and go in and out of doorways. At least all the walls were not yet enclosed, giving us bee lines through the buildings. Michael and Alfonso were willing to join me on site for a small anniversary service, with songs and prayers, taking their flexibility to new levels. On that day we had about ten different crews on site, so I quickly ran through the project, calling everyone to meet me near the door of the infirmary. Curiously, they all came.

"Thank you all for taking a few minutes from your day," I began. "I know this is probably not what you want to do right now, so thank you for doing this for me. This day, one year ago we began the project—only one year and look how far we have come!" I welled up, "Please, take this song sheet, even if you are not Catholic. I tried to make the words common to us all." Everyone received a copy of "Holy Ground," a charismatic song easy to sing.

I began with a few words of prayer. Then with the strap around my neck, my fingers began strumming, Alfonso holding the music for me. "This is Holy Ground. We're standing on Holy Ground," he and I were the only voices singing, but sing we did with full voices. I looked at everyone after that, "Thank you all, thank you. Thank you for being here. Thank you for making it possible for us to build our home. Thank you for your patience as we depend on donations and for working with me even though I have no experience. Thank you for all your love..." my words trailed away with emotion.

After a few minutes of silence, we ended. Most everyone shot back to work, like stones released from taught rubber bands. A few stayed. Michael's men were some of them. Harry, Polly's brother and Michael's right-hand man, said, "Sister Mary, we didn't know you could play guitar," it was his turn to embarrass me.

Later that day I could hear from the distance, "Sister Mary, Sister Mary," it was Polly coming with a plate of homemade food. "You could eat a little something today, you need it Sister Mary," she sweetly pushed me to take the plate. Almost every day Polly would make me lunch and almost every day I would not be hungry. There was a way Spirit was filling me through the project that took away my appetite, but this was so hard to put into convincing words. Polly offered me this kindness every day she was there, regardless of whether I took her up on the provision. Her steadfastness was nourishment itself.

One evening, while working until matins, I offered to help Sister Catherine make fast day bread. It seemed easy enough. Turning the broiler on, I lined slices of bread onto a cookie sheet so all could brown. We used to brown the bread, then dry it out completely so it was edible but dry and hard. It would be dipped in our morning coffee during our periods of fasting. I went to my office for a moment to work out the measurements for the large bell tower pieces Rob was going to cut for us. These pieces would weigh over a ton each, so we did not want to make a mistake in the order. He had a copy of the plans, but he and I always mutually verified everything.

My focus turned entirely to the working plans; the thought of bread was forgotten. It was forgotten for a LONG time. A good half hour later some kind of smell came into the office, *That smells like something is burning*, I thought. But the smell failed to jog my memory about the bread. I kept on with my work. About five minutes later, *Oh my gosh! The bread!* I ran to the oven where smoke was billowing out.

Pulling back the door quickly let the cloud of dark smoke escape, like a pent-up prisoner, and it rushed into the whole kitchen. *Ccchhhh, chcccchhhh, cchhchhccchhh* I coughed. It took me a bit to find the potholder and pull the cookie sheet out. What was on the sheet looked like flat blocks of charcoal. Even though only one side had been exposed to the broiler, the heat had burned the pieces completely through from side to side.

It took about half an hour, with door and window open, to fan the air clear of smoke. All the bread went into a Tupperware, so I could kneel in the refectory to acknowledge my mistake. After the public acknowledgment, which was met with a few giggles in the community, the bread sat in front of my place setting so I could slowly eat it. This is what we normally did, and even though I was told I didn't have to, I felt a bit adventurous thinking it would be good for my digestive tract.

The next morning, I pulled a small piece of the charred nuggets to eat it. First, I tried to just take a small bite, but it was so hard it seemed to be like petrified wood. There was no biting this bread. So, I tried soaking it in the coffee to soften the edges, but the hot coffee did nothing. Then I resorted to trying to gnaw at the edges, a little bit of the ash came off, and my stomach revolted. I drank a little water and tried again, eating a little ash which came back up shortly after swallowing. So, I skipped eating anything. The following morning, I tried again but there was no consuming the black, hardened ash. The morning after that I dreaded going into the refectory to try again. Later that day I admitted to Mother Therese that I didn't think I would be able to eat my mistake; I knelt down and apologized. I wasn't sure if she would say I had to keep trying, but she didn't.

"Oh, thank goodness," she said with a sigh of relief, "Please throw it all in the compost."

Another day, another friend. Michael took me to see Bobby Peiser, a well-esteemed and sought after carpenter, just to check out the quality of his work and see what was possible. Bobby was a true artisan and had built a reputation for the highest quality of work. He could dream creatively for his clients and produce more than what they could have designed themselves. And every ounce was worth it.

The home was only a few minutes from our place, so it was easy to drop by one morning. We made our way up the driveway where two of his male assistants quickly turned their dust-inducing saws off motioning to come, come. One quickly retrieved Bobby from the back section of his garage that had been turned into a workshop. A tall thin man with warm eyes that look like a deer greeted us kindly. We were instant friends.

During this first visit he insisted I see his greenhouse, just to give me a sense of who he was. He told me that he was too expensive to book to do all our cabinets, and that City Cabinets would be a good bet, and would do a very fine job. He did, however, agree to create our large mahogany doors with the smaller inset door for the main chapel entrance and to complete the cabinets for the priest's sacristy for us. We tried to put the greatest quality in the chapel places and then a good quality throughout the rest. We followed his advice. Through the project he checked in, came out to the jobsite to say hello, and even answered questions I had about various carpentry details. His friendship was for life.

In one way our project was like the ocean. If you look at the ocean and see how fluidly it moves, the water seems one with the currents, and while there is momentum and surge and ever brimming life, there is also a sense of all converging where individual momentum is free to express and remains part of the whole. There was a certain outpouring that happened continually, and all the players arose like individual currents as the inspired moment struck them, which always seemed to be in the flow of the larger work being accomplished. I was lost in that flow; the feeling of the Divine was so strong there was nothing to do but be lost in the movement.

Those of great purity, like Bobby and Michael, witnessed over and again the answer they gave to the inspiration of Spirit. They, along with all the others, were my teachers; I bowed before them.

About that time the pillars we had ordered through Mexican "Blue Eyes" (the man from Guadalajara running a shop in Nuevo Laredo), had arrived to his shop. There were twelve of them, all made from a sienna shade of volcanic ash, matching our copper roof and stained doors. Michael offered to make the trip with us, bringing his own flatbed. Each column was cut into four pieces, making them easier to transport. Taking extra pains to confirm the weight, Blue Eyes got back to me immediately. Fortunately, it tallied up to much less than the weight limit of Michael's rig. Plans were made to go down the following week, with the intent to get over the border by one, load up, and be back home by compline.

Providence had other plans.

The drive down was delightful, another joyful venture where Mother Therese rested and Michael and I laughed our way along, forgetting about time. Before we knew it, we were there; this was Michael's one and only time to go to Mexico with us. Blue Eyes took us out back; the entire side of his building was a sea of sienna column pieces. *How exciting! They were perfect,* I thought, until both of us noticed how wet they all looked. We cast worried glances to each other asking Blue Eyes, "Have the columns been sitting in the rain? Did you tell us the dry weight or the wet weight?" The weight he told us was dry, which meant the columns would be much heavier than anticipated, most probably too heavy for Michael's flatbed.

Arrrghhh, what should I do? I wondered. Blue Eyes pressed us to take them all as promised, though we knew he would have to concede if we let him know the weight was too heavy. What an inconvenience. Michael initiated, "Well Sister Mary, let's give it a try." We loaded them up, but you could see his tires weighing down. The situation did not feel good, so to help bolster our hopes, Mother Therese and I said a bunch of prayers.

We made it over the border and made our way onto the highway, keeping a good forty miles an hour pace. I felt so bad for Michael and so bad to be imposing this upon him.

BAAAMMMMM, kaplunk, kaplunk, kaplunk, we blew a tire, about two hours into our drive. "Oooooohhhh," we couldn't help but groan. We sidled to the shoulder and jumped out to see the back right tire completely shot.

"It's okay," Michael assured us. "I have plenty of spares, just give me a little time to change it." The trailer could not even be lifted without removing almost all the pieces of volcanic stone. Michael, the only one capable of budging the wet possessions, poured sweat as he lifted them off, one by one. The flatbed was only about eighteen inches from the ground, but this was too high to shimmy them off with ease; they required lifting.

About an hour later, new wheel in place, new optimism on our faces, columns resituated, we headed out again.

BAAAAAAMMMMMM, kaplunk, kaplunk, kaplunk, we blew another tire about an hour into our renewed drive home. *Ohhhhhhh,* our morale sank a little lower this time. Same scenario as above, poor Michael lifted all those columns off and on the trailer, again, his shirt soaked with sweat and dirt formed on his brow.

About two hours later, new wheel in place, fading optimism on our faces, columns resituated, we started home again. The sun had set, and we moved about thirty miles an hour, holding hope in a suffocating embrace.

An hour later, *BAAAAAMMMMMMM, kaplunk, kaplunk, kaplunk.*

"We have to leave them here, Sister Mary. We are not going to make it home before dawn at this rate, and I do not have another spare," Michael sadly directed.

"Will they be okay? And will your trailer be safe?" I asked.

"We don't really have a choice. I will come back tomorrow with my boys and get them," Michael assured us.

A police officer pulled over to our broken-down trailer. "Hello there, oh, hello Sisters," he quickly switched from an authoritative tone into one of deference.

"How can I help you tonight?" he kindly asked. We laid it all out.

"Do not worry, I will put this orange notice on the trailer which will alert our force to keep an eye on it as they drive by and warn anyone coming close of the penalty if anything happens to the contents," he confidently guided.

"This is great!" I wanted to hug him in gratitude. About half an hour later he had made all his phone calls and we were on our way.

Tensions increased at home. It was unclear why this was happening, other than it seemed Mother Therese's internal struggles were growing. Daily life was generally flowing, and I shouldered the building project, handling the normal stressors of a massive project on my own. I strove to see the face of the Beloved in the workings and challenges. *Maybe there is a way we are all being prepared for this next step in our new home?* I wondered with my waning hope.

About this time, I learned that the community had almost come to an end. No one had told me three years ago when I had been invited to join them. The former prioress who was the founding prioress, Sister Angelica, had come to believe things were not healthy enough to continue and it all needed to end. Plane tickets had been bought and plans made until Mother Therese was elected prioress in North Dakota and stepped in to see about the community continuing. I realized that this was the reason she was considered a savior in the North Dakota community. Learning about the pending dissolution this many years later, my heart just ached. The sisters had been through so much.

There was an ever-widening chasm between life with friends in the building project and life with my sisters. My love was my vocation, my service was for the sake of the community; but my service led me into life giving experiences that I could not bring into our cloistered lifestyle. The project filled voids in me, like support, laughter, and kindness amid friendship; something I had gone without for quite a long time.

This didn't mean that miracles were not still abounding through our consecrated life. The Face of the Beloved still shined through our ministry.

It was a dark evening, even darker for the two women that came to our speakroom. Mother Therese and I went together, sitting opposite the mother and her daughter. The daughter tightly clasped a crumpled, wet Kleenex as her mom told us, "I have cancer and am going to die." The diagnosis had come to them a few months prior, and the disease had spread like wildfire. Teary eyed as she shared the details, the daughter flung her arms around her mom, hoping to lighten the words as they poured forward in hope toward us.

Mother Therese and I asked if they would like us to pray with them, with a few of our relics. The slight relaxation of their bodies was enough of a yes and I bolted out the door. For years they had been stored in envelopes with their papers but now they were appropriately displayed in a decorative five-sided aluminum case with large glass panels. It was a gift from Fernando from our recent trip.

I pulled the Veil of Mary, the Bone of Therese (of Lisieux), and the Cross of Jesus, and quickly brought them to the speakroom. There was a small space in our grille where we could hold hands. Their fingers reached for ours, all fingers touching the relics. Mother Therese asked me to begin.

"Holy Mary, we love you. Holy Spirit, we ask you to flow through these prayers and bring healing to Guadalupe; Jesus, we know that with you all things are possible," I began.

As the words came forward the familiar feeling of Spirit moving in my heart spontaneously stepped up the power of the words while my voice became the messenger. Heart pounding as the words came forward it felt like honey rising in my throat and an inner confidence consumed me, inspiring me to put all my emotion into the words coming forward.

Mother Therese could feel the movement and once I finished, she joined in as well. We never talked about it, but I wondered if she felt the rise within her in the same way, and if we had participated in the Spirit healing together. Spontaneous healing was a part of my family upbringing; however, it was new for her from what she shared with me.

That very night Guadalupe and her daughter were headed down to San Antonio for the final stage of her cancer care and to be readied for passing from this life. I wished we could hug them, but our prayers were probably enough of a hug. During the inspired words their own tears copiously ran down their faces onto their shirts. Their faith was the propelling force bringing forth the prayer as an answer to their devotion.

A week or two later they came back, and we readied ourselves to pray again with them, assuming she was getting closer to her day of transition. "She is healed! God healed her through your prayer!" her daughter jumped up and down. Guadalupe sweetly and steadfastly nodded.

We were beside ourselves, "We are so happy for you. This is the result of your own faith!"

So many miracles abounded in our lives of prayer. This one was dramatic but there were many others with equal magnificence, impressing upon me the words of Archangel Gabriel when speaking to Mary in the Gospel of Luke: "Nothing is impossible with God." (Luke 1:37)

Within the same month Guadalupe had come to us, another woman had come for prayer as well. She too was dying of cancer. Mother Therese had asked me to spend time with her alone, so we met once a week for prayer and sharing.

The first prayer, adorned with relics as well, brought words that came forward not fired with radical healing for her body, but were fired with radical healing in her family. She shared so vulnerably about the division her cancer was bringing up among all her loved ones. This woman was only about fifty years old and something within her felt it was time to let go and transition. Her eyes were so very clear, and even though she wasn't Catholic, her soul soaked up our conversations filled with sayings of my favorite Carmelite mystics who experienced being consumed in Divine Love. It all made sense to her.

We prayed for her inner fortitude as Spirit arose within. I could not seem to pray the same type of prayer for complete healing; it just wasn't there. In a flash I saw that every path is so unique and even if life is sacred, its sacredness is honored when the path of life is given recognition. It seemed her life as she knew it was coming to an end. Most in her family were beside themselves because of her refusal to receive more treatment, but in the process, all the hidden tensions between members were being played out. It seemed like her cancer was there to be an instrument of healing for her family, a true interconnected sacrifice, not chosen like a stoic, but accepted as part of a bigger plan.

The two women with cancer stood side by side and my role was to trust the movement of Spirit, to never push an idea of what is best, or hold to a notion that may not be the plan of the Ineffable. The unfolding of what is meant to be is a natural process that emerges. If we had tried to force prayers with notions that she was not meant to die because she was too young, only resistance would have filled our hearts, possibly leading to unhappiness as her natural purpose and unfolding, like water released from a dam, would finally move to the end it sought.

Destruction of Form by the Formless One

This new year coming upon us was significant; it was the last year of this decade and century. Even though we were not part of the technology of the world, we quickly learned of Y2K worries through our friends. I have no idea if this mass worry consumed most of society, only that some of our friends became incredibly worried, convinced that all was going to go haywire since computers were not set up to adjust to the new digits of *00*.

The DeLaughters, who had agreed to be our caretakers until my mom and Lewis moved, were preparing for the worst by developing plans with other families to live self-sufficiently on a piece of land, buying provisions and generators, and creating water sources.

We were not worried. There was a moment when I asked myself, *Should I be more concerned about this?* The reasoning of the DeLaughters was very thorough and convincing: "Breakdown in society would be certain," they insisted. I decided to trust my gut.

We set about to design the caretaker/chaplain quarters while the phases of the monastery continued. Drawing up a few floor plans by hand, I submitted the ideas to our Dominican chaplain and to the DeLaughters. My mom had deferred all to them in this regard, feeling confident that whatever we built would be perfectly fine.

They made a few suggestions and ultimately, we came to a final plan. It was this very hand sketch that served as our working print!

The first need was to get power from our main pole to the new building site. Jim Martin, from the Texas Southwest Electric Co-Op, donated the time of one of his men who came with a trench digger rigorous enough to break stone. The ditch for the wires was done within two days. This man, just like Jim, was so thrilled to be a part of the project. The orange digger caked in dust and mud moved slowly—so slowly that it seemed progress was non-existent. This man, however, was undaunted.

Once power was there, the construction flew forward before our eyes. I stood and looked on. "Michael, building houses is so easy compared to a monastery!"

"Yep, Sister Mary, it is all the same process, just a different scope," he responded. The glint in his eye was unmistakable as he saw me learn from his own years of successful building and resulting wisdom. Within a month the building was ready for a masonry crew to tackle the facade stone. This could come at any point of the project, so we did not worry about pulling our crews from finishing the chapel and administrative wing.

We had another new stone quarry provide for the walls between the hermitages. They were huge limestone pieces, difficult to maneuver but beautiful in texture and color. We decided to lay them on their sides, which were easily eighteen inches thick. The air conditioning units sat between each hermitage, so the wall was designed to be like a wave arching higher at the center point.

The gentle undulation of the stones would move from three feet at the side of the hermitage wall swelling upward to four feet at the center then back down to three feet to meet the wall of the next hermitage.

We used some of the Continental Cut Stone pavers, donated by Rob, to create a smooth top surface. The beauty drew the eye, like a jeweled necklace strung between each dwelling. This part of the monastery was a perfect symbol of our life together, that is, hermits living in community, tied to each other as Brides of Christ, yet communing in the silent Sounding.

It was also at this time our first shipment of sandblasted pavers arrived from Paul Vricella. One of Rob's trucks picked up about ten pallets, piled high with each paver cleanly boasting a donor's name. Our system was loosely organized. Since Mother Therese kept the forms, they were all put into a file cabinet without any order. I trusted since she collected them that the one-hundred-dollar payments were recorded between her and Elizabeth, our bookkeeper. Once the pavers started arriving, I needed to be able to check them off so no duplicates would be made.

Chad unloaded the pallets for me and one by one I took pavers off, placing them in large gatherings under each letter of the last name. Once my eyes could size up the number of pavers per alphabet letter, I placed them in long lines alphabetizing them as I went. This required a lot of time, but once done was almost foolproof, giving anyone who had a comprehensive list the ability to check what was there.

Since more shipments would be coming, I decided to start separate *A-Z* piles, to save me the time of having to move all the pavers to fit in the first listings. This proved to save countless hours when it came time to lay them out and choose who would be placed where. The system worked flawlessly.

It was now time to act upon the merlons. For a while Michael and I had been talking about this traditional Mexican fortress feature. Even though they were part of our conceptual design we were not sure they would end up as part of the final monastery. The main reason was that they were symbolic and decorative and would add complications in how to engineer the design and have our copper standing seam roof work with them.

Mother Therese, Sister Elizabeth, and I all loved the merlons. They were block style shields jutting up from the main exterior walls, probably serving as workarounds in times of attack. Over time they became a symbol of fortress architecture indicating a place of protection and strength. We learned that Christian priests converting the Mexican culture paid attention to translating the symbology to a Christian reference, so the locals could relate meaning to elements that were a part of their culture. The merlons were kept and became a symbol atop God's house, in this case the mission as a place where true eternal protection and safety could be found.

I could only imagine how deeply the indigenous culture would have been influenced to have their own icons, symbols, and even materials given additional or even new meaning. *Did these new definitions and uses console them? Confuse them?* I reflected. *It would be so easy to project my own ideas oriented toward eternal ideologies, but I know this may not be the sentiment of the locals whose cultural lenses are radically different.*

It was time to cast them or cut them. We decided to go forward; the powerful detail would add beauty to an already beautiful chapel. The question turned to *how* to create them. Talking with Rob Teel from Continental Cut Stone we figured the actual dimensions and weight. Each merlon would be about one ton. Even if we were to cut stone, we would still have the challenge of figuring out how to anchor them, so a thought came to me and my main construction crew. *Why not cast them?* Then we could work out all the structural details ahead of time and tailor the frames to the need.

This created a whole series of fun challenges to solve. Michael and I decided to have a meeting on site with the key project leads that would be involved with these merlons. We gathered Alfonso, the lead chapel masons, Greg and Juan, our project lead for Harrison's copper roofing, Michael, and me.

My blood pulsed with excitement. One by one everyone arrived, enjoying the walk from their cars through the monastery rising all around them, at different stages around the site. We circled around the architect table in the novitiate which had become our meeting hub.

The merlons would sit on top of the walls, which meant they needed to go through the standing seam copper roof. If they were positioned over the internal faux pillars, they would have to sit upon the solid oak trusses inside. The trusses were exposed so the engineering had to create a way for the merlons to be solidly supported in a way that was hidden to the eye.

We all came up with different ideas, and various opinions on what would work, what would *not* work, and why. It was true creativity in the human spirit at its finest.

In the end the two challenges were identified: How do we anchor them into the wall by straddling the trusses? How will we flash around them through the roof, so leaks are avoided?

We decided to have an iron mold constructed in two parts that would bolt on each side and have three holes drilled, one at the top for rebar to extend far enough out that our crane could use it to lift the merlon from the ground up to its resting place; and two at the bottom, carefully measured to extend wider than the truss but within the frame of the open cinderblock. Alfonso ran the specs and confirmed our final design. The execution of supplies was now in my hands. I stopped by the blacksmith that had not been able to create our chandeliers for us but had graciously given me the advice to turn to Fernando in Mexico.

"Sister Mary, so great to hear from you!" he happily started. "How is that project going? Did you ever go to Mexico?"

"Oh, Bob, your advice made all the difference. We never could have said yes to building mission style if you had not provided Fernando," I confided with a bit of emotion. I went on to tell him all he was doing for us.

"Well, that is truly good news, Sister Mary. So, what can I do for you today?"

"Bob, we want to create merlons to line the chapel walls. We decided to cast them ourselves so we can tailor how they anchor into the building," I started in.

He asked me to break the idea down, so I showed him my pencil sketch on a six-by-six scrap paper. He chuckled as I explained the two iron pieces that would form the mold, how they would be bound together, and the three holes needed for the rebar to be placed.

"This is brilliant, Sister Mary. I can do this for you and am happy to donate my work since I haven't been able to help in any other way," he took my hand as he spoke. "Now let me have that working drawing," he said with a little wink.

About a week later they were added to my supply route. Since they were too heavy for me to move, the men placed them in the back of the truck, alongside the normal scrap wood, blueprints, extra tools, and a host of miscellaneous supplies. We also decided to put a fleur-de-lis in the center as a symbol of our devotion to Mary. Michael had the great idea of having Harry, his brother-in-law and right-hand carpenter, craft one with plywood to the specifications needed.

Our sidewalks to the hermitages had been poured months earlier, making them the perfect workstation to cast the merlons. Laying them out, thinking of how we would move them after they set, the first pour began. White masonry cement was mixed and gently poured to the brim of the mold. The rebar had been placed through the holes, but they were carefully adjusted and leveled and then strategically supported so they would set straight.

Our plan looked like it would work, but we wouldn't really know until they went up, which would be at the end of the project. The merlons, laying side by side, looked like strikingly white angels taking naps.

We turned to Ava one last time for a donation, offering her a dedication of the chapel as a living remembrance. For some reason Mother Therese, who was our main contact with Ava, asked me to go. While I was a bit nervous, I welcomed the opportunity to meet her.

At the same time, I was required to write the requisite yearly report for the grant received from the Kennedy Foundation. It gave me a relished moment of pause to recount the great work being done. So clearly a miracle. So evident as an example of the Form of the Formless One. The report felt like it wasn't complete enough, but I figured they would let us know if they needed more information. Not only was our report accepted, but our request to be the recipient for the year 1999 was awarded without need for a new application. We were given another fifty thousand dollars.

That same day, I got into the car to meet the mysterious Ava Decker for the first time, taking with me the plans so she could enjoy what was happening. What a delightful lady. We spent a good hour going through her photo albums where I learned of her work in the school system. She was a true pioneer as a young African American woman. Our conversation turned to the building project.

"Ava, you said to turn to you if we needed more help, and we do. I know you do not know me, but I am the one on the site every day and it is a miracle of a project. Our cost for the chapel will probably be about nine hundred thousand and we wondered if you would want to donate up to 50 percent of that cost for us. I have been organizing a lot of donations to help with the cost as well and think that it would be fair to give you the honor and credit if your donation was about four hundred fifty thousand." She sat placidly listening, I had no way of knowing how she really felt other than the kindness in her eyes.

"I can give you one hundred thousand now," she stated in a matter-of-fact tone, "Then another fifty thousand next month, how would that be? My trust has me set up to donate in increments." She was asking *me* if it was okay, while her level of generosity created a cavern of silence. It was this easy, *Ask and you shall receive*, the words of Jesus rose within me to direct my awareness to what was happening.

Before we left, she wrote a check. We hugged and mutually said we would talk soon. By the time I got home exuberance built and just like Mother Therese I waved the check as we all jumped in gratitude.

It was not long after she called. "Sister Mary?" her quiet voice inquired.

"Yes, that's me, is this Ava?"

"Yes, how are you? I have something for you for the project, can you come over?" she said eagerly.

"Of course, Ava, let me find a ride."

Michael took me over the next day. On her porch was a four-foot by four-foot hand painted tile rendition of Our Lady of Guadalupe. It was beautiful and fit perfectly with our theme. We agreed to put it in the foyer of the people's entrance to the chapel. Since Michael had a big open bed, we loaded it on the spot, and hauled it to its resting place in one of the hermitages for the next year and a half.

Another work visit from my mom and Lewis was timely worked in so we could get to Mexico for another delivery. This time it was the pews and of course the random other pieces that always seemed to find their way as donations to us.

What a site it was to see Lewis eagerly moving through a busy street, hugging a statue of Mary! It was just as delightful to see my mom witness him throw caution to the wind and abandon himself to the magic of the project. When she came, her days were so full. Somehow, she was able to support the driving for the project and fit in all the community's needs.

One day, coming home from the building site, I heard a scurrying behind the door. Opening it, two boisterous Labradors leaped toward me to say hello. "I was going to get us another dog," Mother Therese started, "but these are brothers, and I just couldn't separate them." She was filled with joy. We already had one dog that had been part of the community for many years. This one was especially endeared to Sister Elisha and would sit beside her as she worked and lay outside her door at night as she slept.

One was blonde, named Antioch, and the other was black, named Polycarp, named after two early Christian bishops whose writings we enjoyed. Even though she planned to train them, it never happened so they brought a certain chaos. This meant we had six sisters and three dogs fitting into the tiny residence. We didn't have dedicated spaces (like a living room) where pups could hang out.

About two months later I came back from the building site to find Mother Therese had just adopted two more dogs. Two pugs. I felt mortified at the prospect of what our place was going to become.

"How are we going to take care of so many dogs?" My question was met with resistance.

They made her feel good, however, that part was undeniable. Almost immediately the four of them became a pack. Everywhere Mother Therese went they went, and sometimes you could just about get knocked over as they raced to follow her from one place to another.

They were named Timothy and Titus after the New Testament epistle authors. Titus was much more resistant to new experiences, but Timothy loved going to new places, so sometimes he would accompany us to the building site.

Not long after, another challenging day arose at home. I was in Mother Therese's office going over a few building details, delicately sharing what had to be shared as she sighed loudly with a mix of impatience and fatigue. My stomach churned hoping to be through this quickly but something I said triggered her. She shoved me angrily. At first, I was stunned and just stood there in disbelief at what had happened, then I said I was sorry and moved quickly out of the office.

The next day she called me into her office and apologized with so much sincerity I felt a mix of compassion for her, which washed away the hurt, and guilt for wanting us to get help.

"Please, Mother Therese, let's reach out for help. This is too much," I cautiously yet emotionally asked. For the first time she was willing. We called Father Tomas, who gave us the name of a psychologist known for his work with religious people, Miguel

Perez. Tomas said this man was a friend of theirs and had helped them often.

We made an appointment to go together. She was nervous, as was I, so we entered the place with linked arms. We laid it all out to him. He confirmed what we wondered. She was suffering from depression, so she planned to put into practice the ideas he put out there, and an appointment was made for about two weeks away. In the process, she began talking about all the problems that were in her mind about the other sisters, focusing most of the session upon Sister Elizabeth. Turning the session in that direction left me feeling very uncomfortable, like blame was happening for her own internal struggles. I decided to keep my own perspective to myself. He suggested his colleague, Clara. They became our angels offering us friendship, guidance, and support.

My lingering concern was that Mother Therese held a steadfast belief that everyone else was the problem and she was making great sacrifices for her endurance.

Unfortunately, little changed. She did not experience healing which led to fear growing in my heart. I was deeply questioning my own perception, confused as I was by the influences of my formation, cloistered life, weaknesses of self-blame, and desire to see only the good in others. What gave me comfort was the relationships outside the monastery. They became my reality check. I decided to write a letter to Clara, the one helping Elizabeth. I thought, *I'll lay out all my thoughts and perceptions and ask Clara to help me see if I am delusional or sound and how I can move through the inward and outward difficulties.*

She came to the speakroom where we met in private, the letter in her hand. I prepared myself to hear the truth, to hear whatever I needed to hear, to change in myself anything I needed to change, or do whatever I needed to do.

"Sister Annunciata, you are NOT delusional, you are not crazy, you are okay," she insisted. "I promise you that I am not just trying to make you feel better. You asked me for my honest feedback, and I want to assure you that what you have shared here is worthy of deep concern."

I started to cry and relax. All the years I had been holding it all in, going over it in my mind, wondering how I could act out of charity, and avoid making any kind of judgment upon anyone but myself. She sliced through all of this, and I saw everyone, including myself, with eyes of compassion.

I began to think about my formation. *If my formation is healthy, wouldn't it have supported me in coming to inner freedom and not lead me into this level of inner weakness where I doubt every-thing?* The years of silence plunged me into a kind of dark night, wondering where God was in the moment. God was in Clara's words, for they consoled and gave gentle light. But I had been weakened over the years.

I made the decision to write to North Dakota for help.

The time came to pick up the bells that had been cast in Monterey. It seemed so long since we had ordered them, which made it feel like a Christmas gift to receive them! They offered to bring them over the border and transfer them for us. Even though they did not take up much room, the sheer weight required us to bring a flatbed. Again, equipment abounded, along with volunteers, and not long after, the shiny bells made it to the site. I decided to work with Paul Wilkerson and Bob, the blacksmith, to design the arms that would hold and swing them each into melody.

One sunny day on the site, deep in the heart of the chapel, poring over floor plans with Greg O'Brian I heard, "Sister Mary, Sister Mary," Bobby Castillo's normally quiet calm voice sung through the echoing walls around us. "Sister Mary, do you have a minute, I really want to show you something."

"Of course," Michael and I nodded to each other and parted, leaving the plans there for later discussion. Bobby's step was quick; *it must be important*. He led me through the corridor, out the door of the inner cloister, down the walk, to the closed door to the refectory. "Okay, close your eyes," he boldly encouraged.

I put my hand over my eyes, always happy for a surprise, and let him lead me into the refectory. "Okay, now open!" he said.

"Ooooooohhhh," I gasped. All around me was a sea of radiant red granite, its deep tones seemed to pulse an earth force upward filling the space. It was the most beautiful floor I had ever seen. We just stood there in silence. Bobby had taken great pains to break the stone into large flag pieces, taking him hours to prepare.

"Bobby, this is unbelievable," we took hands for a brief moment as a way to express the union of our hearts. "You are an amazing artist, and this floor will always be a tribute to you," I continued. This is one of our most important community spaces, sharing meals and celebrating feast days. It would be one of the main spaces where we would talk with each other.

Not long after, Harry surprised me as well. This part of Texas is in the tornado belt and even though Pierce's sections in Schleicher County had never been hit directly, Frank and I had planned early on to create some sort of shelter for the nuns. It took quite a bit of dialogue to come to our final design, a round, aboveground room, placed at an angle to the large chapel walls that would shield most directions of wind. We toyed with how strict to be with the room. "Should it be windowless?" we pondered over and again. After all, what good would it do if windows could be blown in on us during a storm.

The final choice was to build it endurable to elements but keep it pleasant for daily use. The community decided to make it the recreation room, and I was able to easily obtain a donated new wood stove to make it homey.

Just like Bobby's surprise, Harry was ready to reveal his own surprise. This man was a true artisan and rarely had the chance to use his skill since most of Michael's jobs did not give him the chance to create such artistic accents. Michael had privately told me of his carpentry skill and we both surprised him one day by offering him the project of creating the ceiling for this round room. He smiled inwardly, looking downward to the toes of his work boots, then looking up directly in my eyes, "Yes, I'll do it."

Shortly after Bobby's floor, a similarly eager voice sought me out, "Sister Mary, Sister Mary, do you have a minute?" Harry unassumingly interrupted a short consultation between me and our painters.

"Of course!" I knew what was coming but I had no idea what it was actually going to look like; my curiosity was piqued. We almost ran to the room. Harry did not ask me to close my eyes, but just the opposite, he flung the door open, and we bolted into the space.

The ceiling was breathtaking. It had hand-culled tongue and groove, starting atop the walls with each interlocking panel stretching up to the center point about three feet higher than the perimeter. He had hand stained the wood before setting, and applied finishing touches once all was set in place.

"Harry this is a true work of art! I will think of you every day we are in this room." He accepted the praise humbly.

We were coming to our last days of needing to go to Mexico. I had grown to love Fernando, Ana, and Mateo, and I imagine Mother Therese felt the same way. It was so hard to believe our time with them was coming to an end. The last two trips were set up once we knew my mom's planned visits. We had secured from them all our lights, pews, armoires, small accent items, sanctuary crucifix, and lights for the altar along with so much more.

We pulled a flatbed for this final pickup, stocked with Mom's special treats which we ate in rest areas along the way.

Our Brothers and Sisters at Holy Spirit Retreat Center invited us to join them for Exposition of the Blessed Sacrament once we got to them, so after a quick meal we made our way to a room of the women's part of the complex. Opening the door, I almost passed out from sheer grace. Music was playing, voices were singing charismatic songs, the Eucharist was front and center, and about fifty young zealous lovers of Jesus were in all positions of prayer and praise throughout the place. It brought the charismatic living memories of early childhood with my family, through to university, within me into THIS moment. This time of prayer was the first since I had entered the monastery eight years ago that let me expand into all the charismatic gifts with liberality. Mother Therese stayed for about two hours, drinking it up as well. She let me stay for as long as it continued. The gathering ended about midnight, and like light bulbs, separating out from a common, generated Source, we made our way to our private rooms once the last song and prayer were said.

The next morning about 7 a.m., we all got into the truck and proceeded over the border. Just like normal we flowed like an unobstructed river to Fernando's place. My mom took pictures so we could remember everyone, and not long after, goodbyes were in order.

"We can keep in touch," Ana's teary eyes asked or proposed.

"Yes, yes, let's do that, and maybe you can even come to the Dedication," I invited. We promised them we would refer them and once their shop on the American side was open, would send their address out to people we know.

I was not ready to say goodbye. We had created together, learned, and laughed, and it was ending because the need ended. But beginnings always have an end and so this one did as well.

Tearing ourselves away we made it to the border, and like a book ready to be closed our last drive was like an iron gate closing upon us. Pulling over to go through the normal check, the police officer proceeded, "So what are these items going to be used for?" His voice was tight as he began an interrogation.

Wow, I thought, *what a sign for us right now. Clearly the golden portal that had remained open for these past couple years was just now closing.* I knew we would make it through this last time.

After an entire sheet of notes were taken, writing down each of our informal answers to all his questions, he went on, "Have you filed a report with our main office? You know you need to do that to bring such quantities over the border."

We had not known but told him we are happy to do whatever he asked.

Off we went, Mother Therese and I, to the main office to fill out paperwork. We were told there was a state government office from which approval had to be received before they would let us over the border. My inner sense guided me to keep it simple and to answer what was asked openly and succinctly. While all we did was legal, there was no need to create a difficult process.

Spirit had given us a beneficent officer on the other line of the phone, so two hours later we were permitted to cross. "From here on out, though, you need to obtain some sort of permit *first*," he counseled. I took all the contacts he gave to me so we could put them on file.

A door of magic had opened for as long as we needed it, almost like Moses parting the seas for crossing. Once we were safely crossed with all that was ours, the waters resumed their normal course.

Arriving home that night a call from Fernando awaited us. We had forgotten all the outside sconce lights! He needed us to get them as soon as possible and offered to bring them over the border to save time. Thank goodness, little did he know the easy door to him had shut for us.

Mother Therese and I accepted Lewis's offer to drive back down early the next morning and come back the next day. We planned to go with him since it would be a strain on him to drive twelve hours in one day. My mom was going to run errands for the sisters who had been building it to quite a large list.

This night we realized there were feast day decorations we needed to cut. We brought supplies out into the speakroom since there was a large table and a light hung brightly in the middle of the room making it easy to see.

This night changed everything.

Mother Therese looked so tired, and when she was tired, she also hated to be bothered. I felt torn, *Do I offer to take over for her so she can go to bed? Or do I leave?* I did not know what to do, and both options felt like a possibly good choice. The offer to relieve her won out, persuaded by the voice in my head that reminded me to be of service to my leader.

If only I had followed my gut instead.

"Mother Therese," my voice wobbled a little bit as she looked up with darts in her eyes, "do you want me to finish that for you so you can get some rest?"

As I said it, I could feel anger arise from somewhere deep within her.

Barely had the words trailed off than she threw the scissors furiously at me across the table. Fear absolutely gripped my heart, and I stood stunned as she raced toward me. "Yooo—uuuuuu!" She shouted at me, her fist shaking close to my nose and her face getting redder by the minute. I was terrified. It was the first time I really thought she was going to hurt me, and I froze. She said some harsh words that no longer remain in my memory and ran out of the room.

I was shaking, trembling. "Calm down, Sister Annunciata," I began to say over and over. "You are okay, nothing happened. She is just in a lot of pain. She doesn't mean it."

It was in that moment my heart felt and believed I was not safe. Up until that point I was able to hold onto hope. In this moment something shifted. I genuinely believed that she would eventually really hurt me and that if I was going to stay, something truly needed to change.

The form of religious life is being destroyed before me. I don't know what to rest into anymore; where is God, where is my Beloved? I lay in bed restless that night.

The Dance of Dissolution and Emergence

The next morning, we were both supposed to go with Lewis. I was too afraid to ask her anything, so I slid out the door, making apologies for her to Lewis. We never rode alone with a man, so it felt unusual even though he was family. It was a first for Lewis and me to spend one on one time together. On top of the unusual circumstance, I was still reeling in shock.

Where is the Beloved?

In this kind man, Lewis; in the ever-solicitous care of Fernando; in the emergence of all the lights we needed for the outdoors for this new monastery. They were symbols of light that were there in the dark.

Arriving home late everyone was in bed. I hoped not to see her, and my prayer was answered. But this could not last, we would have to talk again at some point.

The next morning after terce I proceeded to knock on her door. It was the normal time for our construction discussions. She was peeved at me, and I trembled. She treated me like I had been entirely out of place in offering her help the night before last. Her look triggered an element of guilt and insecurity. My words were hard to find, and I spoke with great hesitation.

"Mother Therese," I added at the end, "we need help. We really need help. Let's ask North Dakota to help us."

Her eyes boldened with indignance: "Sister Annunciata, if you EVER reach out for help, I will convince everyone that you are a problem here and get you kicked out of the Order." The fear from two nights ago resurged in my heart, gripping me as I found a way to back out of the room.

From that point onward, many mornings when we went through details were mornings when she criticized me. Somehow this seemed to abate her inner anger and she increased her happiness toward the rest of the community. I asked her if she wanted me to just take care of construction without turning to her since the details were overwhelming, but she said no, as she usually did.

How can so much good and so much pain coexist? How can both realities be a part of my life right now? Experiencing the miracle of the project before me, running through me, while simultaneously being in this painful relationship with my leader is excruciating. My thoughts moved in a vain circle, leaving me without insight and with increasing pain. I reflected more deeply, *If I wasn't in vows, I could have walked away a few years prior, but my commitment to what I saw to be my calling kept me here.* I thought more, *If this is a gift from my Beloved, what am I meant to learn, heal, or change?*

The thought of leaving seems impossible, I thought again, *for all the people of the project would be let down. There was not the money to replace my donated efforts, nor an obvious choice of another sister in our community to take over my responsibilities.* My thoughts circled.

It was not long after Father Tomas and the brothers wanted to come out and be toured through the site. Mother Therese wanted me to go with her, so we all went. It was a return to some of the joyful moments from four years prior, when we all laughed together on our way from the airport.

The four of us Carmelites walked through the construction, Therese inviting me to share the project in detail and at length. Since the two hermits were builders as well, we relished all the hidden aspects. I found myself relaxing into the rare opportunity to praise the workmanship happening before our eyes. Once through the main buildings, we made our way along the hermitage path, coming to the final pad. We had decided to leave one pad un-built to reference for the additional hermitages we hoped to build as the community grew.

On this pad Mother Therese asked for Father Tomas's blessing. Like the day of my arrival when we knelt outside the speakroom, we both dropped to our knees and Father Tomas extended his hands. His words left me feeling drunk in Spirit, as they wove on in every direction like swelling billows of incense moving up and out. Toward the end, he spontaneously began to consecrate me with a simple word as a future leader of the community. I could feel the blessing run through my body but felt very embarrassed that he was not consecrating Mother Therese. As the words poured through him, our eyes still closed, I was desperately praying he would turn attention to Mother Therese, but he did not. Just moments after we opened our eyes, I looked to her, her eyes darted back at me fiercely. There was nothing I could do, it felt like she was blaming me, so I simply looked down and kept quiet from there on out.

Just a few months later our Carmelite provincial, Fr. John Bailey visited the building site as well. What a glorious moment, couched in a sunny day with work crews spewed across the landscape. Mother Therese and I walked with him as he asked questions.

"Just remember when you are here, Sister Annunciata, that you will need to keep all the sisters close in relationship. You will be living very rurally, so pay attention to build love," the provincial counseled looking directly at me, as Mother Therese looked at him with surprise.

"Mother Therese is the prioress," I reminded him, trying to avert focus from me. I had never thought I would be a leader of the community; I had always wanted to finish the project and then sink back into the embrace of silence as a nun scrubbing floors.

The project took all my attention, so this small disturbance passed, but the larger one remained. *Are we going to get through it? Will things really fall into a rhythm that supports our lifestyle once we move in? Or is this just me being hopeful beyond hope?*

I asked to see Clara as she had become my friend; I leaned into her and occasionally wept which always left me feeling refreshed and supported.

Clara counseled me that I was very wise to write to North Dakota. I had been trying to take this step for quite a while. The letter was written but I still did not have the courage to send it.

"They see her as a savior there; in their eyes Mother Therese can do no wrong. In fact, she is the only one who gets to speak with them, so they only have information about how we are doing from her perspective," I told Clara. I knew they would be completely surprised if I wrote to seek help.

The paradox was not lost on me, the paradox. As the monastery rose high with beauty and inspiration, the tension and negativity within our community at home rose equally. The incident with the scissors shifted me. It released me from my blind belief that my vows were a direct channel I could trust of God was working *through my leaders* to show me love in their role and through their presence. This was profound, as it did not lead me to the opposite belief, that God *isn't* working through my leaders and my order. It led me to understand that mysteriously God *was* working through my leaders in order to bring me to a more subtle experience of grace.

Shortly after our meeting with the Provincial, Casey, one of our beloved volunteers, had arranged to help Mother Therese with a day of errands since needs arose outside one of my mom's visits. It was a Tuesday morning, and the doorbell rang after terce.

"Hi Casey, how are you?" We chatted for a little bit.

"Mother Therese called, I have the entire day to help in any way you need," she confided.

I had not known she was going to help us on this day, "Let me ask Mother Therese. She was not feeling well today and is lying down."

I made my way quickly to the dormitory and knocked on the door of Mother Therese's cell. Half asleep, she invited me in but asked me to keep the light off. She seemed relaxed even though she was drained, so I kept it brief.

"Casey is here. She said you asked her to help today with errands. Could you let me know what to tell her? Maybe there is a list somewhere?"

"I don't know," she despondently said. "Just tell her to go home today, that I am not ready."

Immediately I felt guilt around the inconvenience we were causing Casey, and I felt tension because it was falling on me. "Mother Therese, she took off work today just to help us, can't we give her some things to do?" I inquired.

"No. I said I cannot remember, so ask her if she will help us on another day," her voice had an edge which let me know not to pursue any further dialogue.

Opening the door to the speakroom Casey sat there eagerly. "Casey, I am so sorry. Mother Therese asked if you could help on another day, I am so sorry, she doesn't have the list ready, and I do not know what she had in mind," I said, trying to fill the awkward space with ease.

"I took off the day from work," she was frustrated, and fairly so.

"I know, I am so sorry. I feel terrible and do not know what to do." At a complete loss to console her I also felt angry at the injustice into which I was implicated with this good friend of ours who just lost a daily wage for nothing.

This was enough to move me to send that letter. I had written a rough draft a month earlier and shared it with Clara so she could give me feedback. When I shared it, I asked with open heart, "Please tell me if I am overreacting. I am open to any feedback you will offer to me as I want to be true to Spirit."

After she read it, she looked at me with such tenderness, "Sister Annunciata, you are *not* overreacting, what you are saying here is said with such love and is worthy of serious support and concern." I wept to have someone on the outside of cloister witness what had been so painful for me to navigate the past years.

All I needed was to have an injustice present itself toward someone else. If I couldn't do it for myself, I could certainly do it for the sake of the community and our relationships with our friends.

I was so scared of what would happen from that moment forward that I made a copy so I could refer to it if needed. *What if something terrible happens to me? What if Mother Therese's threat is carried out,* I thought. Mother Therese was our leader. She was convincing, captivating, and beloved. She was also twenty years older than me; I realized there was a good chance North Dakota would disregard me.

As I wrote I reflected on my relationship with Mother Maria Teresita. We had grown close when I was in the Novitiate, and she had seen me as an honest, stable human being. *I have been faithful to my vows,* my thoughts relaxed me, *and there is no reason to think I would not be believed.*

The letter went out the next day. Mother Therese had skipped prayer again and was resting in her cell. I knocked on the door. She kindly invited me in so I went close to her bed where she could see me. My body took me to my knees. "Mother Therese, I wrote to North Dakota for help. The letter went out today," my heart was so heavy and scared as I spoke.

Softly and with great sadness she responded, "How could you do this?" Her tone was heavy leaving me feeling like she felt betrayed.

"We are not functioning well as a community, I needed to reach out for help." She was feeling so low I felt torn about my action but held hope that reaching out would provide us with support.

About a week later a phone call came in, I could hear it from my office, as Mother Maria Teresita was yelling through the receiver. My heart was beating out of my chest with fear and hope. I sat praying ardently. About half an hour passed before Mother Therese knocked on my door. Emotionally she looked like her clothes had been torn and she had been through a battle.

"Mother Maria Teresita is on the phone for you, she wants to talk with you privately," and she handed me the phone. My palms were sweating; I was so scared that Mother Maria was going to yell at me. I was terrified at having reached out for help.

The door closed and I sat alone on the phone. It had been so long since we had spoken, and I had no idea over these past years if our relationship had changed, or remained the same, or if Mother Therese had spoken about the community or me in an unpleasant light.

"Oh, Sister Mary Annunciata, I am so sorry," she tenderly said. "Are you okay?"

Tears started streaming down my face as I felt her kindness. I started shaking at having carried so much for so long. I trusted her.

"Yes, we just need help and I have wanted to write for so long but was afraid," I sensed it was okay to open my heart.

Just then Mother Therese opened the door with a pleading look on her face. Guilt arose but I tried to remain steadfast.

"Do you think Mother Therese should come back here to rest for a while?"

Mother Therese was close enough to hear and began ardently shaking her head, silently mouthing, "Please, no, I don't want to go back there."

I did not want to be in this position, to be deciding what should happen. It was too much for me. Sitting frozen and offering no response, Mother Maria Teresita picked up on it all, "She is there isn't she? Trying to influence you."

"Yes," I said, hopeful Mother Maria would see this action of Therese's and take me out of the equation. "Please, I don't know what is best, that is why I am reaching out for help," I went on. This was such a moment of relief, at least things were not hidden anymore and surely, we would all move to a better place.

"Okay, put Mother Therese back on," she guided. They went back to talking for a while. Once it was over, I was called into her office.

"Well, Mother Maria yelled at me, she told me I could be excommunicated," Mother Therese said, a bit angry but also cautious now that I had drawn a line. "I told her I would see someone professional and report to her each month so she could see how things were going. So, will you call Miguel and set up an appointment?" she said flatly. At least she would hold back on angry outbursts, knowing she would be accountable to someone.

The next week required my full attention on the building site, giving me a welcome amount space from the situation at home.

Progress continued at a monumental pace, and I really needed to move pallets and supplies around the land and to get my crews lined out for the next stages. Pierce had a front-end loader that could be turned into a forklift, so he came up to the jobsite one day once all the crews had left. We worked for about three hours reorganizing everything: moving granite for the kitchen to its place, stone for the admin to its place, freshly cut windowsills donated by Rob to their place, and the last bit of drywall to its installation location, the sewing room. Any supplies not needed were moved to the furthest end of the fence line to stay out of the way. While Pierce drove, I stood on the small metal bar behind the seat. A cool breeze began to blow through the jobsite as the pinkish golden tones of the setting sun cast its blessing upon all around us.

We drank it in. Silently we became absorbed in nature. After a few moments Pierce confided, "This is why I am here, Sister Mary. I wouldn't trade this moment for anything." He didn't need me to speak to know I felt the same way. His presence was my peace. The miracle of the project within us and before us was the utterance of Spirit taking on new form in the world, the steady sunset casting its glow every evening was the assurance of the ever-present embrace of God. Beauty took us upon its wings. Spirit beckoned without force, loudly invited without coercion.

Going home that night my worry felt lighter.

It was not long after a stone Carmelite shield we commissioned Paul to carve was done. This emblem would sit in the finished facade of the entrance to the monastery. Paul called us to pick it up, so Mother Therese and I made arrangements to go the following Wednesday. We would be getting it before the feast of Our Lady of Mount Carmel. Maybe we would even place it in the wall by then. This would not happen; in fact, it would be about a year before the shield would finally make its ascent.

The Vricellas had us come to their house which sat upon a river, where Paul did some of his carving. As we arrived, we jumped out of the vehicle. (The reason we jumped out of vehicles is not as much for exuberance as height; all these pickup trucks were Texas style: LARGE.)

"Sister Mary is here! Sister Mary is here!" a young voice shouted as running steps made their way to me. Matthew, their youngest son, ran into my arms as we hugged hello.

"Hello, Sister Mary!" he said, still shouting with excitement.

"Hello, Matthew, I am sooooooo happy to see you," I swung him around a few times making him laugh. He stayed in my arms the entire visit.

The shield sat in the sunlight, on a flat wooden worktable. It was absolutely perfect. Paul talked to us about how he carved it while

Matthew held one of his tools, waving it around my head to imitate his dad.

"May God reward you," we said upon our leaving, giving big hugs to all.

A check was sent in the mail the next day for Paul, and I outlined the accounting for our record. Sister Elizabeth was in charge of all the accounting, but I did not want anything with the project to chance getting lost, so I had obtained permission to file the records in two portable file boxes in my office. That way I could easily check payments for crews, reference questions, or even get a business or invoice number if asked.

Each time I wrote a check was pure joy. It was one of the main ways I could show gratitude for our team. It left me desiring more money so I did not need to lean continually into charity. As much as I made sure all were appreciated, there was always a niggling desire to pay more. It was humbling to see how much was given, and to see the resulting joy in the exchange. Even Michael and his men, who were my main crew from beginning to end, charged so little and gave even more over and above the long hours of labor. Towards the end of the project Michael wanted to give even more and sponsored the inspired icon of Jesus the Teacher that sits in the podium to this day.

My dad planned a visit along with my young brother, Adam, and my sister and her two girls, Andrea and Monica. It all got worked out around his birthday in July. They gladly drove me to the site where everyone hung out. All I needed to do was keep things rolling smoothly so after the morning ordering and lining out, I could spend time with them. Everyone wanted to help, my family has always been of service. We gave them paint rollers and brushes and pans filled with white wall paint. The Novitiate slowly got covered, since laughing created delays in brushes running against walls. The girls were so cute, running around holding hands. While my dad is meticulous, my little brother was a bit messier, and had just as much paint on him as on the wall.

It was no problem keeping Dad busy so we could set things up, he was intent on finishing the high ceiling before the visit ended. Unknown to him we converted one of the bare bedrooms into party central, the girls writing fun messages on the big cardboard with markers and Kelly loading up the cake with candles. Mother Therese had made it possible to pull together birthday party balloons, plates, cake, watermelon (for my non cake eating brother), and candles. "Da-yad," we called to him as he stood close to the ceiling on the scaffolding.

"Just a minute," he responded. We knew he was dedicated to finishing before he stopped.

We occupied ourselves in a distracted way, checking in until he had to get another can of paint. As he shimmied down the scaffolding the girls grabbed him and we quickly lit the candles. "Happy birthday to you!!!!" we started up. Sweets were a welcome deterrent from a moment of work, and we hung out for as long as we could. I knew once the monastery was done these sorts of visits would be over and cloistered life would resume, so I relished every ounce.

The following month the chapel ceiling would be enclosed. Up until this point only the walls were being finished, casting long hours of light into the space. Even though months of finishing still needed to happen, the trusses were done in San Antonio, and we were ready to complete this portion of the project on every other end. August was one of the most dependable months too. Mark from Texas Timber Frames arranged to do a site visit the month before.

This joyous friend ran up and gave me a big hug. It felt like we had just seen each other even if it had been a good year and a half since that long ago meeting in San Antonio. He confirmed we had done everything to specifications, calling his office to set a date on the schedule. "Okay, how about next week Friday, which will be August 21st?"

Michael and I looked at each other. "Perfect," I said, and we were set.

We decided to have both masonry crews and his carpentry crew (even though they were on another job at this point) on site that day just in case. The sun seemed a bit brighter on that day, if that is possible in the heat of summer, and Mark's men arrived on site early in the morning. Extra magic tinged the air making us all giddy. They were such a tight company. All they needed came with them, including their own crane. This way, they could ensure the setting was to their own level of perfection. It took all day, but one after the other the larger-than-life red oak trusses were lifted and placed and anchored. The only metal used were braces lodged into our block on either side of the trusses to keep them steady.

The sun at all its stages shined brightly upon the warm toned wood. I wished we would not need to cover them; having the wood jutting up into the open air made the chapel feel more heavenly than earthbound.

"Now Sister Mary, this wood is fine outside but we do suggest that you move toward getting the roof in place this month," Mark suggested.

"No problem, we already have the use of a crane next week to set the merlons in place," I let him know, happy to be doing things in a timely way.

It was one of the days my mom was helping which meant many pictures would be taken, such an incredible history she provided. By now she had gained approval through both Mother Therese and her dissertation board to switch her topic to the study of how a community is educated when a religious community is present. She gained approval to let our project be the study.

Many of the companies with whom we worked welcomed my mom's interest. She was so careful to ask up front who wanted to be involved in her research and who did not and was even more careful to frame all she did with the professional ethic that defined her life.

Everywhere we went she would spend the day writing notes. I never asked her about them, my own stress had increased, and I was keeping my emotions to myself. Each day she would take me out to the site, the door would open for me to get in, she would greet me with a big smile, pull out a diet Pepsi (funny that I would drink soda after all these years without), and put some nuts or some other healthy snack in the drink holes for me to take as I wished.

With an unspoken acceptance, she allowed me to be consumed in my work, never pushing to find out how I was doing.

Mother Maria Teresita called to check in monthly, to see how things were going. However, she chose to check in only with Mother Therese, and not with all of us. Therese did not share with me or anyone else what she told Mother Maria. I had hoped she would ask to speak with us all, so each of us would have a voice in the process.

My letter had failed.

In September Mother Maria asked to speak with me, four months after the letter had been sent.

"So Mother Therese says she is doing better, and there is nothing to worry about. I am happy to hear that, Sister Annunciata."

"Why are you only talking to her?" I timidly asked. "Of course, she is going to paint a picture that is comfortable, because she doesn't want to have to spend time back in North Dakota." I was so raw that there was nothing much to lose in being direct.

"Well, has she had any rage lately?" she asked.

"No, she has been calm and is going to prayer too, but it doesn't feel like change is happening, I can't tell you why, only that the air is not cleared," I confided.

"Sister Annunciata, this doesn't seem a good reason not to give her a chance to prove herself," Mother Maria insisted.

"I don't want her to need to prove anything to anyone, but only that we are all supported to change and create a healthier community," I was no match for her reasoning as she saw only that these couple failings were changed, and not for learning the *what* and the *why* of what was happening. There was something in the air that was not right to me, and at least I could speak out loud about it at that time.

I had been given special permission to leave for the building site at 7 a.m. the day we set the merlons. We saved a thousand dollars by my being there for the donation of the crane and all the activity that would happen. We saw this as worthy of missing lauds and Mass that day.

At eight o'clock in the morning we all heard the rumbling of our crane, coming like a monster queen upon her throne, ready to anoint our chapel walls with the fleur-de-lis merlons that had sat upon our sidewalk for endless months. This was the day. This was the big day! All our planning and creating and brainstorming would also be anointed by this crane ready to make the walls into symbols of spiritual fortress.

Juan Navarro with a big smile and ready hands got his men into place. He had so taken our project to heart by then that this day of construction would dub him as a knight at the service of the queen crane, wielding the machinery and intellect that made him head manager of his crew. The day before, we had moved each merlon to the ground just below its final resting place. Michael brought his bobcat from the other job to give us two, and all the other supplies needed were purchased by me. We were already prepared for battle, so to speak. I was not really needed but could not resist jumping onto the lower roof line of the admin building and following every step. I had the plans ready just in case, *What would we need them for?* Not only had we rehearsed this the day before, but also, there was nothing else to work out. The blocks for each placement were the only ones left unpoured and the trusses provided the exact location for the rebar to straddle. Somehow it felt comforting to hold my small thirteen-page chapel architectural set; it let me participate vicariously.

The first merlon was raised into the air like a winged angel in flight. With minimal breeze that day, and the clasp of the metal cable running through our homemade rung extending out the top of each piece, there was not a chance of dropping any of them. The risk was little to none.

It was still a feat to lift them above the twenty-two-foot walls and guide them to the position where they would be anchored. Juan was on the ground preparing for the lift, then he climbed the scaffolding like a billy goat to get onto the chapel wall to guide them to safety. He became *the knight that mounted the merlons* in my mind.

Within six hours the job was done!

Before Roberson Rent-All closed, I was able to call and give the great news. "We did it! The merlons are all in place!" Cheers went up on the other end from all the men in the store.

"Whoo-hoo! Sister Mary way to go!" I loved these men.

Most all our major artistic accents were either done or in process; however, two remained without a subcontractor. The first was our grille, the one that would sit between the nuns and the sanctuary and the second was the sanctuary dome. Michael had spent quite a bit of time thinking about how to build the internal dome. Even though we did not have the money to create an external dome, it was easy to keep the roof line externally then build a dome on the inside composed of metal, wire, and stucco.

"Sister Mary, I got it. I was thinking about this for a while and here is what will probably work," he started as we stood looking up to the high twenty-eight-foot point of the sanctuary. "If we get an I-beam and run it from the floor to the center, my men can use that point to build a self-sustaining arch extending to the four points," he went on to show me how it would anchor, with ties to parts of the inner unseen side of the roof and drilled rebar extended into each corner of the block of the sanctuary space. Michael stood there, joy lighting up his face, revealing the years of developed construction understanding enough to bring his own form of creativity and provide practical application.

"What would I do without you?" I told him, "That is a brilliant idea!"

We got the post ordered as quickly as we could so it could be placed inside, in the natural light, before all the roofing was completed as we got it anchored to the floor. While that was happening, another surprise came our way. An unknown pickup truck rumbled its way to our jobsite and a young man with long blonde hair pulled back into a ponytail jumped out of the driver's seat.

"Hello, can you tell me where to find Sister Mary," he asked my electrician who was working in the speakroom.

"Sure, let me take you to her," he dropped what he was doing, and they made their way—now a maze—through the various passages until the door to the Novitiate opened. I was leaning over our drafting board taking some measurements for the oculus window to be set in a few months.

"Hi there, Sister Mary?" he bowed his head a little. Here was a truly peaceful man standing before me. "I am Tommy. Bobby Peiser is one of my friends. Well, he told me what you are doing out here and I wondered if I could be a part of it? Maybe donate some of my handcrafted iron work?"

"Of course!" I said. "Do you want to know what we still need? Or did you have something in mind?"

"Could you tell me what you are looking for, and I can decide if it fits what I can donate?" he responded in a way that was open to the point of sounding indifferent. But I knew this man was nowhere near indifferent.

We walked over to the chapel.

"Bobby is making our mahogany doors and we need hardware for them. We are really open to whatever style you would want to create; they need to hold the large doors in place with the ability to open them in, and one smaller inset door to open out. Now, right here we will have four layers of arches," I went on just to give him a sense of the scope of the entrance.

"Sister Mary, I would be honored to donate the hardware. Let me show you some of my work." He pulled out a laminated binder and slowly flipped pages showcasing his large array of iron pieces that were clearly works of art.

"Oh, Tommy, we have been hoping to find the right person for this other need. Can I show you?" I ventured.

"Of course, let's see it," he picked up his step as I cascaded in my full habit toward the front of the chapel, sweeping around the corner a few feet before stopping.

"This spot is where we plan to have a grille. It is a symbolic gate, not to keep us in or others out, but to signify our consecration to God in our cloister. What we are longing to create," my hands and arms spread open and wide, "is a large arch, imitating the arches that will be in the sanctuary, where the grill will shoot up the sides until you get about fifteen feet high, then span the width. This large arch will be all vines and grapes to symbolize the line, 'Vine Blossom Laden,' spoken of Mary in our traditional chant called the 'Flos Carmeli.'"

I sang the chant for him,

> Flos Carmeli
> Vitis florigera
> Splendor Caeli
> Virgo Puerpera
> Singularis
>
> Mater mitis
> sed viri nescia
> Carmelitis
> esto propitia
> stella maris

"The bottom piece of the grille," I went on, "would be like a fence with a center gate and have a different design. So, what do you think? Does this project interest you?'

"Sister Mary, I cannot tell you what an honor it would be to create this piece. And I insist on donating it; will you let me donate it?"

"Tommy, you have no idea how much you are an answer to a prayer," I told him, "Not only because we were in need, but because we wanted someone of your caliber to create these iron pieces for us. You have been an answer to two prayers, thank you, thank you!" I poured upon him.

We had little contact after I gave him a copy of the plans and the finished wall measurements. He worked out structural details with Bobby, so it was not until the time for installation that he and I met again. A couple months later I let him know where we were in our progress, and a couple months after that, he called to keep in touch as well. The conversations were sincere, warm, and brief.

As the roofing was being completed the O'Brian crew began to stone the inside. By this time the stone Sister Catherine and I had chosen was stockpiled close to the chapel so they could choose the best way to get the stone into the chapel and keep laying it at a consistent pace. So often on the project I stopped to marvel at the work happening. Only a year and a half earlier we were rejoicing in the underground and, because of all those that brought their expertise forward, we kept a steady pace. Even my electricians and painters were in the administrative wing, the air conditioning units were being finished for the hermitages, lights were being hung from the beams outside the Novitiate, roofers every day, masons every day, and another few crews flowed in and out. I felt so utterly blessed, almost like I was watching a valley fill in with trees and lakes and wildflowers before my eyes.

After the scissor incident, however, I withdrew more and more emotionally. Things didn't get worse, but they didn't get better either and I just wanted to protect myself. One way was to just be alone in my work and open to whatever was asked of me in community. My heart could not muster the same enthusiasm in the community anymore, could not be the joyful young religious who would keep her heart open no matter what the response. My presence became very serious as a result. I loved everyone, but my love needed to be quiet and alone, or I did not know if I would be able to finish the project with the level of quality it deserved. In addition, there was a sensation of not wanting to be touched. If I had been touched, I would have started crying, and if I started crying, who knows if I would have been able to pull myself together.

I held tight to being faithful to my word as though it were a mast of a ship on a stormy sea. This coupled with a waning hope. I had given myself a concrete plan. My plan was simple. I will finish my role as general contractor, get my community moved out to our new home, and see if things shift. If peace returned and we settled in, then I would stay, happy to have made it through our community's dark night of the soul. If things did not get better, I would ask to either explore another community or leave altogether.

Mother Therese's feast day came, and we celebrated as we always did, with zest and love. Not long after, it was time for our elections. I found it so hard to believe that three years had passed so quickly.

Sister Felicity had not taken solemn vows yet, so she could not vote. She gladly prepared the meals while we prepared for the voting process. There were only five of us, and the vote would be for a prioress and two counselors.

Shift was in the air. I could taste it and feel it, like the coming of a storm system to shake things up. On election day every atom seemed a different color. Into the moment, I poured prayer. I poured my heart in prayer. I was absorbed in deep consolation and presence. I didn't even know what to hope for, only for change that would lead to peace.

Once the logistics were set up for the ritual of our voting, we awaited the hour of the bishop's arrival—about 1 p.m.

Mother Therese spent the morning talking to Mother Maria. My one contact with Mother Therese was brief but in it, she told me she was asked how she felt about the elections.

"I am a shoo-in," she related her words to Mother Maria to me, "there is absolutely no one else who could be elected, so I will call you tonight to confirm my position," she confidently told them.

I had to reflect; *Is she right? I mean who else could be prioress?* Sisters Elisha, Elizabeth, and Catherine were all candidates; I was not since you needed to be thirty-five. Not one of them had ever been in leadership; it would be such an adjustment. However, the shift in the air was undeniable. SOMETHING was going to change. I had already resolved that I could not vote for her even if everyone else did.

My compass was to vote for the sister who would be open to getting help. If I had been old enough and happened to be voted in, that is exactly what I would have done.

There were free hours before us as we waited for the bishop, so I found myself back in the chapel. Sister Elisha was there as well, and we nodded to each other then went our own way into private prayer. The quiet was so very full of presence. At a certain point I opened my Bible and read these mysterious words from John 15:7-11: "If you abide in me and my words abide in you, ask for whatever you wish, and it will be done for you. My Father is glorified by this, that you bear much fruit and become my disciples. As the father has loved me, so I have loved you; abide in my love. If you keep my commandments, you will abide in my love, just as I have kept my father's commandments and abide in his love. I have said these things to you so that my joy may be in you and that your joy may be complete."

I had no insight, only that the phrase consoled me and brought me to the familiar place of bliss. To the invitation of Jesus, I gave the largest YES I could possibly offer.

Mother Therese rang the bell letting us know the bishop had come. The lights in the Chapel flicked on and he walked into our small space with Mother beside him. It was awe-inspiring to have him in our small space. We each kissed his ring and took our spots, kneeling at our stalls. He spoke to us, giving us a short inspirational talk.

It felt like angels and guides filled the space with us. We were only six women living lives of prayer in a Diocese of thousands and here was the bishop serving our need. What a living symbol of care he embodied.

Since I was the first counselor, elected last time to the position, it was my job to read the opening words that inaugurated the elections. As the passage was read every sister was relieved of her role.

Until the new roles were determined, we were in flux, and the flux could be felt. The air around us felt surreal to me. *Guide me*, I begged the Holy Spirit.

I tried to think it through.

If I vote for Sister Elisha who knows where her pent-up anger will go? And she is the only sister that has no idea what is happening with the building project since she doesn't like working with me. Plus, she is almost always sick due to her debilitating MS; who knows if she would be capable of being present daily. On the positive side, I wonder if her health would return if she was esteemed for what she wanted to be in community, but is that a solid reason to vote for her? Inwardly I continued to another sister. *Sister Catherine is the sweetest soul, but her memory has faded at seventy-four years old, and she is simply not a leader. She loves to support leaders but has expressed little interest in guiding community toward decisions. She would have to manage so much correspondence, something she had never done before, and it felt it would be unfair to her.* And last I reflected, *Sister Elizabeth, she was the best choice. I will vote for her. She is happy, would work hard to serve, and even if she does not seem to be a natural leader, she would truly have a listening heart to others.*

So I did it. I voted for Sister Elizabeth.

The first vote went inconclusive, there needed to be three votes for one nun to determine the prioress and the votes were all over the place. The second vote went inconclusive, leaving us in great division.

The bishop stepped in; he was aware it was not going well. "Sisters, pray, pray, open to the Spirit. You need to be united for the sake of community." I was amazed that I was clearly not alone in wanting a different prioress. The third vote was cast, Sister Elizabeth was elected.

The air did not move to peace, it moved into chaos.

I cannot explain what happened, only that the community was not at rest, and I did not know what to do with myself. It felt like I had followed Spirit, but the result was a feeling of everything moving into a stormy space. We all hugged Sister Elizabeth and bid the bishop goodbye. He was only required for the election of the prioress; next would be the selection of the counselors.

Everything changed.

Ending Message to the Reader

Thank you for walking with me on this journey, what a journey has begun! And just like the first book, this second book leaves you hanging. I can tell you this, everything changed. The project finished. The third book will continue the journey with more unexpected miracles and explosive events that led to my own final days as a Carmelite monastic nun.

As I wrote the manuscript in its entirety there were numerous reflections that came to me that I wish to share with you here.

The first is how humbled I am to have participated in such a project. How inspired I am, even to this day, when I recall a story or a person who participated in the project. I proclaim from the rooftop the song of Spirit that sang through us those three and a half years. I hope all that participated in the project feel the gratitude for them that is expressed in the story here.

The second was the utter miracle of grace. It was that I was so young and found myself capable of holding all—in moments of sheer magnificence and in moments of challenge. There were times I was completely undone by the immensity and beauty of this project, and there were times my heart and spirit felt crushed. In latter moments you could see that I asked for guidance and most often did not know what to do. Staying the course was the natural choice.

In my entire gift of self to God as a Carmelite, like the many hundreds of thousands of women and men that give their own assent into religious observance and spiritual communities, there is a formation that happens. It leads to an entrusting of self in or to your order. Eventually, I believe, these structures, these assents and even ourselves go through some kind of destruction so that we can emerge and awaken even more fully.

One of the fruits for me is a penetrating compassion for all humanity. Each one of us is moving through layers of trauma and conditioning back to our essential wild nature, and our service to each other is walking with compassion and kindness alongside the path another may be navigating. What greater friendship could we offer to another?

The third reflection that happened then and happened even more for me as I prepared this manuscript is how little support there was for us women. It was not an easy choice for me to reveal some of the challenges that existed inside our monastic life, after all, these are very private and deserve respect. But they are also integral to my own experience of everything as Grace. They are an important part of the entire miracle.

Every nun in this story had given her entire life out of love for God, had left everything to spend herself in prayer and meditation for the world, and every nun did so from a place of humble gift of self. I saw it over and again in each one of my sisters—their sincerity, their commitment, their goodness.

I am committed to taking personal responsibility in life. This is the way we discover paths to wholeness and healing. In personal responsibility comes the ability to look at the effect of our environment. I believe that our formation and our observance were the principal reasons we did not have the resource or skill to move through a time of challenge, individually and communally. This does not diminish the faith and grace existing within each one of us, and within our Order, but rather shows how the structures fell and can fall short of being a support towards compassion, healthy practice, and solid growth. Our order did not have the skillfulness, our community did not have the under-standing, and we, as nuns, were conditioned in ways that made it difficult to know how to help ourselves.

I was sad to see how often we were judged or treated with harshness within the hierarchy instead of being offered a helping hand. It was a bit like a catch-22. In the text you will see that I inwardly wrestled, as a young, newly professed nun, being asked to assent to practices that I wasn't sure were of God. I know that I am not alone. I have not met one human being that has not given their heartfelt assent in some way to hierarchy or authority for all the best reasons. The unfortunate result here is that, due to the cloistered nature of our life, we were even less resourced when we needed more support to navigate a difficult time.

I was also sad to see that my status as a *young* nun reduced kindness and support for me within my order. There were moments that a genuine word of kindness from someone in authority, or an invitation to dialogue, would have made all the difference. But I understand why this could not be so, given the practices in religious life.

There was one sister who shined for me at all times. It was Sister Catherine. She acted with a level of freedom and kindness that will inspire me for the rest of my life.

And everyone, *everyone* is doing the best they can.

Miracles are happening within everything: that which is birthing, that which is destroyed, and everything in between. And everyone, without exception, is doing the best they can.

There is much for us to grieve and change within our structures and in ourselves. There is much for us to celebrate in the human spirit that opens to experience unconditional love and freedom. There is much for us to learn in order to heal the collective consciousness. There is great ignorance that longs for the light of Spirit to awaken and there is reason to rejoice in the dance of this awakening happening.

Miracles are happening in the naked light. When we let go our defenses which keep us cloaked, when we get naked, we discover the grace in each moment. Each moment becomes a miracle in and of itself.

How Can I Support You?

There are many ways you can engage with me. If you are feeling an urge to step into the fullness of your life with greater audacity and authenticity, or if you wish to book me for your group or organization, I am here for you.

What is possible with me?

- Join my newsletter for monthly inspiration and announcement of events.
- Sign up for one of my online courses.
- Allow me to provide companionship through personal healing sessions, meditation coaching, intuitive and spiritual guidance, and even Reiki training.
- Join my online spiritual community called EssenceTribe which offers monthly mystic meetings with others around the world, two multi-week meditation series per year, a two-week mystic immersion, inspired videos, articles, and a meditation library.
- Book me to offer the inspired message for your conference, spiritual community, or summit.
- Allow me to lead your retreat or attend one of mine.
- Hire me to design and provide a corporate training or group event.
- Secure my services to assist you to create and act as officiant for your meaningful ritual, such as wedding, funeral, or any special moment.
- Purchase one of my books or CDs.

You can reach me here:

Acknowledgements

Thank you to my family who witness to me kindness and love. Thank you to my friends who share your hearts and lives with me. Thank you to my colleagues who are spanning the world working to live a life of inspiration and assist others in their journey. Thank you to the sky that raises my eyes to see beyond boundaries. Thank you to the ocean that stirs my soul with its beauty. Thank you to the air that refreshes me and blows new life into my heart. Thank you to the mountains that make me wish I were a leaping mountain goat upon the slopes, and leave me feeling it is possible. Thank you to the trees that speak to me. Thank you to the animals that seem to serve us as messengers of consolation and create such a wonder-filled world to the eyes. Thank you to the plants for sustaining this earth we call home. Thank you to my many friends and guides who are not in form that stand beside me and remind me that I am loved beyond this world—thank you for the insight you whisper into my being, the compassion you let me taste directly, and the courage you infuse me with to open myself again and again to learn how to live fearlessly.

Thank you to my friends at GracePoint Publishing who are a skilled team and helped make this book possible. You have provided happiness for my heart through your expertise, your personal care for each of us authors, and your commitment to raise consciousness through the medium of communication. Thank you to Linda Maree, accomplished writer and friend, who read the full manuscript for all three books, pacing me as I wrote it uncensored in 2014. Our weekly conversations still inspire me. You were the perfect companion for my process and part of the reason this book is published today.

Thank you to all those I have forgotten or do not know personally that have influenced my life for the better. We are parts of this constellation together and I bow in gratitude to the ways my life is touched by yours unseen.

Thank you to the Beloved who is ever emerging within me, teaching me and transforming me. You have rooted me in the ever-growing aspiration to look with Your Eyes to see Your Face in everything.

Kimberly Braun

Kimberly is passionate to answer the call at the center of her being, to be and become the embodiment of Consciousness, to know and be Love, to discover what it means to be fully alive. She believes the unceasing unfolding of the eternal is at the center of every person's being, which is to her the essential foundation of human nature. She is equally passionate to help people connect with and live from that part of themselves.

In her early childhood she oftentimes had the experience of veils pulling back to reveal intimate experiences of reality where everything was pulsing of Divine Presence. This formed in her a cosmology and worldview which has remained the lens through which she looks at life. Her mystic adventure and self-discovery continue even today, for the eternal moment has not faded.

When she was sixteen, she entered a state of extreme challenge, a dark night of her own soul. Doubts clouded her vision. After two-and-a-half years of struggle, she experienced Divine Love in such a way that shadows and edges were illumined then dissolved, and she found herself taken even more deeply into an experience of the Eternal in and as all things.

While phenomena, considered extraordinary by some, became a daily occurrence for her, the driving force in her life was the healing and transformation that happened. She found she could do nothing but surrender to Divine advances that would take her into states of ecstasy for long periods every day. Life became, quite clearly, a miracle, and she was naked and unguarded experiencing it.

Desiring to be with the Beloved in solitude, she entered a Carmelite monastery. Her first book, *Love Calls: Insights of a Former Carmelite Nun,* along with this book and the forthcoming third one, take place largely during her time as a monastic.

This fire of Love continues. For the past twenty-two years she has traveled the world, serving others to help them discover and live from Source, which resides at the center of their being.

She has moved from one *yes* to the next. Upon leaving the monastery, she was given a scholarship to complete a master's in theology with a concentration on the adult spiritual journey. Her desire was to learn how to hear the language lying at the heart of others' experiences. To serve is to be able to walk with, grasp, bring compassion and insight to, and inspire individuals along their path, as every path is unique and individual.

She graduated with double distinction, having passed both sets of her oral comprehensives without flaw. Kimberly also obtained a certification as a spiritual director through the well-known Shalem Institute for Spiritual Direction.

She is an ordained minister through the Church of the Creator (COTC), a Certified Speaking Professional (CSP) through the National Speakers Association (NSA) offering keynotes internationally, a meditation coach, Reiki master, retreat leader, and fellow mystic adventurer on this journey called life.

Her style is playful, deeply inquiring, and intelligent in the synthesis of not only how to access the deeply Resourced part of ourselves, but also in how to live from that place more consistently.

Kimberly has seen in her own life that the more we open to the potential within ourselves the more we manifest beyond what we could have imagined. Evidence of this is the truly miraculous project where she built a 17,000 square foot monastery led by faith alone, with no money or prior experience (see her TEDx talk here: https://www.kimberlybraun.com/).

Her pioneering manifestation may have begun in elementary school but continues today at fifty-six. With faith and trust, she initiated a forty-acre wellness festival in her city raising awareness of holistic modalities along with building an interdependent economy. She organized all parts of eighty stops on a national book tour for her first book. Kimberly served at Omega Institute on the meditation faculty for seven years and started a multi-lineage spiritual community called Theikosoma (Divine Body), bringing together local community and college students in services that merged all traditions. She also formed mystic workshops exposing attendees to a wide spectrum of paths. She recognizes and trusts there is much more magic awaiting her in the next half of her life. She hopes to enlighten readers to their own miraculous innate nature and union with the Beloved.

Other Books by Kimberly Braun

For more great books from Empower Press
Visit Books.GracePointPublishing.com

If you enjoyed reading *Miracles in the Naked Light*, and purchased it through an online retailer, please return to the site and write a review to help others find the book.

www.ingramcontent.com/pod-product-compliance
Lightning Source LLC
Chambersburg PA
CBHW020049170426
43199CB00009B/222